Children of the Welfare State

Anthropology, Culture and Society

Series Editors:
Professor Vered Amit, Concordia University
Doctor Jamie Cross, University of Edinburgh
and
Professor Christina Garsten, Stockholm University

Recent titles:

Children of the Welfare State

Civilising Practices in Schools, Childcare and Families

Laura Gilliam and Eva Gulløv

With contributions from
Karen Fog Olwig and Dil Bach

PlutoPress
www.plutobooks.com

This book is adapted from *Civiliserende Institutioner: Om idealer og distinktioner i opdragelse* published by Aarhus University Press, 2012.

First published 2017 by Pluto Press
345 Archway Road, London N6 5AA

www.plutobooks.com

British Library Cataloguing in Publication Data
A catalogue record for this book is available from the British Library

ISBN	978 0 7453 3609 1	Hardback
ISBN	978 0 7453 3604 6	Paperback
ISBN	978 1 7868 0000 8	PDF eBook
ISBN	978 1 7868 0018 3	Kindle eBook
ISBN	978 1 7868 0017 6	EPUB eBook

This book is printed on paper suitable for recycling and made from fully managed and sustained forest sources. Logging, pulping and manufacturing processes are expected to conform to the environmental standards of the country of origin.

Typeset by Stanford DTP Services, Northampton, England

Simultaneously printed in the European Union and United States of America

Contents

Series Preface

Anthropology is a discipline based upon in-depth ethnographic works that deal with wider theoretical issues in the context of particular, local conditions – to paraphrase an important volume from the series: *large issues* explored in *small places*. This series has a particular mission: to publish work that moves away from an old-style descriptive ethnography that is strongly area-studies oriented, and offer genuine theoretical arguments that are of interest to a much wider readership, but which are nevertheless located and grounded in solid ethnographic research. If anthropology is to argue itself a place in the contemporary intellectual world, then it must surely be through such research.

We start from the question: 'What can this ethnographic material tell us about the bigger theoretical issues that concern the social sciences?' rather than 'What can these theoretical ideas tell us about the ethnographic context?' Put this way round, such work becomes *about* large issues, *set in* a (relatively) small place, rather than detailed description of a small place for its own sake. As Clifford Geertz once said, 'Anthropologists don't study villages; they study *in* villages.'

By place, we mean not only geographical locale, but also other types of 'place' – within political, economic, religious or other social systems. We therefore publish work based on ethnography within political and religious movements, occupational or class groups, among youth, development agencies, and nationalist movements; but also work that is more thematically based – on kinship, landscape, the state, violence, corruption, the self. The series publishes four kinds of volume: ethnographic monographs; comparative texts; edited collections; and shorter, polemical essays.

We publish work from all traditions of anthropology, and all parts of the world, which combines theoretical debate with empirical evidence to demonstrate anthropology's unique position in contemporary scholarship and the contemporary world.

Professor Vered Amit
Dr Jamie Cross
Professor Christina Garsten

Acknowledgements

This book is the outcome of the research project 'Civilizing Institutions in a Modern Welfare State', financed by the Danish Council for Independent Research, Social Sciences. The analyses were first published in Danish in 2012 by Aarhus University Press and translated into Norwegian in 2015 by Fagbokforlaget. The present text is an updated and reworked version of the Danish book directed towards an international audience.

The analyses that we present in this book are based on ethnographic fieldwork in families, day-care institutions and schools in Denmark where we have explored ideas and practices concerning children, their upbringing and proper behaviour. We are deeply indebted to the many children and parents, pedagogues and assistants, teachers and principals who have allowed us to gain insight into their everyday lives in the various institutional settings. We are very grateful for their patience and cooperation and for allowing us to interview them and observe their everyday practices and conduct the sometimes peculiar practice of anthropological fieldwork.

During the analytical phases, we have profited immensely from informal as well as organised discussions with close colleagues on topics related to children and education in contemporary society. In addition to the inspiring conversations we have had regularly with our close colleagues within the fields of educational anthropology and child research at the Department of Educational Anthropology at Aarhus University, University of Copenhagen and Roskilde University, we have benefited a lot from comments given at national and international seminars. In this regard, we would like to thank Allison James, Richard Jenkins, Bradley Levinson, Robert van Krieken, Noel Dyck, John Gillis, Susan Brownell, Liisa Malkki, Anne-Trine Kjørholt, Jan Kampmann, Morten Thing, Paddy Dolan and Norman Gabriel for their thoughtful comments and reflections at various stages in the process. Special thanks should be given to our two husbands and fellow anthropologists, Henrik Vigh and John Gulløv, who throughout the process have supported and inspired the work with thoughtful comments and ideas.

In the process of adapting and revising the Danish text into the present English version, we have also been helped by several skilled translators. Initially, all the chapters were translated into English. For this comprehensive effort we will like to thank Amy Clotworthy and Luci Ellis (chapters 1 and 9), James Bulman-May (chapters 3, 5 and 7), and Simon Rolls (chapters 2, 6 and 8). Yet, as we have subsequently rewritten most of the text, the present version is at once sharpened, shortened and extended compared to the Danish manuscript. In this phase, Simon Rolls and Nicholas Wrigley have done a fine job correcting and polishing the English text. The financial support for the process and translation was generously donated by the Department of Education, University of Aarhus and Lademann's Fond.

Finally, we must compliment each other on the teamwork involved in this project. It has been an exciting yet also challenging task, not least to translate a complex concept such as 'civilising' into an analytical tool useful for understanding everyday practices and notions in day-care institutions, schools and homes. This exercise would not have succeeded had it not been for the exceptionally fine, inspiring – and, not least, 'civilised' – cooperation.

Laura Gilliam and Eva Gulløv

Introduction

Laura Gilliam and Eva Gulløv

Anthropologists have generally understood civilising missions as imperialistic practices, and thus associated these missions with a colonial logic of the past. In this book we argue that civilising missions are as much practices of the present, taking place in formal and informal children's institutions in a welfare state. Focusing on schools, day-care institutions and families in Danish society, we explore their civilising ideals, aims and practices. Based on ethnographic observations and interviews with children and young people aged 1 to 22, parents, pedagogues,[1] teachers and school principals, the book analyses the everyday practices and internal conflicts of these public and private institutions, and discusses how norms of civilised conduct are negotiated, standardised and disseminated. Moreover, by exploring children's experiences of and reactions to their institutional upbringing, the book also points to ambiguous outcomes of these civilising projects for children who differ in age, gender, ethnicity and social class. On the one hand, children are treated with considerable regard for their personality and sensitivities, and taught about equality and inclusive behaviour towards others. Yet on the other hand, though characterised by a strong egalitarian ideal, the institutional upbringing creates subtle distinctions between social groups, teaching children about moral hierarchies in society and prompting them to regard themselves as more or less civilised citizens. Illuminating these dynamics, the aim of the book is to shed light on the ideals and practices of children's upbringing in a welfare state and to discuss their social and cultural embeddedness and consequences.

Civilising Institutions in the Danish Welfare State

By focusing on children's institutions in the Danish welfare state, the book addresses the general issue of society's interest in the upbringing of new generations, while also presenting a specific case. All societies engage in some kind of shaping and socialisation of the new generation (Durkheim 1975 [1922]; Levinson and Holland 1996), but one distinguishing characteristic of the Danish welfare state is the amount of time the majority of

Danish children spend in public institutions from an early age, the extraordinary amount of attention and effort put into this process by the state, as well as the widespread cooperation in this endeavour by parents of different social backgrounds. In 2015 89.7 per cent of all children aged 6 months to 2 years in Denmark attended out-of-family care in public-funded nurseries or small at-home day-care facilities, while 97.5 per cent of all 3–5-year-olds were enrolled in public kindergartens. Whereas day-care institutions for younger children are optional, school is compulsory from the age of 6. In 2015 81 per cent of all Danish schoolchildren attended state comprehensive schools catering for 6–15-year-olds,[2] and 81.6 per cent of all 6–9-year-old children frequented after-school clubs in the afternoons (Statistics Denmark 2015).

Though recent developments in global relations and contemporary political priorities have altered many premises of the classic welfare state, the focus on children's institutions and educational efforts has not declined. In fact, investments in this area are greater than ever before. Children have moved into the centre of political concern, with the consequence that the educational system is expected to prevent or even contribute to solving the main challenges of Danish society (declining market shares, competition with other countries, unemployment and social exclusion, immigration and social segregation). Thus, rather than leaving the upbringing of children to families or private agents, the Danish state has intensified its civilising efforts by striving to get all children into public care from their first year of life in order to ensure a proper and effective socialisation process and educational development. The result is an integrated and finely tuned system of public children's institutions which cater to the working parents' need for care and education for their offspring, but also, not least to society's need for new generations of citizens of the right mould. So this massive effort is not merely a practical arrangement demonstrating concern for the nation's future workforce. The extensive focus on children and the investment of time and money that is made in their care and upbringing bear witness to the fact that the Danish welfare state does not leave the practice of childrearing to parents alone, but plays an active role in the proper upbringing of the next generation of citizens.

An Eliasian Approach to Childrearing

The institutional priorities and practices in relation to childrearing will be examined using the concept of 'civilising', inspired by the work of sociologist Norbert Elias (1994 [1939]). In Elias's work, the concept refers to culturally specific norms of proper and cultivated behaviour, which evolve through changing power relations and processes of integration between social groups, yet contribute to cultural distinctions and social hierarchies. Unlike related concepts such as socialisation, upbringing and disciplining, 'civilising' applies to both formative efforts and the social processes of integration, distinction and psychological change which make people strive for certain forms of behaviour which they regard as appropriate and distinguished, while discarding others which they regard as inappropriate and degrading (see further discussion in chapter 1).

We are aware that the concept of 'civilising' – and especially 'civilisation' – is controversial due to its historical baggage and evolutionist ring. We will, however, argue that it is precisely its focus on social distinctions and human hierarchies that gives the concept its analytical potential, as long as it is not used to make normative judgements about people's behaviour but is employed to understand their behavioural norms.[3] Hence, it is important to stress that the term 'civilising' does not stand for specific universal values, or for a set of universally applicable norms of conduct. Societies and their populations differ in terms of which forms of conduct are considered civilised, and even within individual societies there will be different and changing understandings of what this entails. It is a subject under constant negotiation between different social groups. However, it is a central point in the work of Elias that some groups have greater opportunity to impose their understanding of what is respectable. When this influence persists over longer periods it often appears as an almost natural perception. One of the aims of this book is to illuminate how civilised conduct is conceived of and negotiated in a welfare society which strives for equality, yet is based on norms reflecting historically produced power relationships between social groups. In our view, Elias's theory of civilising is analytically useful for this, due to its focus on the relationship between power, behaviour and moral judgement, and its ability to illuminate the relation between cultural values, social interdependencies and subtle processes of distinction. By applying this discussion to Danish institutions for children and young people, the book addresses how the encompassing institutionalisation of children relates to changing group relations and extensive processes of integration in wider society, necessitating children's transformation into civil persons capable of engaging in public spheres in ways considered non-offensive and socially acceptable. In a further perspective, we find that this approach contributes to more general theoretical discussions of the relationship between educational institutions, cultural norms and processes of distinction.

The Role of Institutions

Part of the negotiation as to what is civilised takes place between parents and childcare professionals. What should be prioritised in childrearing? Who has the right and the authority to decide how the child should be brought up and what it should learn? Danish society is interesting in this regard because the extensive institutionalisation demonstrates that public institutions for care and education are, to a great extent, given the right to raise children from a very early age. By analysing everyday situations and practices in families, day-care institutions and schools, we will examine the negotiation of roles, authority and priorities in relation to children's upbringing which takes place in and between the private and public spheres, but also examine recurring features of the formative work with children across the different types of institutions.

A main tenet in the following analyses is that day-care institutions and schools are central civilising and integrating organs in the welfare state. They are constructed to ensure that new generations are cared for and civilised, yet at the same time they also contribute to the very ideas of what civilised behaviour and a civilised society entail. We will thus argue that behavioural norms are both 'institutionalised' through children's institutions – in the sense of being routinised and disseminated – yet also become 'institutional' that is moulded by the conditions and social relations of the institutions. The analysis of everyday life in such institutions can therefore provide insights into the values and norms that are prioritised to such an extent as to be part of the institutional arrangement, while at the same time revealing how these values are interpreted, negotiated and moulded by the institutional structures and personal interactions. With this approach it is also possible to look into why some groups of children and some types of behaviour fail to meet the relevant standards and are therefore perceived as wrong and not measuring up, in moral terms, within a social hierarchy.

The Ethnographic Approach

As mentioned, the book is based on ethnographic research. This entails that, over an extended period, we have conducted participant observation and gathered material regarding everyday life in the institutions that were included in our study.[4] We have observed both daily routines and unusual incidents, paying attention to what children and adults do and talk about, and we have interviewed children about their experiences and understandings, as well as interviewing pedagogues, teachers and parents about their practices and notions of children, upbringing and institutional tasks and settings.

Studies of this type probe into everyday life, but, of course, our material is not representative of all families, day-care institutions and schools in Denmark, nor does it reveal all aspects of institutional life or touch upon all issues relevant to the discussion of civilising. Nevertheless, we find such studies well suited to produce a more general form of knowledge. Although the ethnographic approach is local and situated, our research interest is general and directed towards society's underlying values and multiplicity of rationales. As a result, we have attempted to understand why people act as they do in concrete situations and contexts, but, at a more general level, we have also tried to shed light on the cultural understandings and values and social dynamics behind the childrearing practices and institutional priorities we have observed. We aim to understand both local practices and a national case, but also to explore the relationship between welfare institutions, parents and children on a more general and theoretical level. Our ambition is to provide insight both into underlying cultural values of Danish society, and into the social processes which continuously either challenge or corroborate such values, and which provide a basis for self-perception, social cohesion and hierarchy.

In this endeavour, we not only draw on the sociology of Norbert Elias but also on insights gained within the fields of anthropology of children and sociology of childhood, the anthropology of education, Bourdieu's praxeology, the sociology of institutions and ethnographic studies of Scandinavia. In these different academic traditions, we find overlapping and parallel interests in exploring the relationship between childrearing practices, processes of enculturation, notions of what it means to be educated and the impact of institutions on social stratification. Inspired by these studies and analyses concerning children, educational institutions and upbringing practices in various cultural settings, we aim not only to present a study of a specific national setting, but also to contribute to a more general theorising on the cultural foundation and social implications of civilising institutions.

The Book's Structure

The book is an anthology in the sense that the chapters are written by different authors and are based on several studies carried out in various institutions. As such, each chapter can be read in its own right. Nevertheless, the studies were conducted as part of the same project, and it is our ambition that the book can be read in its full length as an aggregate analysis. In this sense, we regard it as a monograph. The four authors are all anthropologists, and ethnographic methods and descriptions are at the core of the book's analyses. This also means that, particularly in the book's six empirical chapters, we have given priority to the empirical material and made frequent use of situational descriptions, transcripts of conversations and direct quotes.[5]

The first two chapters by Gilliam and Gulløv frame the following empirical analyses. Chapter 1 introduces and discusses Norbert Elias's notion and theory of 'civilising' and the book's theoretical perspective on institutional childrearing. In chapter 2 the historical background to and development of the institutionalisation of childhood that has taken place in Danish society over the last century is described and analysed, as well as the different conceptualisations and practices of childrearing, civilised conduct and societal forms that these convey. After this introduction, the book's six empirically based chapters present studies of different institutional settings and groups of children. Chapters 3 and 4 discuss the efforts to civilise children in the first public institutions they encounter as autonomous agents – that is the day-care institutions of nurseries, kindergartens and integrated institutions for 1–6-year-olds. In chapter 3, Gulløv analyses the prevailing ideal of the young child as a flexible and socially balanced person able to adapt to shifting situational requirements. This ideal allows for many interpretations giving children a certain leeway, which, however, not all children are able to handle in acceptable ways. In the following chapter, Olwig examines the kindergarten as a site where young children experience early forms of sociality and how their position as 'not-yet-civilised' within the institution influences the way they interact with others, form groups and assert themselves.

After these chapters on early childhood institutions, the next three chapters address society's primary civilising institution: the *folkeskole*, that is the comprehensive Danish state-funded school. In these chapters, Gilliam examines children of different ages and of various social and ethnic backgrounds. Based on fieldwork conducted in grade o classes at two *folkeskoler*, chapter 5 illustrates the work involved in teaching the youngest schoolchildren – aged 5–6 – to be 'social' and in moulding good, civilised communities. It explores the institutional logics of this, and the consequences that the school's ideal for civilised conduct has for different children's identities and practices in school. In chapter 6, the focus is on 10–12-year-old children in an ethnically diverse school in a former work-ing-class urban district and the extensive civilising work directed towards especially immigrant boys, who are considered problematic and uncivilised. The analysis demonstrates how these efforts, and the social dynamics of countercultural forms to which civilising projects may contribute, teach children about the social categories of gender, class, ethnicity and religion. This theme is continued in chapter 7, which analyses the final grade 9 in a financially and educationally privileged suburban environment. This chapter analyses how affluent young people – aged 15–16 – come to see their own position as morally superior by the way teachers describe them and the surrounding world through categories and narratives loaded with moral evaluations.

In chapter 8 the focus turns towards families and their upbringing practices. Based on fieldwork carried out in a number of homes in an affluent residential area, Bach shows how parents – particularly mothers – are engaged in close regulation of children in order for them to interact in appropriate ways with others and to build up their social capital. She further explores children's role in parents' social networking and in their demonstration of their own civilised capacity and position. The book ends with more general and theoretical reflections on the relation between children's institutions, the welfare society and contemporary understand-ings of civilised conduct. In chapter 9, the concluding chapter, Gilliam and Gulløv examine the civilising projects across the various institutions and discuss how they relate to and reflect dominant cultural norms and social hierarchies in Danish society, as well as their implications for children of different social and ethnic backgrounds.

1

On Civilising

A perspective on childrearing, conduct and distinctions

Laura Gilliam and Eva Gulløv

In this chapter, we present the theoretical framework of the book; that is, the way we have adapted Norbert Elias's theory and concept of 'civilising' to the study of upbringing ideals and practices in the institutions of the Danish welfare state. In Elias's work the concept of 'civilising' is used to denote both visions and ideals of cultivated conduct and ambitions, as well as the process that over time creates changes in the way people feel, think and behave. These visions and ideals reflect relations of interdependence and social domination, and give way to processes of distinction. Applying this notion of civilising to the way Danish families, day-care institutions and schools bring up children, and exploring how civilising projects unfold in the everyday lives of these institutions, grants us a better view of the social and cultural embeddedness of formative work and its implications for children and childrearers. As we will argue, the approach also opens up insights into how children's institutions contribute to the social and moral hierarchies of welfare society, not only in Denmark but also in contemporary welfare states in a more general sense.

The Civilising Process

Norbert Elias elucidated his theory of 'the civilising process' in a complex and comprehensive work containing an in-depth examination of the relation between the formation of Western European states and what he describes as a 'civilising' of behaviour and personality since the Middle Ages (Elias 1994 [1939]).[1] According to Elias, civilising processes take place in all societies, but the civilising process of European societies has a particular character, due to the central role of the state (1994 [1939]:379; Mennell 1990:208). Using France and Germany as his empirical cases, he describes a lengthy historical development from the establishment of courts in the Middle Ages, towards an increasingly integrated state society in which the state gradually gains a monopoly over taxation and the use of violence.[2] This consolidation of the state reflects a process of greater population density and a division of labour and functions, leading to a high degree of internal dependence between members of society, or what Elias calls 'chains of interdependence' that become longer and more differentiated over the centuries (1994 [1939]:289).

Elias argues that the combination of state monopolisation and increased social integration has led to greater physical security for the members of a society and, over time, a general aversion to and heightened 'threshold of sensitivity' towards violence (Elias 1998a:182–93). In order to live in mutual interdependence, members must develop a high level of self-control, avoid aggression and other behaviour that may offend others, and seek to adapt their behaviour to other people's expectations (Elias 1994 [1939]:366–9, 429). This necessitates a certain standardisation of conduct and coordination of interactions – not least through increased temporal regulation (Elias 1992:118–19). In a societal organisation based on members' mutual dependence, control of drives and predictability becomes central. Over time such adaptations are integrated into well-established patterns for interpersonal interaction. A central point here is that through this process, what were previously external requirements are gradually internalised as 'self-restraints' associated with feelings of shame or disgust over the uncivilised behaviour of yourself or others (Elias 1994 [1939]:365). The genuine fear of other people's use of violence and reprisals is transformed into a fear of other people's judgements: a fear of being excluded or losing face. Thus, self-control and shame become psychological mechanisms that replace the fear of aggression from others. In this way, behaviour becomes the basis for assessing status and respectability.

Elias illustrates this via a historical review of rules for etiquette and manuals for childrearing aimed at raising young boys in the German and French court societies. He describes how norms slowly spread from these court circles to the rest of society and became integrated in social interactions. Using examples from these manuals, he shows how physical restraint and the restricted expression of emotions in particular became markers of social distinction gradually changing the make-up of the individual psyche. Whereas, for example, in the fifteenth century, spitting on the table when eating was described as being merely bad manners, over time spitting has become something which is generally repellent. However, this is not simply a change in practice, but also a need that is eliminated or at least suppressed via a gradual transformation of feelings (Elias 1994 [1939]:131–6). Using several body-related examples (e.g. table manners, bed sharing, sexual relations, toilet habits, and fights), Elias illustrates how, over the centuries, an increasing suppression of drives and a detailed division of public, private and intimate behaviour has developed (1994 [1939]:160). He argues that a person's social reputation and interactions with others necessitate an intensified awareness about which forms of expression and ways of behaving are appropriate in different social contexts. Corporal punishment of children in Denmark may serve as an example. From being a normal and widespread practice, adults' right to hit children was first problematised, then forbidden for authority figures in children's institutions, and finally in 1997 – after substantial controversy – made illegal also for parents in private homes and, in addition, fraught with shame. In this way, behaviours that were previously widespread in the public sphere have gradually become socially degrading, even within the boundaries of the home.

Figurations and the Relationship Between Sociogenesis and Psychogenesis

As this shows, the norms of conduct that people must observe to be accepted as civilised persons change over time. Elias's point is that they change in relation to alterations in social power balances between social groups, and via complex processes of social mobility, social struggles, integration and distinction. He describes, for example, how the growing bourgeoisie of the seventeenth and eighteenth centuries in Germany and France, in their striving for social elevation, adopted part of the court's etiquette and symbols of distinction while dismissing other aristocratic manners as decadent in an attempt to establish their own code of conduct as morally superior (1994 [1939]:387, 433). Such social dynamics and changes in power balances are decisive not only for which norms become dominant, but also for the individual's personal conduct and perception of social relations. They influence what Elias terms 'human figurations'; that is social networks of interdependent actors which form the outset for individual reasoning, self-awareness and orientation (Elias 1970:127–

33). It is a key point in the theory of Elias (also named 'figuration theory') that it is not possible to understand the actions of a person in isolation; their meanings are fundamentally social and must be grasped in relation to the webs of interdependences and structures of dominance within the figurations which all individuals and groups are situated in.

In this way Elias systematically links the acts of individuals with changes in social dynamics or what he terms 'psychogenesis' and 'sociogenesis'. It is through interactions with others – especially in childhood – that each individual's 'habitus' is formed into what Elias calls a 'second nature'; that is, the social adaptation and suppression of the 'first nature' – an individual's immediate drives and needs (Elias 1994 [1939]:369; Wouters 2011:148).[3] Due to this social base, people's innermost feelings are inextricably linked to the power balances between social groupings and societal norms and values. From this perspective, important changes to societal structures (industrialisation, urbanisation, commercialisation, democratisation and, not least, monopolisation of violence and the formation of the state) influence both interpersonal relations and individual people's innermost orientations, perceptions and judgements. Likewise, historical transformations of behaviour, psyche and norms are caused by changes in human figurations and will follow these.

Elias stresses that this dynamic reveals that the civilising process is not a planned process, though it does have a certain structure and causality. It develops without a goal, though not without the will of humans. It is driven by historical changes that appear to have a particular direction, but are actually just the result of many individuals' acts, choices and plans:

> This basic tissue resulting from many single plans and actions of people can give rise to changes and patterns that no individual person had planned or created. From this interdependence of people arises an order sui genesis, an order more compelling and stronger than the will and reason of the individual people composing it. It is this order of interweaving human impulses and strivings, this social order, which determines the course of historical change; it underlies the civilising process. (Elias 1994 [1939]:366)

Self-Regulation and Informalisation

Although Elias emphasises that the historical development of manners never was linear, and that there has been an easing of behavioural norms in the period following the Second World War, he nevertheless concludes that the psycho-social development of Western Europe generally has been characterised by an increase in self-restraint (Elias 1994 [1939]: 413–14, 1998b: 235–8). With an unmistakable Freudian inspiration, Elias describes the development of a more distanced relationship to the body, and repression of impulses and drives (Elias 1994 [1939]:409).[4] Though drives have always been socially regulated, along with the increased social integration of society, bodily urges and natural functions are pushed behind the scenes of social life. However, this does not mean that violence, bodily secretions, sex and intense affect have ceased to be part of social life. On the contrary, as anthropologist Mary Douglas also elucidates, taboo marks phenomena of key cultural significance (Douglas 1966; Elias 1994 [1939]:439–45).

This process has been accompanied by new thresholds for feelings of shame associated with transgressing social norms and breaking cultural taboos (Elias 1994 [1939]:415; Engebrigtsen 2006:110; Scheff 2004). Shame comprises a fear of losing esteem and of social degradation, arising from what Elias describes as 'the constant pressure from below', and may thus be considered a strong driving force which increasingly character-ises social interactions (1994 [1939]:424). The more people depend on each other and the evaluations of others, the more expectations will be related to behaviour. Therefore, an ever greater number of factors become associated with the risk of social blunders and linked to feelings of shame. At the same time, shame itself becomes an indication of social respect-ability. Feeling shame – or at least expressing that one knows one should be ashamed – becomes a way of demonstrating an awareness of social requirements, a way of showing that one is a trustworthy and accountable person. According to Elias, this development culminated in the moral code of the Victorian era, followed by a relaxation of self-restraint and a – selective – loosening of taboos within the last century (Elias 1998a:206). Elias's point is, however, that the interpersonal dependence of the present day does not require a lesser degree of self-control, and that shame is still an important mechanism of social regulation – just in different ways.

This point is further elaborated by sociologist Cas Wouters when discussing 'the informalisation process' which has unfolded in European societies during the twentieth century (Wouters 1977, 2004, 2011). As more rigid forms and authoritative societal structures were left behind, emotional expressions that were previously repressed and associated with shame became more widely recognised. Wouters argues that despite the seemingly less restricted style of interaction, emotional expressions have not become more in tune with 'the first nature' – the immediate drives and needs. Rather what comes to the fore is a new form of personality – a 'third nature' (Wouters 2011:152–6). The current form of expression is still socially regulated; it has simply been adapted to a more individualised societal form in which the individual cannot rely on standardised forms. Instead, he/she must flexibly and reflexively express and conduct him/herself in ways that are considered to be respectable, credible and sincere in a variety of social contexts (Wouters 2011; Elias 1998a:206). The result is thus heightened demands in terms of the individual's social sensitivity and tact, and what Elias has described as 'controlled decontrolling of emotional controls' (quoted in Wouters 1986:3).

The Social Dynamics of the State

In Elias's analysis, it is particularly in relation to the historical reduction of violence in Western European societies that the significance of shame and self-regulation is revealed. In most circles, physical aggression is now perceived as unacceptable – an essential breach of self-control and therefore socially degrading and associated with shame. He relates this development to the emergence of the state as a mediating authority. The state's monopolisation of violence and punishment has resulted in the criminalisation of all forms of physical violence, and it is no longer acceptable for individuals to solve conflicts between themselves in a violent manner. This has led to a general decrease in the levels of violence in society. However, people are well aware that violence may occur and that the civilised order could erode. This fear is latent and functions both as a regulatory mechanism in interpersonal interactions and as a legitimisation of the state's authority to mediate, judge and punish. Sociologist Loïc Wacquant articulates Elias's point in the following:

> Elias places violence and fear at the epicenter of the experience of modernity: together they form the Gordian knot tying the outermost workings of the state to the innermost makeup of the person. The expurgation of violence from social life via its relocation under the aegis of the state opens the way for the regulation of social exchange, the ritualization of everyday life, and the psychologization of impulse and emotion. (Wacquant 2004:112)

In this way, the state plays an important role in Elias's argumentation. However, it should be noticed that Elias regards neither the state nor society as distinct entities in relation to other entities: individuals (Elias 1970:14–16). The state and society are made up of people who act and reproduce the societal order via their actions and social interactions (see an elaboration of this point in Bourdieu 1994, 2004). Thus, the state's function is indeed regulatory, but this is only maintained by many individuals' acceptance of the specific understanding of order that the state enforces. In this context, the regulating and detail-oriented Scandinavian welfare states can be regarded as a special case. The increasingly refined institutional structures that incorporate people of all levels of society, have turned security, predictability and equality into key concerns of the state. However, it would not be possible to exercise this regulatory function without acceptance by many individuals who acknowledge the core values of the welfare state in their daily activities. For instance, most people refrain from violence, pay taxes and send their children to school not just because they have to, but also because they feel that these are the right things to do (see a related discussion in van Krieken 1986). Societal order cannot be reduced to supra-individual functionality or external regulation; it is upheld by a pronounced moral dimension and influenced by psycho-social mechanisms, such as shame and trust, a sense of the appropriate, a striving for respectability and fear of social degradation.

The Civilising of Children and Childrearers

According to Elias, one of the changes that the civilising process in Western Europe has brought about is a change in the conceptualisation, treatment and rearing of children. Although he did not conduct empirical analyses of childrearing, childhood and children were central themes in his discussions of the civilising process. As mentioned above, he studied the inculcation of manners through etiquette books for young boys, and he analysed the relationship between generations as well as the formation of the individual habitus in childhood. He points out that each generation will bring up the younger generation according to the norms its members deem important. Elias underlines that this 'civilising of the human young' has become increasingly comprehensive and the focus of planned interventions, in line with the increasingly extensive standards for what is considered shameful and offensive (1994 [1939]:367, 376–7). The more the codes of civilised conduct are refined, and the greater the demands made on the individual, the longer the transformation process becomes that the individual must undergo from child to adult (Elias 1998a:200).

According to Elias, the civilising process does not only lead to a growing preoccupation with teaching children how to behave properly, but also involves what he sees as a classificatory distinction between children and adults, and thus an increased distance between generations. Based on historical sources, Elias portrays how children in medieval society participated extensively in adult life. They often slept in the same room or even in the same bed, and were not kept away from adult knowledge or activities (Elias 1998a:197). Discussing the argument of the French historian Philippe Ariès (1962) that childhood was 'discovered' between the fourteenth and sixteenth centuries, he argues that the perception of children's distinctness has further developed up till the present time just as the distance between the generations has grown since the Middle Ages (1998a:190). In line with Ariès, he sees this as a process accelerated by schooling, but also by the industrialisation and urbanisation of Western Europe, which through the nineteenth and twentieth centuries gradually reduced the economic function of the child and thus altered the pattern of interdependency within the family figuration (1998a:208).

The distance between the generations seems to have reached something of an apex in the Victorian period in the latter half of the nineteenth century among the privileged and therefore normative classes (1998a:206). Strong contrasts between classes, increased social mobility and mutual dependence necessitated greater attention, at least in bourgeois circles, to class affiliation and stratification. As Cas Wouters points out in his discussion of social changes in the Netherlands, this created greater demands in terms of presentability and moral solidity and thereby a greater focus on the family, on women's respectability and a close monitoring of children and their 'indecent' behaviour (Wouters 2004:202; for a parallel discussion from Sweden see Frykman and Löfgren 1987 [1979]). One consequence of this was that children were gradually moved from public and adult life into homes, schools and institutions (Wouters 2004:202).

Describing the picture with broad brush strokes, Elias argues that these changes not only altered the position of the child in the family as well as in society, but also led to a 'civilising of parents' (1998a). As birth rates fell and children became less useful as workers, and as the family lost many of its former functions to the modern state, the individual child grew more valuable for its parents and the emotional functions of the family grew stronger (1998a:206–8). This changed the power ratio in families between parents and children, leading towards the democratisation and emotionalisation of the adult–child relationship. One important aspect of this is the curbing of the use of violence by parents, a more egalitarian and informal relationship between parents and children, and a raised awareness of children's needs and particularities (1998a:190).

The civilising process in Western Europe has thus generally implied greater separation between the generations yet also an increased emotionalisation of the relationship between them. Childhood has increasingly been conceptualised as a period of learning the civilised behaviour of adults. In the light of Elias's reasoning, educational institutions for children can be seen as purpose-built for this learning process: it is here that children, who are vulnerable, and inept in terms of impulse regulation and respectable behaviour, are transformed before they can take part in society's interactions. Or in the words of Ariès: 'the child was not ready for adult life, and [...] had to be subjected to special treatment, a sort of quarantine, before he was allowed to join the adults' (Ariès 1962:412–13).

Civilising as a Theoretical Concept

As is clear from the presentation above, what comes to the fore in Elias's historical analyses is how norms and ideas of civilised conduct and proper relations can change substantially over time. Elias also emphasises that there is 'no point at which human beings are uncivilised and as it were begin to be civilised' (Elias 1992:119). Nobody lacks the ability to practice self-restraint, and all societies have different understandings of civilised behaviour, reflecting changes in social figurations in their own ways. Likewise, civilising processes do not have a fixed route and are often interrupted by periods of war or decivilising 'spurts' (Elias 1994 [1939]: 157). Neither do they have a particular end goal, but are instead initiated and kept going by a web of relations and social collisions (1994 [1939]:65–7).

Yet it has been discussed whether the concepts of 'civilisation' and 'civilising' nonetheless have an evolutionary and Eurocentric tone (see, for example, the discussion in Goody 2002). This controversy may be due to the fact that Elias himself uses the concept both empirically and theoretically. He investigates the empirical context in which the concept of 'civilisation' was formed and became an expression of 'the self-consciousness of the West', and, in this context, he investigates how the term 'civilised' has been understood in different countries and periods (Elias 1994 [1939]:5). At the same time, the idea of the civilising process is fundamental to his theory of the development of Western society towards increased social integration and non-violent relations. This duality creates ambiguity, at least if the two ways of using the term are confused. We are of the opinion that one should avoid the teleological and evolutionary connotation so often attributed to the concept in a great deal of everyday usage as well as some academic usage (i.e. that it ranks societies or conduct according to developmental level), as well as avoiding the Eurocentrism from which Elias is not entirely free, despite his best efforts. Instead, one should focus on the theoretical premise of the Eliasian approach: that all societies have – and dispute – standards for interaction and behaviour, and that these refer to perceived hierarchies of humans and human behaviour. Thus, rather than using the term to evaluate behaviour normatively, one should seek to gain insights into the normative – and often evolutionary – meanings that are empirically attributed to the concept (i.e. to study a specific society's changing and often contested understandings of what characterises civilised behaviour) and the resulting locally defined hierarchies of societies and individuals. Used in this way, the concept of 'civilising' is valuable in anthropological analyses as it affords a theoretical tool to understand a society's moral cosmology, local perception of norms and the social relations, struggles and hierarchies that these ideas both derive from and produce. As a processual concept it is particularly suitable for exploring the interrelatedness of these dimensions in contemporary society, but it can also be used to shed light on the historical processes that have led to present figurations, distinctions, norms and understandings. In this way we find that it can be used to reinvigorate anthropological analyses of cultural norms, giving a vital focus on history and social processes of distinction, dominance and inequality (Ortner 2006).

A Perspective on Civilising Projects

With regard to our focus in this book, this theoretical basis provides a perspective that we can use to elucidate the phenomenon of childrearing in relation to the values, norms and standards that underlie the requirements, prioritisations and evaluations of children in families and in public children's institutions in contemporary Danish welfare society. This complex analytical approach can show us something about children's upbringing in institutions that is different than the perspectives afforded by related concepts such as 'disciplining', 'educating', 'childrearing' or 'socialisation'. We do not reject these concepts, which include discussions that are closely linked to those that the concept of 'civilising' aims to illuminate. As we point out below, 'disciplining' focuses on the aspect of power that is key to every type of transformation of oneself or others, and 'educating' describes the intentional transformation of the individual into a culturally informed and skilled citizen. 'Childrearing', on the other hand, encompasses the general and deliberate project of moulding the child, but does not explicate the relationship to other individuals, whereas 'socialisation' focuses on any process by which the individual acquires certain social forms and becomes part of a social context or group. We consider these aspects of formative processes to be important dimensions of civilising projects and processes, and will therefore make use of these concepts in the following chapters whenever relevant. However, we aim to focus in particular on ideas of 'civilised conduct', and thus on ideals which both set goals and mark social and moral boundaries, as well as showing the consequences of such ideas for the childrearing, formation and socialisation that take place in Danish children's institutions.

In other words, we use the concept of civilising to pursue a specific interest which is not covered by other concepts. The concept of 'the civilised person' overlaps with the concept of 'the educated person', coined by Levinson and Holland (1996) in their important work. Yet the notion of 'civilising' focuses particularly on the moral and hierarchical dimensions of the culturally produced notions of the educated person. In similar ways, the concept has another emphasis than the concept of 'socialisation'. A person may be socialised into just about anything – even asocial behaviour – while the goal of civilising is not arbitrary but reflects what dominant social groupings regard as respectable, cultivated manners and behaviour, in contrast to what is locally perceived as the tacky, barbaric, vulgar or uncultivated. In this way the concept systematically addresses central oppositions between what is appropriate and what is inappropriate, between selfishness and sociality, between nature and culture, animals and humans integrated in the social configuration of the society in question. Such cultural schemes of classification and distinctions are often overlooked, but can provide insights into fundamental cultural ideas about human hierarchies and value judgements. As we conceive it, the concept of civilising highlights how everyday formative practices such as childrearing are inevitably related to – and thus provide us a window on – more pervasive cultural values and cosmologies.

As we have already stated, this does not mean that specific understandings of the civilised are universal in nature, or that it is a concept that people use in everyday language. What is considered distinguished behaviour, how it is expressed and, not least, what aspects of behaviour these norms do not attend to, differs from society to society. But it is universal that people place themselves and others in social and moral hierarchies: that some people are considered to be cruder than others who are seen to be more refined, and that some people act in accordance with or in opposition to what is perceived to be respectable. And it is universal that people seek to bring up their children in consideration of such understandings. Therefore, civilising is a theoretical concept that is aimed at understanding what is considered to be the correct form of behaviour, relationship and coexistence in a given context, that is, the culturally dominant vision of the respectable person and society. We thus regard the concept of civilising to be a way to theoretically comprehend these cultural values, the way they are taught, as well as the social relations of interdependence and dominance that have led to their naturalisation.

In this respect, our intention is somewhat different from that of Elias. Whereas Elias's historical-sociological approach looks at civilising processes as elongated social movements, we primarily employ an ethnographic approach which looks into current outcomes of historical processes and the everyday practices and perceptions of individual actors. Second, we investigate civilising projects or missions: that is, the intentional programmes and institutionalised contexts that adults – parents, pedagogues and teachers – place children in, in order to make them into people of a certain calibre. Though he did not explore this empirically, Elias also recognises civilising intentions in relation to children, lower social classes and colonial relations. He thus stresses: 'it is precisely in conjunction with the civilising process that the blind dynamics of people intertwining in their deeds and aims gradually leads towards greater scope for planned intervention into both the social and individual structures' (Elias 1994 [1939]:367). Several of his followers also discuss deliberate interventions, termed 'civilising offensives' (see discussion in Powell 2013). In his use of the term, Robert van Krieken describes it as a concept that: 'take[s] account of the active, conscious and deliberate civilising projects of both various powerful groups within societies and whole societies in relation to other regions of the world' (1999:303). Our concept of civilising projects is closely related to this, but aims to describe the planned interventions of societal institutions – which we describe as 'civilising institutions'. In other words, civilising intentions and practices that are not necessarily directed at specific groups understood as uncivilised, but take the form of more generalised and institutionalised civilising efforts (Gilliam and Gulløv 2014). In this way, we describe the more widespread and generally accepted task of moulding every child in accordance with established understandings of social conduct and the way these projects unfold and sometimes run aground in everyday institutional life.

Civilising and Disciplining

In a number of ways, Elias's theory of civilising can be compared to Michel Foucault's discussions about discipline and self-discipline (see for example Foucault 1977). Foucault also shows how individuals deal with increasing demands regarding their behaviour, and gradually internalise these requirements in the way they perceive themselves. And, like Elias, he investigates the basis of self-control and social adjustment. Despite this similarity, there are also several marked differences between Elias's and Foucault's approaches to the internalisation of external requirements (for further discussion, see Dolan 2010; Smith 1999). For Foucault, internalisation refers to a logic of power, whereby the individual is formed by the 'power knowledge' that describes normality and the individual as a subject, and how he/she internalises the behavioural requirements associated with the subject position to which he/she is assigned by discourse (Foucault 1982). For Elias, internalisation is inextricably linked to social relations and interdependencies (Elias 1994 [1939]:70–1), which, in contrast to Foucault's notion of self-perception (see for example Foucault 1980:155), includes a constant awareness and observation of others in order to assess oneself, adapt and, in some cases, demonstrate superiority. In this sense, observation is more a source of social positioning than an expression of passive internalisation of dominant ways of thinking (see discussion in van Krieken 1986, 1998).

In relation to our investigation of childrearing in children's institutions, we find that Elias's and Foucault's approaches complement each other. Discipline is genuinely exercised because institutions always draw upon what Foucault calls 'regimes of truth' (Foucault 1980), and, as such, they strive towards normalisation, requiring a structure of authority and monitoring of the children. And these institutions have a dominant influence when it comes to how children form their identities and identifications: how they perceive and think about themselves and the world, as well as how they deal with their own feelings and actions. At the same time, it is important to understand that the adjustments and adaptations that individuals undertake are also an expression of the individual's strategic interpretation and consideration of the social environment as well as his/her own position and status.[5] Here Elias's focus on power balances and interdependencies sheds light on the fact that, even within an institutional structure, the exercise of power takes multiple directions and may have different outcomes. Although structures of authority are rarely fundamentally changed by challenges to power, it is nevertheless evident in our material that negotiations, adaptations and power struggles give rise to dynamics which have social and cultural consequences. Thus, dominant discourses are influential, but individuals' interpretations and actions may lead to quite different understandings. The attention to social conflict in Elias's notion of civilising emphasises this dimension.

Integration and Distinction

The theoretical ambition of Elias is also similar to that of Bourdieu (see for example Bourdieu 1984), in that he aims to illuminate how social structures are reflected in individual taste and dispositions for behaving, doing so without descending into structural determinism (for a discussion of this, see Paulle et al. 2011). To this end, both theorists use the concept of habitus.[6] Yet, whereas Bourdieu is preoccupied with investigating the forces behind social distance – expressed symbolically through physical distance, levels of contact, cultural distinctions and economic stratification – Elias, with his concept of 'figurations', offers an important insight into the significance of social dependence for social stratification. He focuses on the integrative processes that, over time, have increased social interdependencies and necessitated the adaptation and internalisation of particular forms of interaction and behaviour. He describes how contrasts between people are gradually evened out – partially by dominant groups deliberately transferring behavioural norms to other levels of society or colonised groups, and, as we have already touched upon, partially by dominated groups striving to gain influence and social elevation by adopting distinguishing codes (Elias 1994 [1939]:430).

As described, Elias illuminates how these processes also reflect Western Europe's demographic development, with its increased population density, urbanisation and more differentiated yet also more mutually dependent divisions of labour. Up through the twentieth century such conditions necessitated more flexible interactions between people from different social levels who now met in business life and work processes, as well as (we would add) in institutions of the welfare state. Describing this from the Dutch context, Wouters (2011) shows how it became increasingly important to avoid any marking of superiority and class difference. He notes how these new dependencies meant a wider use and tolerance of behavioural norms and emotional expressions hitherto associated with lower social classes (Wouters 2011). While upper-class codes for distinguished behaviour had previously spread to the expanding middle class, the social empowerment of the lower classes led to a spread of their characteristics, in particular a wage labour lifestyle and more informal manners. Thus one can discern a certain democratisation or 'commingling of patterns of conduct deriving from initially very different social levels' (Elias 1994 [1939]:383). This informalisation of social forms became particularly pronounced in the protests against formalised norms and established authorities in the 1960s and 1970s (Wouters 1977; Elias 1998b:235–45). Wouters argues that the ability to demonstrate indifference towards established markers of superiority or class gradually became a social requirement (Wouters 1977:437–56, 2004, 2011). Or one could say that the informal code of conduct (for example swearing, showing affection publicly, dressing in a relaxed manner and adopting a more informal attitude towards authorities) became distinctive in itself: a subtle yet socially appropriate way of expressing social status.

Over the past 25 years, the work of several anthropologists has demonstrated that such downplaying of differences is particularly pronounced in the Scandinavian countries (Gullestad 1992; Salamon 1992; Liep and Olwig 1994; Lien et al. 2001; Jenkins 2011; Bruun et al. 2011). Although the avoidance of differences and aspirations towards equality are a more general phenomenon, this seems to especially characterise Scandinavia as a cultural region. Here, equality is both a matter of a levelling out of economic differences and legal justice and, to a great extent, a matter of social parity or what the Norwegian anthropologist Marianne Gullestad calls 'sameness' (Gullestad 1992:185). We will argue that welfare institutions have played a particular role in this process, with children's institutions not least contributing to the development of a pronounced sensibility towards expressions of difference, authority, social exclusion and inequality (Gilliam and Gulløv 2014). However, the presence of integrative processes that downplay differences does not mean that distinctions have been eradicated. Rather, a change has taken place with regard to how differences are marked: the demarcations and distancing practices have become more refined and subtle. Elias shows that this is a general characteristic of civilising processes – greater social integration leads to more refined practices of distinction (Elias 1994 [1939]:385, 424, 430). From his perspective, the progressive levelling out of markers of strata and the homogeneity of forms of expression do not indicate the absence of conflicts. On the contrary, they are the result of tensions between groups and individuals who, with varying degrees of influence, have found ways of relating while being mutually dependent on each other.

The Established and the Outsiders – Class, Dominance and Social Conflict

Dominance and conflict – especially between social classes – is a recurring theme in discussions about civilising. The whole idea of class is based on the concept that people can be divided into higher and lower, more refined and cruder, classes of people based on their level of cultivation and livelihood. Here, we – like Loyal (2004:122–39); Bourdieu (1987); Elias (1994[1939]:382–3) and Faber et al. (2012) – stress that there is no one-dimensional stratification and that classes are not empirically identifiable entities. Yet this does not mean that no hierarchical structure exists. Rather the basis of this structure is variable, and cannot be reduced to predetermined or universal parameters such as people's financial situation, job or level of education. Class demarcations and relationships continuously evolve due to tensions and conflicts between individuals and different groups. Thus, there is no stable class structure; rather, there are numerous shifting relations of dominance that are expressed and maintained through various markers of distinction.

This discussion is relevant here because, as we will see, social distinctions – and the more-or-less subtle ways in which they refer to and co-construct social-class positions – play an important role in institutional childrearing, even in Danish children's institutions where everyday life is characterised by pronounced efforts at social inclusion and equalisation. The norms that children encounter in institutions reflect particular understandings of what constitutes good behaviour, and how one should express and conduct oneself. As Bourdieu and Passeron (1990 [1977]) demonstrated in their influential study of the French school, such understandings will always be related to social hierarchies. Though reflecting the notions of dominant groups of society, these understandings are presented as universal and incorporated into the institutional structure: sanctioned and standardised by the state and, thus, accepted as reasonable educational requirements for everyone. Hence the educational system reproduces the hierarchies of the social world by:

> transform[ing] social classifications into academic classifications with every appearance of neutrality and establishes hierarchies which are not experienced as purely technical, and therefore partial and one-sided, but as total hierarchies, grounded in nature, so that social value comes to be identified with 'personal' value, scholastic dignities with human dignity. (Bourdieu 1984:387)

In addition to this dynamic of social and cultural reproduction, we find that dominant groups have a tendency – as well as the necessary symbolic power – to monopolise recognised forms of behaviour and to maintain this monopoly by way of categorical inclusion. In our material this is illustrated when a child with a lower social or ethnic minority background behaves in an exemplary manner, or stands out by being academically accomplished. In such cases, the behaviour will often be interpreted as the lower-class child transgressing class boundaries or as an expression of the ethnic minority child's integration into Danish culture, rather than an occasion to review the relationship between higher classes, majority ethnicity, skills and civilised conduct (Gilliam 2009). In this way, such behaviour does not challenge the hierarchical classification or dominant groups' monopoly of appropriate and acknowledged manners. As we will show in detail in the empirical analysis of this book, this relationship between dominance and behaviour is crucial for understanding children's willingness to live up to institutional educational requirements. It is also relevant for interpreting parents' attitudes towards children's institutions and the civilising projects of teachers. Parents, teachers and children may all have different ideas about correct behaviour than those that prevail in society as a whole. And in this respect the rejection of established indicators of civilisation, such as what is seen as 'good manners' and 'nice language', can serve as markers of opposition towards those who monopolise the civilised forms of interaction.

It is precisely these relational, subjective and cultural aspects of class relations and identities that interest us here. Both Elias and Bourdieu describe how class positions are maintained, reproduced and challenged in ongoing symbolic struggles over whose understanding of reputation and norms of behaviour is valid (Bourdieu 1987; Elias 1994 [1939]:382–3). Using the concept of 'spurts' and 'counterspurts' Elias (1994 [1939]:382–3) epitomises these tensions, which are fuelled by power imbalances between different segments of society. Similarly, Bourdieu (1977: ch. 4) uses the dual concepts of 'orthodoxy' and 'heterodoxy' to indicate how an existing but rarely discussed order (doxa) can be the object of conflict between different social groups. In these conflicts class structures are consolidated as the dominant views (orthodoxy), formulated by groups who aim to uphold them, while other – previously dominated – groups challenge them by trying to make other views valid (resulting in a state of heterodoxy).

The mutual positionings can play out between groups that are defined in other ways than class – ethnic groups, age categories, gender divisions, groups of neighbours and so on. Using the concepts of 'the established' and 'the outsiders', Elias introduced general terms for the relationship between those who master or establish the codes in a specific context, and those who do not do so, which stresses its processual and hence precarious character (Elias 1994 [1977]). Moreover, these terms indicate the boundary demarcations that individuals and groups conduct in relation to others while they attempt to attain or maintain affiliation, influence and social legitimacy. Approached in this way, our material from Danish children's institutions shows several forms of social-boundary demarcation, such as stigmatisation, marking of similarity and exclusion. This bears witness to latent conflicts over group affiliation and the power to define behavioural norms, social distinctions and cultural values.

Disintegration and Decivilising

As we have already noted, one of Elias's key points is that integration processes are always an expression of a form of imperialism, whereby a dominant group incorporates culturally, politically or socially subjugated groups via the dissemination of standards and ways of living. Thus, he does not consider a well-integrated society to be necessarily an expression of equality and harmony, but regards it as a result of asymmetrical relationships that have settled into undisputed dominance relations – similar to what Bourdieu calls 'doxa'. Conflict and stability are interwoven in historical developments, with changes taking place due to tensions between social groups. This social power play is the driving force behind the civilising processes, but it is also what can shatter the veneer of civilised interaction.

Neither civilising nor social integration are processes that take a single progressive direction. Elias – and several of his successors – point out that there is always a latent possibility of disintegration or even 'decivilising' (Mennell 1990; Elias 1996, Dunning and Mennell 1998; van Krieken 1998; Swaan 2001). In his view, the Second World War confirmed that 'the armour of civilised conduct would crumble very rapidly' if there are changes to society that amplify a fear of the unpredictable in other people's reactions (Elias 1994 [1939]:532). Decivilising is a destructive reaction to instability and unpredictability, whereby trust in civilised interaction (which is the basis of social order) ceases and is replaced either by violent forms of regulation or by strict systems of control and surveillance that replace shame with fear and trust with control. Both civilising and decivilising tendencies are always present (Mennell and Goudsblom 1998:20). Therefore, conflicts between different groups in society not only represent a challenge to the dominant position; they also have the potential to undermine the dominance that ensures predictability and stability, and which forms the basis of the civilised order. Any power challenge involves a real risk of disintegration, as does any manifestation of power – including the power established to crush the challenge.

Thus, integration and disintegration, assimilation and distinction are some of the key dynamics in civilising processes. These aspects are also central to the analysis of childrearing practices in the Danish welfare state. As we will show, day-care institutions and schools attempt to integrate and assimilate children into the society in which they grow up; but these institutions also give rise to distancing, social tension and the risk of disintegration. In this sense, the institutions' educational priorities reflect relationships of dominance in society as a whole and, as a result, these institutions are also scenes of social tension, compromise and conflict, even though dissent is seldom articulated explicitly.

The Influence of Children's Institutions

It follows from the discussion above that we regard children's institutions as highly important sites for understanding social dynamics and cultural values in society. A main assumption in the book is that institutions like day care, schools and families are civilising institutions which mould children and their interactional forms in accordance with norms of what is regarded as civilised conduct, at the same time as they influence, reproduce and disseminate these norms. In our view, this means that these institutions are particularly suitable venues for anthropological and sociological explorations of cultural values, dominant perceptions and social hierarchies.

In order to follow this interest, we draw on and aim to contribute to the points made within the sociology of institutions, in particular the perspectives raised by Peter Berger and Thomas Luckmann (1966), Erving Goffman (1961), Mary Douglas (1986), Richard Jenkins (2004), Jaber Gubrium and James Holstein (2001) and Richard Scott (2001). In accordance with this, we regard institutions as predictable and well-established practices, routinised as 'how things are done' (Berger and Luckmann 1966:59–60). They can be formal institutions upheld by law, buildings or economic structures such as day-care institutions and schools and other public institutions, but they can also be informal institutions maintained through incorporated and repeated practices, roles and tasks such as the family. Either way, activities and behaviour are regulated and coordinated, routines establish a predictable structure of events and norms, and categories uphold a social order. In this sociological sense, institutions establish notions of the way things should be done and are – although this is often unacknowledged – highly influential in defining people's social orientation and the way they interact and see themselves.

As we will discuss further in the concluding chapter, this influence of children's institutions also stems from them being part of the state apparatus. According to Bourdieu, the school system is one of the main channels for the state to impose the categories through which we understand the world (Bourdieu 1994). While Bourdieu thus points to the cultural integrative force of state institutions, Elias emphasises how the evolving state agencies contribute to the social integration of individuals and groups into the institutional organisation of society (Elias 1994 [1939]:273–7). In his view, this has led to an extensive coordination and standardisation of people's interactions, which, yet again, enforces a high level of stability in terms of power and in relations between people (1994 [1939]:369). As such, state institutions such as children's institutions play a key role in the cultural and social integration and reproduction of the state.

It should, however, be noted that institutions do not simply reflect or transmit a dominant set of values. We will argue that social institutions in themselves influence notions of what it entails to be civilised. Through the daily formative work with children within specific institutional structures and according to institutional logics, norms of civilised social interactions are institutionalised in a dual way. They are *institutionalised*, that is, presented and routinised as the normal and proper way to act. But as we will argue, they also become *institutional* in the sense of being shaped and defined by the conditions and functionalities of everyday institutional life. Once incorporated into children, such institutionalised and institutional norms of civilised behaviour are disseminated in wider society as well-established understandings of how to behave and evaluate the behaviour of others. We will argue that this applies for all welfare societies with a comprehensive institutional structure of childcare and education. When a huge number of children spend their weekdays in nurseries, kindergartens and schools, the routines and functionality of these institutions will come to shape perceptions of what is appropriate behaviour for the individual and civilised interaction in groups. In this way, children's institutions are highly influential in constructing and spreading notions of what is civilised. The following analyses will demonstrate this institutional dominance, but also the interplay between different notions of what is best for the child, for the institution, and for society. One of our ambitions, as such, is to examine the link between everyday life in institutions on the one hand, and the societal context and cultural concepts of children, citizenship and notions of the decent and proper human being on the other. We do this by taking our point of departure in the specific context of Danish welfare society, as we find that this society provides a particularly illustrative case due to its high degree of institutionalisation of childhood. Yet we see in the approach a more general contribution to anthropological and sociological studies. The dual focus on everyday interactions and negotiations between various actors in and across society's main socialising institutions and broader social processes opens up insights into the establishment and dissemination of specific cultural understandings, values, moralities and distinctions. In this regard we find that the notion of civilising provides a useful analytical contribution to the existing literature on institutions, as well as on social and cultural reproduction within the field of education, with its particular focus on the moral dimension and social distinctions embedded in societal upbringing.

The Paradox of Civilising

The elements of dominance, integration and assimilation that we have outlined in this chapter point to an important dynamic in civilising projects, namely that integrating and marginalising processes are present simultaneously. One particularly important aspect of Elias's approach is the duality of the civilising concept, referring to both a prescriptive, universalist effort and a normative creation of distinctions and hierarchies. In his discussion of the history of European societies, he shows how groups with higher social standing have always been concerned with both subjugating and educating 'uncivilised' groups – children, other ethnic groups, lower social classes or colonised populations – according to their own world view, and in maintaining their own elevated rank by marking their superiority and distance (Elias 1994 [1939]:382–6).[7] As we have noted, the relative levelling out of social differences – which, for example, occurs when marginalised groups are included via schooling or other formalised educational initiatives – does not necessarily lead to an equalisation of social strata. As Elias stresses, groups of higher social standing will often refine the markers of distinction and find new ways of reproducing their social status, thereby undermining the equalising effects of any movement towards greater integration (Elias 1994 [1939]:382–6, 424).

Although Elias does not describe it as such, this process seems to represent a paradox which becomes particularly salient in children's institutions (Gilliam 2010). The very attempt to integrate the 'uncivilised' into the civilised way of life simultaneously has an exclusive or indeed counterproductive effect. Or, in other words, the monopolisation of the civilised ideal of specific categories of people may lead those who are not included in these categories to refrain from using the specific forms presented as civilised, and even to end up identifying themselves as being outside or in outright opposition to the civilised category. This kind of 'cultural inversion' (Ogbu 1987) often happens among young people who identify with marginalised social classes, subcultures, ethnic groups or gender positions. But it is also seen between parents and children, in which case adults monopolise the civilised position in relation to the uncivilised status of the child. Thus, as we describe in chapters 3, 5 and 6, the dual nature of civilising – as practices of inclusion and markers of distinction – means that civilising projects do not merely teach civilised forms. They also mark – and produce – 'uncivilised' physical and social behavioural forms, people, categories and symbolic figures which connote lower social standing in human hierarchies. Thus, the paradox entails that those concerned with civilising and integrating others simultaneously stigmatise and exclude many of the very people they aim to civilise and recruit into their own civilised category. In contrast to what is intended and expected, being brought up in families or attending day-care institutions or schools does not necessarily result in everyone behaving in a 'civilised' manner or regarding themselves as being included in the community. One of the contributions of this book is to show how and why teaching civilised behaviour sometimes fails and even has the opposite effect to what is intended, namely that some children use and come to identify with what is considered 'uncivilised' conduct – aggression, violence, bad language, vulgarity and challenges to power. The point is that civilising institutions – because of this embedded paradox – can both succeed in promoting certain ways of interacting and sow the seeds for the exact opposite. The risk of disintegration is latent, and can be the result of the integrative and civilising efforts of institutions.

Children's Contribution to the Social Dynamics in Institutional Childrearing

What the civilising paradox demonstrates is that adults' education of children – and, more specifically, society's and the state's intentions for new citizens – do not have known or unambiguous results. Elias alludes to this when, in the quote above, he states how 'the many single plans and actions of people can give rise to changes and patterns that no individual person had planned or created' (see p. 11). Taking an ethnographic approach that focuses on daily life and the actions of situated individuals instead of long-term historical processes, we try to unfold the way such patterns are formed, and show their ambiguity as well as their trends. Through the focus on everyday interactions we see how individuals and groups on different levels, interpersonal as well as organisational, struggle over and negotiate ideals, social order and cultural meaning. In these negotiations, children are both actors and symbols. As stressed by the anthropology and sociology of children and childhood, children are a subjugated and circumscribed group in most societies, yet they also have strategies and ways to influence, negotiate and comprehend their positions and possibilities (e.g. Hardman 1973; La Fontaine 1979; Corsaro 1997 James and Prout 1997; James et al. 1998; Olwig and Gulløv 2003). To understand the shape and outcome of civilising projects in children's institutions, we find it fruitful to add this child-research perspective to the theoretical framework of Elias. As we will see, children are influenced by, adapt to and challenge norms. They have other projects and ambitions than learning the social norms of behaviour and other criteria for status and hierarchies, and by practising these occasionally oppositional forms they sometimes challenge, sometimes perpetuate moral and social hierarchies (Willis 1977).

Moreover, children are themselves active civilisers, nurturing and disciplining one another and sanctioning and encouraging various types of conduct, just as they create friendships and communities on the basis of appraisals of each other's behaviour and social characteristics. As we will see in several chapters, they are often very aware of which norms apply in different institutions and situations; of what is expected of them as children; of which adults value or condone which kind of behaviour; and of how they themselves are seen in terms of their conduct by other actors, adults as well as children. As such, the identities, communities and distinctions they create are both closely related to the civilising project of the institutions and central to the outcome of the institutional upbringing.

At the same time, children have symbolic value for their caretakers. Childrearing is an expression of parents' proficiency as parents and of the professional ability of both teachers and pedagogues. However, these assessments also contain the potential for challenge and opposition, both for individuals (children, parents, pedagogues and teachers) who are marked as being 'not respectable', and for individuals who advocate other views of civilised behaviour than the dominant view. In this we see the micro-dynamics of civilising projects and processes. On a more macro-level, formative ideals and childrearing practices emerge through social negotiations and vary along with changing social balances. Although they are perpetuated by individuals in actual interactions with children, these ideals and educational practices relate to the wider social space and human figurations in which people are dependent on each other and, at the same time, enter into relationships of dominance that influence their orientations. In the next chapter, we will look more closely at these processes in Danish society, with a special focus on the emergence and development of children's institutions and the civilising ideals that these rest upon.

2

Society's Children

Institutionalisation and changing perceptions of children and upbringing

Laura Gilliam and Eva Gulløv

One of the central aims of public children's institutions is to contribute to the civilising, integration and peaceful coexistence of citizens. It is in these extra-familial institutions that children have to learn how to act and cope in contexts outside the immediate family. It is here they are expected to acquire the knowledge and skills that are deemed useful and relevant for them in order to perform and interact with others in educated and appropriate ways, and to participate in society as well-integrated citizens. However, neither ideals of civilised demeanour nor upbringing practices are static: that much is clear when considering Danish society in a historical perspective. Over the course of the past 150 years, changing perceptions of children, childhood, knowledge and behaviour have shaped both educational ideals and efforts and the way children's institutions are organised. Approaches to childrearing have changed and undergone professionalisation. The generation gap has grown at the same time as adult–child relations have been democratised and emotionalised. Various kinds of children's institutions have been established, with responsibility for an increasing amount of children's time and formation. In the following we will focus on such changes and discuss how children, childhood and childrearing entered the centre of public interest in the twentieth century and became hotly debated topics related to the civilising of citizens in the emergent welfare state.

The Introduction of Compulsory Education

In Denmark, the state-run institutional system of education dates back to 1814, when a large school commission initiated a new epoch of universal compulsory education. While these regulations initially received little support among the general populace, and had little effect on the everyday lives of most children, they do signify the first formalisation of the Danish state's influence on childrearing (Skovgaard-Petersen 1985:150–3). The stated objective was to teach all Danish children, including rural children, to be 'good and righteous individuals in accordance with the evangelical Christian doctrine, as well as teaching them the necessary knowledge and skills to become useful citizens of the state' (Danish School Act, 1814). In other words, one of the expressed aims was to ensure integration within the Danish state through the education of skilled, enlightened and patriotic citizens who were assets not merely to their families, but also to the state.

This interest in the new, young citizens was fuelled by Enlightenment ideals, philanthropism and the widespread ideas of patriotism of eighteenth-century Europe. This patriotism changed gradually into nationalism following the British attack on Denmark-Norway in the Battle of Copenhagen in 1801, Denmark's cession of Norway in 1814, and the influence of national romantic trends from France and Germany. The introduction of compulsory education for all children reflects this dawning national consciousness, but it also bears witness to changes in the social figurations in Danish society similar to those that Elias describes for Germany and France. These changes involved the growth of the bourgeoisie in the late eighteenth century, the increasing tensions between upper and lower classes, and the emerging consolidation and centralisation of the state towards the end of absolutism. The emergent state was based on the establishment of a number of administrative and educational institutions which were authorised to determine and regulate relationships between citizens, and between citizens and the state. In this regard, the integrative and civilising objective of compulsory education is very clear.

It is, however, important to stress again that, from an Eliasian perspective, state initiatives and formal regulations are the outcome of ongoing negotiations between different groups and organs of society which have different visions and interests. And formal regulations by the state do not in themselves alter the conduct of civilians – at least not immediately. The introduction of compulsory schooling for all children is indicative in this regard. Despite the royal regulations, it was almost a century before the majority of all Danish children went to school. This process was full of negotiations and conflicts between various religious movements, politicians of different persuasions, bourgeoisie and peasants, parents and state, all of whom had different ideas of children, what they needed, what they ought to know, and how they should spend their time (Larsen et al. 2013: ch. 18). In this way, the establishment of the school as a fundamental civilising institution in society cannot be perceived as an inevitable and intentional project, but illustrates how changes are the result of many single acts within human figurations, by people with their own agendas and desire for influence.

One of the controversial issues concerned who should be in charge of the upbringing of children. Both religious movements and groups of parents openly contested the legitimacy of the state summoning all children to school (Korsgaard 2004:333–6). Particularly in the rural areas, children were part of the household's workforce (or worked outside the home), and managing without their labour had huge implications. For this reason, many parents only gradually and reluctantly entrusted their children to schools (Coninck-Smith 2002:79–80, 219–20). However, there was also a more ideological concern over the kind of formative endeavours that took place in school. Particularly the Grundtvigians, a free-church movement led by the priest N.F.S. Grundtvig, who became a central figure in Danish cultural life, argued that ultimately it was the parents, and not the state, who were responsible for their children's upbringing and education. The controversy resulted in the Free School Act in 1855, giving parents the right to set up their own 'free schools' – although these schools were subject to regular monitoring by state representatives, ensuring that the children were taught the same skills as those imparted in state-funded schools (Korsgaard 2004:335–6). This act specified that in Denmark there was no compulsory school attendance, only compulsory education for children, implying that parents were obliged to ensure the education of their children – a law that still applies.

Despite the controversies, the state ended up having the main responsibility for the education of children. The establishment of regular compulsory schooling (either in the state-funded *folkeskoler* (the people's schools) or in state-subsidised and -inspected private schools) gradually institutionalised a contractual interdependence between parents and the state whereby the parents were expected to entrust their children to the school's project of citizen formation in exchange for formal education and cultivation. Yet it was not until the introduction of a number of worker protection laws (the first in 1873) that the utilisation of child labour was restricted. Thus the school only gradually gained access to more and more of children's time, initially in the cities, but later also in rural communities (Coninck-Smith 2002). Around the year 1900, virtually all Danish children received seven years of schooling. Even though negligence remained among groups of parents, and a number of compromises concerning schooling were agreed in various parts of the country resulting in huge local differences, the school thereby had become the locus of childhood.

The Need for Public Upbringing

The ambition to summon all children to school was partly influenced by philanthropists, who were eager to get children off the streets, away from hard labour and the ruthless adult world. In this we see the spread of romantic perceptions of children inspired by thinkers such as Jean-Jacques Rousseau and Friedrich Fröbel (Sigsgaard 1978), encompassing a new ideal of a civilised childhood. Yet the placing of children within schools also in itself came to affect the perception of children (Ariès 1962; Hendrick 1990). As the extent and frequency of child labour was reduced and school became children's primary occupation, their economic dependency was increasingly taken for granted and began to influence concepts of the nature of childhood. Schooling made children appear both innocent and incompetent, and therefore in need of education in institutions designed to simultaneously discipline them and inscribe them with the necessary and approved knowledge (Hendrick 1990:46). As such, the school institution was both based on, and created ideas of, what proper childhood should be.

Yet it is important to stress that although most Danish children attended school by the turn of the century, these schools were still very diverse. A range of state and private schools divided schoolchildren according to social class and urban and rural areas. As such, it was not a straightforward civilising project that lay at the root of the educational endeavours in various institutions for children in the nineteenth century and the first part of the twentieth century. It was not until the second half of the twentieth century, with the influence of the Social Democratic Party and the expansion of the welfare state, that schools became increasingly homogeneous and standardised in terms of their understanding of childhood and their educational practice.

Yet while the schools across the country slowly became more similar and undivided class-wise, the institutional structure became more differentiated, with various types of educational practices for different age groups and children with special needs. Of particular relevance for our discussion is the gradual establishment and expansion of day-care institutions. From a highly class-divided structure in the late nineteenth century, with asylums catering for children from the lower classes and Fröbel-inspired kindergartens for the bourgeoisie, the institutional division slowly began to dissolve as the contrast between them became too controversial for influential philanthropists. Based on Fröbel's ideas, the 'folk-kindergarten' was established, aiming to cultivate and educate children from the working classes before they entered school. In 1919 the Danish state was one of the first in the world to pass a resolution of financial support for early childcare institutions (Borchorst 2005:133–46). Though in financial terms this was initially a minor commitment, the resolution illustrates how the care of preschool children became a matter for the state. During the twentieth century, early childcare institutions gradually became more widespread and common as they slowly changed from offering support for children and families in need into a universal part of the educational structure offering professional care by staff with professional training (Gulløv 2012). It is noteworthy that these childcare professionals were not regarded as teachers (and, indeed, this is still the case), but constituted a distinct profession of 'pedagogues', who had special knowledge of young children and their upbringing. Through this process the involvement of the state gradually increased, expanding the investment in the general upbringing of children of all ages.

The Integration of Social Classes

As we have seen, the rise of state-regulated care and schooling for children granted the state control of at least part of the formation and education of children, and thus of the definition of what is best for both children and society. However, it is important again to emphasise the Eliasian point that changes in conventions and norms will always be related to changing power relations between social groups. To understand the development of the civilising project of the expanding welfare state, it is therefore important to look at the shifting social figurations in Danish society.

After the peaceful fall of the Danish absolute monarchy in 1848 and the diminution of the country (after the loss of first Norway in 1814 and then Schleswig and Holstein in 1864), Denmark went through a process of democratisation, industrialisation and integration. The constitution was adopted in 1849, transforming the Danes – with the notable exceptions of women, servants, men without property, criminals, foreigners and men below 30 years of age – into voting citizens. The population grew expansively from 1.4 million in 1850 to 2.5 million in 1901, mainly due to a decrease in infant mortality and health improvements. As in other European societies, more and more people moved to the cities to be employed in urban industries, and previously dominated groups such as the peasants and the new class of urban workers organised themselves and gradually challenged the hegemony and norms of the ruling groups. In 1915 women and servants gained the right to vote, and since the 1930s more and more Danish women have entered the workforce. All this amounted to a major process of democratisation and integration of social groups, which accelerated subsequently owing to the increased industrialisation and economic prosperity of the 1960s and the social mobility of the working class, resulting in a huge expansion of the middle class. In terms of norms of conduct, these processes of social mobility and integration, empowerment of the lower strata and levelling of class differences seem to have resulted in two different dynamics. First, the adoption of middle-class manners, lifestyle and aspirations by people from the working class; and, second, in the 1960s and 1970s, the break with formal manners and a less authoritarian and more flexible code of conduct (Wouters 2011:152; Elias 1994 [1939]:428, 430, 440).

Looking across these broader changes, the shifting power balances between social groups gradually, but decisively, contributed to the democratisation of manners and new, more informal norms of civilised behaviour. This also resulted in a change in the concept of children and what was considered the appropriate approach to childrearing. To understand this and the way it has influenced the civilising ideals and practices of the children's institutions of today, it is necessary to look in greater detail at the discussion and changes in regard to visions of childhood and educational practice since the First World War.

Visions of a Better Society – the Social Democratic Party and Educational Reformism

As described above, the changes in demography, interdependence and work patterns had increased the integration of social groups in Denmark and changed the power ratios between them even before the two world wars. This seems to have contributed to the gathering momentum in the interwar phase – the 1920s and 1930s – of two movements which were to become highly influential on the development of Danish children's institutions and childrearing practices. The first was the Social Democratic Party, based on the workers' movement, and the second was the educational reform movement. Though the aims of these movements sometimes overlapped, their projects were also distinct. At the election in 1924, the Social Democratic Party became the largest party in Danish politics and held power – often in coalition with other parties – for two-thirds of the remaining years of the twentieth century. It was this party that stood behind the gradual establishment of the welfare state and was the driving force behind postwar social and educational policy. In the interwar period, their main concerns were to reduce the church's influence on schools and make education less class-divided. Their vision was a free 'unity school' for all children, extended schooling for all children, and equal opportunities for entrance to lower-secondary schooling for working-class children. While the church's supervision of schools was eventually abolished in 1933, the unity school was not established until 1958, and not fully implemented until 1975. Yet the perception of education as a principal motor in the development of an equal and democratic society was expressed in the party's first steps towards the social politics of the welfare state, which were taken in the 1930s and 1940s.

In this period, the Social Democratic Party was influenced in particular by the ideas of Scandinavian 'social engineers', experts and intellectuals whom the party consulted (Thing 1996a). Swedish social-democratic couple Gunnar and Alva Myrdal's scientifically based social analyses were especially influential both in terms of the party's underlying philosophy and in what later became the Danish welfare policy (Thing 1996a). Their work contained reflections on population issues, combining the circumstances of family life and education in an integrated social policy. The central position of small children and school institutions is evident in Alva Myrdal's (1935) book *Stadsbarn* (City Child). Here, she took issue with society's ability to serve the interests of urban children, criticising it for failing both children and society. She presented a detailed argument in support of the idea that community-based childrearing was vital in ensuring future social cohesion, advocating the professionalisation of childrearing in 'collective nurseries' (*storbarnkammare*), while also presenting a vision of a society in which the task of childrearing is attended to communally (1935:80–7). Not only did such ideas strike a chord politically, particularly within social-democratic circles, they were also influential in terms of the educational debate in Denmark (Larsen 2010:279–80). The psychologist Jens Sigsgaard, for example, who was an active participant in the postwar educational debate in Denmark, presented virtually identical ideas about 'the kindergarten of society', arguing that kindergartens and schools should be considered social investments in a new form of citizenship (Sigsgaard 1947). Early childhood education was regarded as an important investment in order to establish a new society (Larsen 2010:280).

This was also a central idea within the educational reform movement (in which Jens Sigsgaard also took part), which became highly influential during the interwar and postwar periods. This national movement with international alliances comprised a wide range of psychologists, pedagogues and teachers, as well as artists and intellectuals connected to the movement of cultural radicalism, the political left wing during the interwar years, and later the resistance movement during the Second World War.[1] The horror and brutality of the two world wars, the spread of fascism and Nazism, and the perceived repression of rationality, humanity and individual freedom caused what can be seen as a 'civilisation anxiety' for the future. Fuelled by this, the movement developed visions of an alternative form of society driven by new generations brought up to believe in freedom, democracy and independent thinking (Nørgaard 2005). Thus they argued for revisions to established modes of upbringing and the need for school reforms. Although the educational reformists were not and did not become politicians, they had a strong influence on the normative agenda and their visions left their mark on much subsequent thinking on education, children's upbringing and what it means to be civilised.

Upbringing and education were not new concerns for those advocating reforms of society. As far back as the Enlightenment period, a number of influential individuals and movements, both nationally and internationally, had been preoccupied with public involvement, education and children's rights; and since the turn of the century some of the private independent schools had adopted a more liberal attitude to children and education, banning corporal punishment and rote learning. The aforementioned Grundtvigian 'free schools' had been especially influential, stressing a focus on the whole human being, enlightenment and teaching through 'the living word'. Yet the reform movement also launched new ideas inspired by burgeoning child psychology and the belief in scientifically based yet child-friendly teaching and assessment methods (Gjerløff and Jacobsen 2014: ch. 17). Inspired by these ideas, the reform movement advocated a liberal approach to childrearing, aimed at encouraging free and autonomous individuals by supporting their natural development and 'self-activity' (Nordentoft 1944:16–17; Øland 2010:72; for a similar discussion of the Germany case see Mannitz 2004). In particular, the authoritarian pedagogy of the school was seen as a threat to the development of the type of person and form of democracy that could protect society against dictatorship and fascism.

Notions of the Free and Natural Child – a New Civilisational Ideal

It is important to note that while educational reformists challenged the bourgeois norms and Christian morality which had hitherto dominated, they did not reject the need for civilising. In their view, forms of childrearing based upon notions of discipline, manners and the suppression of nature were rejected as oppressive and interpreted as expressions of bourgeois conservatism. To the contrary, the locus of the civilised was in the child (and in 'primitive man'), who was seen as closer to an unspoiled, original human nature, not yet destroyed or amputated by society, education and school (Thing 1996b). For the educational reformists, this understanding called for a 'mild' approach to discipline and a focus on the individual child, but also a careful, pedagogically supervised cultivation of the natural, free and rational consciousness (Hoffmeyer 1978 [1952]:112–13; Thing 1996b:81). The seeds of the civilised person lay in human nature, but had to be nurtured and set free through creative expression, enlightenment and personal initiative (Øland 2010). As a result, an early start was necessary in order to both safeguard and develop the child's nature. The child should therefore attend children's institutions not to discipline its uncivilised nature, but to protect and nurture its potential. Good childhood spaces should be created – kindergartens and schools designed for children, and secluded from the more callous (and in that sense uncivilised) adult world.

The reformists shared an anti-authoritarian educational ideal, placing individual liberty, tolerance and a rejection of violence as the cornerstones for a more humane society (Øland 2010). In the words of the pivotal child psychologist Sofie Rifbjerg, the aim was 'to improve people – make them more suited to living peacefully together and preventing a lust for power, bigotry and egoism from getting the upper hand' (1969:12, our translation). It was, as such, a civilising project which was both part of and contributed to the emergent change in and informalisation of relations between adults and children, social classes and the genders. The norms of decency and sexuality, public appearance and propriety, expressions of authority and thresholds of shame were particularly challenged, but a less rigid relationship between children and adults also slowly gained ground. While the teachers' union as well as the Social Democratic Party had been inspired by the reformist thoughts since the outset, it was not until after the Second World War and over the following decades that such ideas gained actual political influence. During postwar political negotiations these pedagogical ideas and a more sensitive approach to children were gradually incorporated into both the legal framework and vision of schools and kindergartens. By influencing the very core of society's formation of future citizens in this way, the educational reformists, with their critique of society, in fact became an integral part of the exercise of state power (Øland 2010:62).

The changes described above reflect how certain segments of society gained the opportunity to challenge existing notions and define and institutionalise new ideas about order, decorum and upbringing in the postwar period. The experience of the two world wars and the resulting collapse of the 'doxic' order seemed to have given this urge for a change of norms a larger appeal. Helped by a welfare state apparatus that was expanded and consolidated through this period, this emergent change of norms received broader support and gained momentum through policies and practice in state institutions. As we will see in the following, these new perceptions of education and children's nature and needs gradually gained authority and were established as doxa.

Educational Optimism and Societal Progression

Inspired by the visions of the educational reformists, a number of alternative kindergartens, schools and teacher training colleges were established over the next decades. Likewise, the vision of liberty, creativity and autonomy resulted in a showdown with authoritarian and passive knowledge transfer. It was particularly the school that became the focal point of the educational debate that followed in the wake of the anti-authoritarian rallying call in the early postwar period. The mantra was that the school should adapt to the child, not the other way round (Thing 1996b:210). The former rural and urban schools were united in 1958, and the 1960 teaching guidelines for this 'unity school' are a milestone in this new educational endeavour. Here, the emphasis is on teaching methods which encourage the enjoyment and active participation of students and which draw upon the child's own life and experiences, unlike the previous focus on rote learning, formal knowledge and exam preparation (*Undervis-ningsvejledning for Folkeskolen* 1960).

The new values are also evident in the description of the disciplines which, by contrast with the earlier focus on abilities, emphasised the self-realisation, imagination and emotional development of the child. This was also reflected in the reformulation of the school's objectives, which underlined that the school should not only improve children's skills and abilities, but, first and foremost, 'further every opportunity for children to grow up as harmonious, happy and good people' (*Undervisningsvejled-ning for Folkeskolen* 1960:29, our translation). The guidelines also stress that learning involves 'teaching students to adapt their conduct to a course such that it becomes natural for them to take into account the well-being of other people' (1960:24). In the burgeoning welfare state, the school assumed a new role. The idea was that it should contribute to a better, more harmonious and democratic society, so it was given a broader remit. Schools were now expected to be concerned with the whole person, ensuring the child's physical and mental health and, not least, its socialisa-tion (Hermann, 2007:71–2).

It should, however, be noted that while this educational approach was influenced by educational reformism, it was particularly its interest in the common good, and its belief in humanity, science and rationality that was adopted; not its faith in the child's nature, perspective and 'self-activity'. The Cold War and economic downturn of the 1950s made politicians eager to accelerate economic growth by 'mobilising the intelligence reserve' of uneducated young people, as a concurrent phrase put it (Gjerløff and Jacobsen 2014: ch. 19). And in the 1960s societal developments such as economic growth and a reorganisation of industry merely supported the new belief in education as a driver of progress and a strong faith in scientific rationality. This had an impact within the field of education, where â positivistic-inspired form of child psychology in particular came to influence mainstream educational thinking in schools as well as early childcare (Kampmann 2007). The idea was that the child should grow up as an informed, rational and well-socialised citizen, and it was therefore the task of the children's institutions to ensure this progress. Thus the civilising project gradually changed in tone over the course of the 1960s from unleashing the child's inherent potential to a greater emphasis on rational learning, applying modern educational methods in order to increase the general level of education and prosperity of both the individual and welfare society. This project, however, required support from the family. Modern childrearing required cooperation and systematic planning, and this demanded the backing of parents – especially the efforts of mothers – to bring up their children in accordance with the latest knowledge on child development and childrearing. The family also had to prove its worth as a civilising institution.

However, one challenge to this cooperation was that women were entering the labour market in large numbers: by 1970 about half of all married women worked outside the home (Borchorst 2000:60–1). This situation depended on the establishment of day-care institutions, the number of which had expanded enormously by the end of the 1960s. Until then, nurseries and kindergartens had only been a growing but relatively marginal phenomenon, but this changed rapidly. For the first time, public authorities became actively engaged in developing these institutions as part of the consolidation of the expanding welfare state. Early and partly state-financed childcare became a matter of state obligation, aiming (at least in principle) to take care of all children while their parents were working (Kampmann 2004:132). Opponents to this development were concerned that the institutional structure would damage the development of the individual personality structure (2004:34). But advocates argued, with reference to developmental psychology, that children were much better stimulated in well-designed environments with specialised staff trained to take care of children's development in ways appropriate for their age. The dispute faded with the growing number of working mothers and the responsibility for caring for, stimulating and socialising children thus became a task shared by parents and the welfare state.

Education for Equality

The belief in education as a relatively straightforward way to ensure progress was challenged as a focus on inequality caught on in the 1970s. The wide-reaching vision for educational policy (U90) launched by the Social Democratic Party states that one of the fundamental objectives of education policy must be to 'smooth out and reduce the major imbalances and inequalities in education' (U90 1978:128, our translation). While reflecting the contemporary Marxist critique of education as reproducing inequalities and the capitalist society, it also shows the persistent belief in social engineering which was a foundation for the welfare state project. Thus, despite the criticism, day-care institutions and schools were believed to have emancipatory potential, offering an opportunity for social change. In a practical sense, these institutions (and schools in particular) were supposed to be a training ground for a better and more just society (Hermann 2007:74–9). The greater awareness of the stratifying function of the education system led to the abolition of the separate academic stream at the lower-secondary level in 1975 and a stronger effort to establish a community spirit, participation and equality within school classes, both to ensure the best possible development and education for all students and as a prerequisite for society's cohesion and functionality (U90 1978:135). Elaborating the earlier educational reformism, a more consistent informal, anti-authoritarian and democratically oriented educational practice took centre stage and came to influence day-care institutions and schools, as well as adult–child relations, from the late 1970s. Free play, non-obligatory educational activities emphasising imagination, group work, voluntary subjects, scheduled weekly class discussions, creative and practical disciplines as well as project- and experienced-based teaching were employed in order to make education more adapted to and motivating for the child (Coninck-Smith et al. 2015). A central tenet was that democracy should not be taught but experienced through participation in a democratic environment, through engagement in pupils' councils and everyday decision-making in groups (Korsgaard 1999:97; Kampmann 2007:408). In this way, democracy was regarded not merely as a form of governance but as a culture; a particular – civilised – way of being part of a community which children's institutions should cultivate and incorporate from the earliest ages.

The Competent and Responsible Child

The democratic project and egalitarian visions were consolidated and further developed in the institutional practices of the 1980s and 1990s. In this period 'the self-management of the child', 'the child as a competent actor' and 'child democracy' became central tenets in pedagogical rhetoric (Kryger 2004:154–5). This focus on the child as an independent and competent actor derived partly from the influence of the educational reform movement, which had stressed the natural curiosity and self-activity of the child, and partly from the critical approach to education of the 1970s. It also stemmed, however, from a new international focus on the individual child as a holder of rights and as an individual with specific needs, illustrated by the UNESCO (UN Educational, Scientific and Cultural Organization) International Year of the Child in 1979 and later the adoption of the United Nations Convention on the Rights of the Child in 1989. As is also pointed out by Elias (1998a), these events illustrate a particular aspect of the civilising process: how the child gradually became a global figure with its own human rights.

Despite the emancipatory drive of this period, however, the emphasis on children's participation also resulted in new expectations for the civilised child: from educational reformism's understanding of the child as an independent being who should be offered opportunities for self-realisation of its natural potentials, to an expectation or even a requirement that the civilised child should be competent and capable of self-government in interaction with others. Thus considered, participation in decision-making, collaborative work and adaptation to shifting social commitments were not only a liberty but became a democratic duty of the child, institutionalised in daily routines in day-care institutions and schools. This gradually came to influence codes of conduct and norms of emotional expression in ways that can be described in terms of Wouters's depiction of the formation of a flexible 'third nature' (see chapter 1 and Wouters 2004:211). As we will see in the following chapters, these codes are still highly influential. The expectation that children should show engagement and commitment, be socially inclusive and responsible, and solve problems and conflicts through verbal negotiations brought an intensive focus on the need to behave in flexible ways, with a specific awareness and adaptiveness towards shifting social constellations.

This priority of social codes and the inclusive child community also placed focus on the parents' role once again, but this time in a different way. As we will see, particularly in chapter 8, parents were and still are not only expected to participate in the school's work as part of a democratic unity comprising school, child and parents, but are also responsible for ensuring that their child is capable of active participation, self-expression and socialising with others (Knudsen 2010).

Anxieties for the Future – Strengthening Academic Competences

By the end of the twentieth century, and in particular after the turn of the century, new expectations for children were added to the emphasis on children's participation and social interaction. Following the international oil crises in the 1970s, Denmark's economic growth and almost full employment were replaced by economic crisis and a big rise in unemployment. This crisis eroded confidence in the progress of the welfare society and in the social project of the school at the same time as it changed the power relations between groups in society. The right-wing liberalist critics of the welfare state and of the educational reformists' influence on the school gained momentum, and, as part of the efforts of successive governments to reform the Danish welfare state in the 1980s and 1990s, the role of the school was challenged. After a report in 1989 described the Danish educational system as the most expensive within the OECD and international tests in 1994 showed that results for Danish pupils' reading abilities were only average, a range of committees were set up, and policies and reports were issued outlining measures to ensure improved economic effectiveness and educational quality. While these policies did not change practice in schools from one day to the next, as the new initiatives were combined with established practices instead of taking over from them, the change does show a new focus in the state's childrearing project at the turn of the century. While the world wars had created an anxiety regarding the civilised state of future generations, and the Cold War had made politicians eager to 'mobilise the intelligence reserve', the acute awareness of competition in the globalised world at the turn of the century – or, in Eliasian terms, the new interdependencies and structures of dominance within the global figuration – made politicians turn to schools and the next generation once again, this time to future-proof the national economy. In the view of the political scientist Ove Kaj Pedersen, this changed the view of the school: it was now supposed to service the labour market rather than the welfare society (Pedersen 2011:186–8). This required, it was argued, a return to a focus on academic skills and new ways to measure and evaluate them.

Since the turn of the century, these tendencies have increased following Danish pupils' repeatedly average performance in the international PISA (Programme for International Student Assessment) tests. In relation to day-care institutions, it has caused a shift in focus, as new policies and technologies have been implemented to mobilise day-care pedagogues in children's preparation for school. This is perhaps most clearly evident in the change in the preamble to the legislation on day-care institutions from supporting the child's development of creativity and imagination in 1997 (Lov om Social Service, LBK no. 454) to promoting children's learning and acquisition of competences and ensuring a successful transition to school in 2015 (Lov om Dagtilbud, LBK no. 167, §7). While nurseries (taking care of children from less than 1 year up to the age of 3) and kindergartens (catering for 3–6 year-olds) had hitherto focused on giving the child time to play and learn to interact with other children, they are now required to focus a part of their time on 'learning', introducing children to numbers, colours, letters and so on. In this way, the youngest children have also become part of the national educational strategy – a priority also illustrated by the political efforts to have all children enrolled in day care as early as possible, and ideally from the age of 1. The need to intensify young children's academic skills is also reflected in a change in the institutional structure. From 2009 it became compulsory for all children to attend school from the age of 6, a year earlier than hitherto. The comprehensive school was hereby prolonged from 9 to 10 years, with an introductory 'Grade 0' (see chapter 5), thereby reducing the time spent in the looser educational programme of day-care institutions (nurseries and kindergartens).

As we will explore further below, the growing number of immigrant children in day-care institutions and schools, and their relatively poorer academic results, also played an important role in this new priority. The political stance taken by the Social Democratic Party, and the right-wing government which came into power in 2001, was to point to the need for a strengthened state intervention in childrearing processes. In this effort day-care institutions were considered of prime importance in order to ensure a proper and timely transmission of prevailing standards and skills needed in school. But, as stated in the legislation, the aim was also to ensure that children develop the ability to be part of Danish society (Lov om Dagtilbud, LBK no. 167, §7(4)). Thus it has gradually become a more explicit objective of early childcare institutions to identify and prevent risks and social problems in children and families as early as possible, and to help all children and their parents to live in accordance with dominant norms. The introduction of formalised assessments of preschool children's social abilities and linguistic skills links to this particular civilising project. In this way institutions for the youngest children have become a key tool of political intervention.

Also in schools, a whole range of new social technologies and practices has been introduced within the last 15 years. These include regular national tests, goal-directed teaching and pupil plans used to assess and increase the academic accomplishments of children. This allegedly reflects an important change in the political approach to schooling, as tests, individual assessments of young pupils and the kind of pupil subjectivity this is associated with had been shunned for decades. Pedersen even argues that this reflects that the purpose of the school is no longer to create citizens of the democratic state, but to equip the individual pupil to become 'a soldier in the competition state' (Pedersen 2011:172).

Yet, as will be apparent in the empirical chapters, this change in the political project has not yet created the massive change in viewpoints and practices that Pedersen and other Danish educational experts expected (Pedersen 2011; Hermann 2007; Moos 2014; Krejsler 2014). The new academic focuses do have an effect on how time and teaching are planned, and may possibly change the norms of appropriate conduct over time. However, when such policies meet the everyday institutional practices of Danish day-care institutions and schools, they apparently become adapted to the existing routines and to teachers' values of child-centred pedagogy, equality, democracy and inclusive communities which are embedded in these practices. At the same time, the policies themselves often stress these established values. One example of this is the latest reform of the schools in 2014. The main objective of this reform, initiated by the Social Democratic Minister of Education Christine Antorini, is to 'challenge all pupils to become as competent as they can'. Yet the aim is also to reduce the influence of social background on academic outcome and to enhance trust and well-being in school (*Aftaletekst om skolereform* 2013). This is to be done by using well-established didactic forms and moral projects such as hands-on teaching and a focus on social relations, indicating that a unilateral focus on academic skills is still associated with a problematic past of rote learning and a hostile school environment for children. Even before depicting the aims of the reform, it is thus stated: 'Our school is among the best at developing students into active citizens and giving them good social skills', 'the students are well prepared for their future lives as citizens in Denmark', and 'the Danish pupils have good interpersonal skills and the culture of debate and the social climate of the school and in the classroom is generally good' (*Aftaletekst om skolereform* 2013:1). The fact that the text starts with these affirmative statements shows that an intensive focus on academic optimisation is only acceptable if it has been firmly established that the school's civilising work is in place and that it is therefore legitimate to embark on a project of refinement.

National Integration and Enhanced Expectations

Simultaneously with these changes to the schooling project, another formative project has been pushed to the forefront by politicians. The educational policies of the period from the 1990s to the present day have been characterised by a more explicit focus on Danish history and culture. In 1993, a new aim was added to the school law, stating that the school 'should make children familiar with Danish culture' (Lov om Folkeskolen, LBK no. 509, §1(3)); and in the first decade of the new century the right-wing government advanced this national agenda by introducing canons of history and Danish literature to be taught in schools (Kryger 2007; Gilliam 2009). In the legislation on childcare, a similar national inclination is apparent. With a clear reference to children of immigrants, one of the stated objectives is that the child should develop 'solidarity with and integration within the Danish society' (Lov om Dagtilbud, LBK no. 167, §7(4)).

From a civilising perspective, these tendencies to prioritise children's academic skills and national identity testify to a shift in the social figurations through the last 25 years, which has made itself apparent in new interpretations of what characterises the well-integrated and commendable individual and society. At a time of increased immigration, international integration and competition (often referred to as 'globalisation'), and the shock of the financial crisis in 2008, the enhanced political focus on learning and cultural formative processes can be regarded as an attempt to curb challenges to the established order and strengthen national integration. As Elias describes in his analysis of 'the Germans' before and during the world wars, 'mobilisation of national sentiments' and 'conformity with [...] national ideals and norms' are often the result of situations of 'mounting threats and anxieties on the international level' (Elias 1996 [1989]:353–62). That the current surge in these sentiments is part of a broader European tendency can be seen in a study by Schiffauer et al. (2004) of what they call 'civil enculturation' in Dutch, British, German and French schools. While the formation of national identities has always been a trait of the school as a national institution, the widespread and recently intensified fear of national and cultural disintegration (not least due to the influx of 'outsiders' in the form of migrants and refugees) seems to have reinforced this effort (for a similar discussion see Jenkins 2011). In this light, the need to ensure and improve the transformation of the new citizens can be seen as an attempt to protect the established order of the nation by upholding and securing particular civilised forms.

However, the field today cannot be characterised by any sort of clear orthodoxy. Various influential groups advocate for their views on the tasks of educational institutions in relation to both children and society, and the battle lines are clearly drawn. Some groups refer to a culturalist understanding that civilised behaviour is a particularly Danish (and Western) phenomenon, best maintained by teaching children about Danish history, culture and norms with an explicit civilising offensive towards children of immigrants or refugees (see discussion of 'civilising offensives' in chapter 1). For others, the task for schools and day-care institutions is primarily of an academic nature and is regarded as providing the basis for both the individual's and the nation's future opportunities within a globalised world. Others again view the focus on tests, academic prowess and 'Danishness' as too reminiscent of rote learning and nationalism, thereby constituting a civilisational retrogression to a more authoritarian and less tolerant society. When taken at face value, the increased focus on academic betterment and nationalistic reinforcement seems to challenge hitherto existing civilising ideals for the child and the community. However, as in the case of the latest school reform, our empirical data suggest that institutional childrearing does not change abruptly. Testifying to the inertness and reproductive logic of institutions, these new priorities rather seem to be added to the existing norms and an attempt is made to incorporate them within institutional practice. As we will argue, the new demands placed on the individual child merely add to existing requirements for the civilised and competent child: academic excellence, versatile individual development, honed social skills and adaptation to the larger community.

Shifting Civilising Ideals for Children and Childrearers

The development we have described testifies to some important changes in relation to childrearing, institutional objectives and the constitution of Danish welfare society, reflecting a changed relationship between adults and children and the role of children in society. While there has been a resurgence of concern regarding a disciplinary crisis in schools and we are presently witnessing another quest to re-establish the authority of teachers and the centrality of academic competences in schools, there is little call for a return to an authoritarian style of upbringing or to the obsequious child of yesteryear. Today children and adults, parents and teachers, engage in informal relationships and communication forms, just as it is widely accepted throughout the Danish society that children should not be beaten, chastened or held down by authoritarian adults, but instead given opportunities for self-expression and self-realisation.

This change is not only a Danish phenomenon. As we have touched upon several times, Elias describes a general process of informalisation of the relation between adults and children in Western Europe. Over time, social regulation and physical distance in the form of increased institutionalisation have been accompanied by a democratisation and an emotionalisation of adult–child relations (Elias 1998a:208, van Krieken 1998:156). The increased focus on the susceptibility of the psyche, and here especially on the developmental, emotional and relational importance of childhood, has changed the nature of the responsibilities of those rearing children. The civilised educator should cultivate, not suppress, and must keep her or his temper and act tenderly and considerately in relation to the child (Øland 2010:79; Hermann 2007:69). In the Danish case, the process of informalisation has also changed the ideals of childrearing from celebrating obedience to an emphasis on participation, engagement and awareness of others. Whereas the function of childrearing was previously seen as the transfer of a relatively clear-cut code of standards, the priority now in Danish families, day-care institutions and schools is that the child should develop the ability to appraise and adapt to shifting social contexts, yet also have the self-confidence to stand up for his or her viewpoints. In this way, the task of childrearing has shifted from knowing the rules to understanding the game; a complicated effort requiring considerable investment of time and awareness. However, as will become apparent in the following chapters, this vague authority structure has made the task of childrearing more complicated. Successful childrearing requires constant attention to and engagement in the individual child through educational practices such as guidance, encouragement and correction in order to establish the child's self-control and independent stance (for a similar discussion, see Bach 2014, 2015). The democratisation of generational relations does not, therefore, equate to a relaxation of the attention paid to the conduct of the child; on the contrary, greater attention is necessary in order to ensure that the child develops social sensitivity and avoids inappropriate verbal and physical behaviour, as well as demonstrations of inequality and conflict.

In this sense, the democratisation of relations implies a new form of social distinction. As Bach shows in chapter 8, parents – and particularly mothers – display conspicuous engagement and an investment of both feeling and time in their children's activities, conduct and relationships. This attention seems to reflect a greater focus on children's well-being, but also that children are part of social stratification processes, both as active participants and as objects for investment and status. As children act on their own in multiple social contexts, they become indicative of their

family's social and civilised status. In a similar vein, children's active participation in association activities and democratic events, for instance, has
become a symbol of a democratic and civilised society (see Kjørholt and
Lidén 2004; Anderson 2008:203–4). In this way the informalisation of
authority structures and democratisation of intergenerational interactions
have turned children into important social symbols, giving civilised status
to those parents and educators (and nations) that know how to include
and listen to children in respectful ways and include this in the formation
of active citizens.

Although these attitudes towards children's voices and democratic participation have become less prominent in recent years, the general picture
points to an unmistakable increase in the attention devoted to children
over the course of the last century. Children and their welfare are now
taken into account in political priorities, economic measures, labour
market initiatives and practical arrangements; they are part of the very
definition of a family, and children's institutions constitute a fundamental
part of the fabric of the welfare society. From being of value as labour – and
economic capital – the child has become a symbolic form of capital which,
through successful upbringing, bears witness to the democratic spirit and
social decency of both parents and welfare society. It is in this light that
society's great interest in children should be seen. Historically, a link
has been established between the education of the next generation and
society's democratic and civilised nature, requiring a strong investment,
both symbolically and practically, in children and their upbringing. In
a certain sense, children and the institutions devoted to their care and
cultivation have become a focal point of the civilising missions and
assessments of civilised society in today's Danish welfare society.

Coexisting Ideals and the Everyday Life of Institutions

As is evident from the historical outline we have presented in this chapter,
the perception of children, the role of institutions for children, and what
characterises civilised behaviour have changed in line with new social constellations, power relations and conflicts. During this time, institutions for
children, especially schools, and their education of new citizens have been
a subject of constant debate and change, as has the form and function of
this education within society. This underlines that the state and politicians
may have a widely accepted right to establish the overall framework for
the institutions of childhood, but that the content remains open to debate

and is regularly adjusted to reflect shifting social and global figurations. In every institution included in our study, we have identified opinions and understandings reflecting the traditional appreciation of formal manners, the humanistic worldview found in educational reformism, the social-democratic welfare project, educational optimism, the focus on the inclusive and democratic community, the new concerns with academic prowess and national values, and the general informalisation of social and generational relations. However, we have also witnessed that these ideals are sometimes conflicting and are therefore often the subject of debate, not just in the long term, but right here, right now.

Ethnographic material of the kind we present in this book can show how changes in educational approaches – seen, for example, in legislation, textbooks and journals – do not necessarily dominate the institutions' practice in the way that discursive analyses often imply. As noted, there is no direct route from educational debate or political ambition to institutional practice (Shore and Wright 1997; Sutton and Levinson 2001). In several of the book's chapters, we will see how different values and educational rationales exist side by side, merge together or compete as the legitimate educational forms and ideals. Borne as they are by individual historical actors – pedagogues, teachers, institutional managers, youth workers, parents and educational researchers – who have grown up through these periods and have encountered and internalised the values during their own upbringing, schooling, education and professional lives, they are often present simultaneously despite historical transformations and political projects.

This means that the educational forms and norms of institutions for children reflect not only current social conditions and dominant discourses, but also various contemporary configurations of the historical accumulation of values, rationales and experiences and the specific institutional structures and practical conditions which have left their mark in this field. Thus, we will argue that it is not possible to understand institutional childrearing and civilising projects purely on the basis of policy and discourse analysis, or as a result of historical processes like those presented in this chapter. It is in the everyday interactions between children and adults in local children's institutions that values are realised, manifested and have an effect – and it is here that political currents and ideological rationales can gain influence or run aground, be reshaped and receive new meanings.

3

Civilising the Youngest

An ambiguous endeavour

Eva Gulløv

This chapter offers an analysis of the civilising endeavours in Danish nurseries and kindergartens. These are the first institutions outside the family that children attend, often from their very first year of life. For about five years, they spend their weekdays here, yet the precise educational goals are not particularly well described. In my analysis I will explore what it is, more specifically, that children are supposed to learn during these early years. What are the civilising ambitions behind the educational priorities?

The material used for this analysis is based on participant observation and interviews conducted during three ethnographic fieldworks in four day-care institutions. The first period of fieldwork (no. 1) was carried out over six months in a kindergarten in Copenhagen in 1995 and 1996. The second (no. 2) was conducted over six months in 2002 and 2003 in two day-care institutions, both with a nursery and a kindergarten section, in a provincial town in northern Zealand. The third (no. 3) took place in a Copenhagen kindergarten over two months in 2007 and 2008, with a short follow-up visit in 2011. The data consist of written field notes, video recordings of everyday interactions and audio recordings of interviews with children, staff and parents.

In a cumulative perspective, the material is based on a total of 14 months of daily observations distributed across three phases spanning 16 years. Over this period a range of new administrative procedures and control measures, including the introduction of learning specifications and language tests, have altered pedagogical working conditions considerably. Despite these changes, I find a high degree of consistency in the civilising work in the institutions; for instance, in the views of proper interactions, child development and ideals of upbringing. Across the three studies, a strong focus on social skills can be identified; however, it also becomes clear that the civilising ideal children encounter in everyday interactions is somewhat composite, aiming both to make them adapt to context-specific social requirements and to express their individuality. As I will show, this complexity in terms of what is considered civilised behaviour allows a certain degree of leeway, which represents an opportunity for those children who are able to decode the norms, but also constitutes a challenge for those who are not, thus making social distinctions an integral part of this otherwise very socially inclusive civilising ideal.

A Short Note on Danish Day-Care Institutions

As outlined in the previous chapter, early childcare institutions have changed considerably during the past 100 years. From offering stimulating pedagogical activities to children from affluent families on the one hand, or childminding and safekeeping to the less privileged on the other, the institutional profiles gradually changed into a project for all children regardless of background. This change was part of the consolidation of the welfare state and can be dated to the early 1960s, or, more precisely, to the epoch-marking law on child and youth welfare from 1964 (Lov om Børne- og Ungdomsforsorg, no. 193, 4. juni 1964), which emphasised the need for universal childcare as a responsibility of the state. The law specified institutional obligations, established a framework for public funding and repealed parental income as a criterion for admission. From this time on, the number of day-care institutions expanded, as did the state's investments in the sector (Bayer and Kristensen 2015; Borchorst 2005). While few parents in the 1950s availed themselves of the possibility of sending their children to kindergartens, the 1960s and 1970s saw an increase in their popularity and a growing number of children were enrolled. Since the mid 1980s, nurseries and kindergartens have been an integral part of a typical Danish childhood. In contemporary Danish society, almost all preschool children attend a day-care institution (see outline in Gulløv 2012). Throughout the period of the expansion of the day-care sector, the upbringing of children has become ever more profes-sionalised and subject to state legislation and authority. In this process, childhood and childcare institutions have increasingly become the subject of political scrutiny and of intense discussions concerning investment and societal outcomes.

Despite the widespread use and acceptance of public care for young children, the overall objective is only described in general terms in formal juridical documents, as well as at the level of the individual day-care institution. There is no formal curriculum and though transition to school is a pronounced focus, in practice planned activities are most often organised around themes considered relevant or of interest to the specific group of children. A more detailed exploration is therefore required to find out what children are expected to learn over the course of the years they spend in such institutions.

When looking at the everyday organisation of activities, in all four institutions where I conducted fieldwork, there is a loose but recognisable structure. There is no fixed registration time and children therefore arrive at a time that fits into their parents' lives: for most children before 9.30 in the morning when organised group activities usually begin. Though children are not required to participate, the older children are encouraged to take part and parents are asked to drop off their children in good time. Lunch is around 11 to 12 o'clock, after which it is outdoor play time for a couple of hours. About 2 p.m., a light afternoon snack is served followed by various activities initiated by the children themselves until they are picked up by their parents. In this structure there are many opportunities for children to make their own decisions with regard to what to do and with whom. However, the loose and rather free structure does not mean that the pedagogy is without norms or intentions, as I will show in the following. As demonstrated in many ethnographic monographs, Scandinavian kindergartens[1] are characterised by an open and child-friendly pedagogical form, with gentle regulations for behaviour. The organised group sessions and the high priority given to the children's own activities are meant to work as a non-regulative way to gradually instil social norms in the children. The open form reflects a cultural idea of children as active participants in their own socialisation process, and the task of the early children's institutions is, therefore, to support and carefully cultivate their autonomy through a soft pedagogy.

'To Be Social' as a Civilising Ideal

This prioritisation of the gentle guidance of children in order to nurture autonomous individuals is, however, only one aspect of the pedagogical project. Another side of it became apparent during my periods of fieldwork, where a recurring theme in my conversations with staff was their emphasis on the importance of making children social (see chapter 5 for a similar focus in school). The term was used in relation to quite different situations and appeared to be a way of assessing the individual child and the forms of interaction in the group. However, it was also presented by staff as a pedagogical objective, as the following excerpts illustrate:

Hanne: Well, we really try to teach them to be social. They should, for instance, learn to empathise with other people's thoughts and emotions. That it hurts when you slap someone and therefore you shouldn't do it. Or that it is not pleasant if someone screams in your face. So, you should try to communicate in more appropriate ways [...] But also understand that it is possible to talk instead of solving conflicts by fighting. (Fieldwork no. 2)

Or as Anette, a pedagogue, explained when I asked her why she had repeatedly urged three children to listen to the others during a recently completed group activity:

Anette: Of course, they are just young children and they are not able to stay in the background and be considerate. But that is what they are here to learn. When they start school, they should be able to sit still and raise their hands when they want to speak, while also listening to what the others have to say. However, that is actually not what is foremost in my mind in such a situation. The point is not to make them obedient or to 'train' them [voiced with an ironic inflection and a smile]. To me it is much more about basic social competences. [...] In fact, that you respect others, show due consideration, and do not want all the attention yourself.

Eva: Yes

Anette: These days it is evident that the parents see their children as projects [...] and allow them to do whatever they want. But this may impair their social abilities. To me it is extremely important that you learn to be considerate and to control yourself. Remind yourself that there are other people in the world.

Eva: Do you experience that this is something you need to teach the children?

Anette: Yes, that is something you need to know. In fact I see it as the most important part of upbringing, to teach children to be considerate and sometimes accept second place. So that is what I work on. [...]

This is what is required to be in a group. If you want to be part of a group, you darn well need to be able to adapt. Basically, it is all about being social, showing respect for others without, of course, repressing yourself [...] (Fieldwork no. 3)

The notion of 'the social' illustrates a clear prioritisation of teaching children to control themselves, suppress their impulses and show respect for others, as these things are perceived as prerequisites for the establishment of a harmonious and functional community. As can be seen from the excerpts, the children should learn not to be too wild and rough towards each other, and not to disturb other people's activities. They should become familiar with conventions for communication and interaction, such as solving conflicts with language instead of violence. In this way, being social is an expression of basic understandings of how the individual's relations to other people ideally should be and, by extension, what the purpose of the pedagogical task must be.

In many ways, this understanding can be seen as an empirical equivalent to the theoretical concept of civilising (see also chapter 5). It reflects the general focus on norms of interaction and the exercise of self-control, which, according to Norbert Elias, have gradually become part of inter-personal relations in Western Europe (Elias 1994 [1939]). As mentioned in chapter 1, interacting with and depending on others in an ever more integrated society increasingly demands that the individual is able to adapt his or her appearance and emotional expressions to ever changing situations and social contexts. In this process, upbringing becomes increasingly focused on teaching children to control their urges, impulses, feelings and inclinations, particularly with regard to physical aggression (1994 [1939]:169–72). Judging from the efforts to regulate children's behaviour that I have observed, it is precisely this type of self-control that the pedagogical work in Danish day-care institutions addresses (see Dencik 1989). The children are corrected when they become too loud and lively – when they storm through the rooms or hit and kick each other – and they are instructed to communicate in considerate and peaceful ways.

Despite the recurrent emphasis on being social, the pedagogical objective appears to be somewhat more complex. While children are taught to control and master their impulses and urges, I have also registered a recognition and respect for the young child's autonomy and not-yet-civilised approach to life (see chapter 4). The dirty child should learn to wash, but the mud on the hands is also recognised as an expression of an authenticity in the contact with nature which the adult has lost. Veneration for lost innocence seems to be part of the perception of young children and is expressed in a number of composite reactions to their dirt, noise and savagery. In that sense, the approach to upbringing involves a certain degree of ambivalence per se. As discussed in chapter 2, this ambivalence must be seen in a historical perspective. Stemming from the educational reform movement, recognition of the young child's naturalness and spontaneity gained ground in the postwar decades, leading to a shift from manifest authority structures to an increased empowerment of the child. This development resonates with a general 'informalisation' in the codes of conduct which, as described by Cas Wouters, led to a celebration or even 'cult' of people from the working class and of children as being more natural, forthright and uninhibited (Wouters 1986:4).

In the material upon which this chapter is based, this informalisation is reflected in the staff's general rejection of obedience and discipline as desirable qualities among children, and their efforts to nurture the children's autonomy and ability to speak up for themselves while at the same time being socially inclusive and responsive to others. The line of thinking is that, while norms of interaction are important, they must not become inflexible or irksome fetters impeding the development of the individual child. There must be tolerance, but not blind adherence to demands. The pedagogical task embodies a complex challenge since the individual's adaptation and regulation to the norms of the group of children should neither limit the potential of the individual child nor suppress sincerity in the expression of emotions. Thus, a systematic intervention can be observed in terms of teaching children norms for communication and social interaction, yet a pronounced resistance to any pedagogical approach regarded as too controlling is also found. Children's behaviour should be balanced, at once enabling them to engage in various social contexts and to express their individuality.

Controlling Bodily Expressions

This balance between the formal and the informal – teaching the children norms of social interaction without enforcing rules – is particularly salient when it comes to children's bodily movements. Explicit directives are a regular part of everyday life, for example when teachers admonishingly say: 'Please sit still while you eat'; 'Do not run around in here. You know very well that you are not allowed to run wild indoors'; 'Keep your shoes off the table'; 'If you need to let off steam, go to the rough-and-tumble room'; 'Please sit still if you want to participate when we read aloud' – to pick out just a few examples from the observational notes. However, more implicit guidance is also part of the daily flow, either in the form of well-established routines (walking in line and holding hands while on excursions; washing hands after using the toilet; sitting down while eating, etc.) or in the way the spatial organisation and the interior design indicate what should and must happen where. For example, the functional sectioning of rooms – dolls' corners, rough-and-tumble rooms, toilets, wardrobes, places to eat – distributes the children and invites them to participate in some activities rather than others (Gulløv and Højlund 2005).

The child is expected to be able to understand and comply with such guidance, preferably without being told. It ought to know that the rough-and-tumble room is for tumbling, the playground for running, jumping and cycling, the lunch table is for sitting down quietly, the dolls' corner is for playing calmly, the small tables are for working with beads and drawing, and role-play games take place in the corners laid out for that purpose. The child is also expected to be familiar with and adhere to the time structure, knowing the specific times for different activities. It is precisely the incorporation of these understandings that is the aim of the staff's efforts: children should know how and when to move and have a well-developed sense of things, places and who is present, for example when to take up space and be the centre of attention, and when to calm down and be quiet.

The requirements regarding the children's movements and behaviour are not solely defined by institutional functionality. The pedagogical project is much more comprehensive, reflecting cultural ways of interacting and communicating. Gunter Gebauer and Christoph Wulff (2001:105) address this dimension of civilising young children, when they argue that institutions of upbringing require and encourage certain body postures and forms of gesticulation that refer to generally acknowledged norms of body conduct (see Palludan 2005). When children participate in daily activities, they are supposed to incorporate the cultural codes of physical proximity and distance, of movements and gestures, in relation to various types of social situations. At least for those children who are met with praise and encouragement, this knowledge gradually becomes a habitual way of moving and interacting, yet also of judging other people's behaviour. In this way, the institutional structure has a strong formative impact on children's bodily expressions, interpretations of others' expressions and understanding of implicitly communicated expectations.

However, children do not always conform to the expectations they encounter. Other impulses can make it attractive to act differently, and adaptation is thus not the only response. Despite the institutional requirements, one can observe children running and shouting, climbing and jumping, throwing things around, tumbling, and dancing. The following example shows how children, despite being aware of the expectations, attempt to circumvent the rules by using objects in ways that are not allowed:

Ahmed and Michael have gathered some pillows in front of a bookshelf angled against a wall in the big room. By mutual agreement they take a good look around, and when they think they are not being observed (in their experience, the field observer does not interfere, so she doesn't count), they get a table, place a chair on top, and crawl on top of the shelf. From this position they jump onto the pillows and repeat the action while alternately laughing and hooting, shushing each other, and scouting nervously for possible interventions. As soon as an adult appears, they freeze and assume innocent expressions. When the coast is clear, they climb the forbidden bookshelf again and jump onto the pillows. This sequence of events is repeated many times. After a while, Ahmed is about to jump when he sees Jonathan.

Ahmed: Jonathan!
Jonathan: [Looks up at him] I will tell on you.
Ahmed: [Jumps down] I won't do it again.
Michael: I will do it again.
Michael climbs up, Ahmed follows him. Gül, a kitchen employee, enters the room.
Gül: Ahmed, no.
She turns her back to take buns out of the oven. Both boys rush onto the bookshelf, jump, and subsequently assume innocent expressions. When she goes to find something in the fridge, they do it again. They laugh conspiratorially. A moment later, the pedagogue Sofie enters, and Ahmed quickly sits down on a chair and smiles at her. Michael climbs the bookcase again.
Sofie: Hey, you cannot climb the bookcase. It could be dangerous. Will you stop at once! It is not a climbing frame.
Michael climbs down. (Fieldwork no. 2)

As demonstrated by this example, the children occasionally bypass rules, as well as expectations as to how the inventory should be used. The staff upholds the regulations, but, like Gül, they also turn a blind eye to many transgressions. As long as nobody hurts themselves or others, the personnel make allowances for minor breaches of the rules and comments celebrating children's creativity in such cases are by no means rare. The following dialogue took place later the same day:

Birgitte: Oh, you should have seen Jonathan this morning. He devised a
   way to use the bookshelf as a springboard. He jumped into the pillows
   and called them the 'pool'. I thought that was quite clever. And he
   succeeded in getting several of the others to join in.

Sofie: Ah, I don't consider that okay.

Birgitte: Well, it went all right. At first I was in doubt about how
   dangerous it was, but nothing happened. And he was really good at
   helping the younger ones.

Sofie: Hmm, I was actually in the room at an earlier stage, and I stopped
   Ahmed and Michael jumping from the bookshelf. I really think it is
   too dangerous, and I find it unacceptable.

Birgitte: Okay, perhaps – yes, I could well imagine that Ahmed and
   Michael perhaps could not control themselves and could not take
   proper care of the younger ones. Certainly not Ahmed. But Jonathan
   could, and it is also important that they are allowed to try some
   things out. I think that, hmmm, perhaps we should distinguish
   somewhat between them as individuals, because we can also become
   too controlling. In fact it is more important that they learn to assess
   whether the situation is dangerous or not, rather than doing precisely
   as we say. We also have to give them the opportunity to be a little
   creative without interfering constantly. In any case, some of them are
   perfectly capable of handling such situations. (Fieldwork no. 2)

Evidently, the attitudes of the pedagogues vary, as do their views on specific situations and interpretations of individual children. Some children can get away with things that others cannot. This variation is, however, neither merely an inevitable aspect of a composite organisation, nor a glitch in an otherwise thoroughly planned civilising project. It is, in fact, part of the ideal. To be flexible and socially inclusive are central aspects of the civilised ideal, as expressed in the following excerpt:

Søren: We are all different, and for this reason I would emphasise rules in a situation which some of my colleagues would reject. The children know full well that nobody is alike. The information they get varies according to the pedagogue they talk to. Actually, I do not see that as a problem. On the contrary, in fact. […] I think it is quite OK that they learn that we all have different limits. […] They should not learn to be obedient. They need to learn that it is nice to spend time together. And that it will only be nice if you are considerate towards those around you, meaning that you respect their limits. The world is not a template, and they must learn to deal with differences. (Fieldwork no. 1)

Søren clearly states that situational adaptation, flexibility, inclusiveness and attention to individual differences are part of an anti-authoritarian, socially oriented civilising project. The project doesn't have a specific formula, nor can it be expressed as a regulated programme for raising children. It instead emphasises ambiguity as part of life, therefore requiring continual interpretations by the adult pedagogue, as well as by the children. In this perspective, the many ignored breaches of rules can be interpreted as a deliberate pedagogical effort to support the autonomous individual in finding its own way without transgressing others' boundaries. Abiding by the rules or submitting to authority are not virtues in this type of pedagogical approach. While analysing the part of the material where the pedagogues discuss or explain their priorities, I detect widespread reservation towards what is regarded as an excess of neatness and conformity, as seen in the following three quotations by pedagogues from two different day-care institutions, the first two addressing the way some of the immigrant children are dressed:

Lone: Well, in my view it is a little over the top. Of course it is fine that little girls want to be pretty and wear dresses, etc. That also goes for the Danish children. But when it comes to long skirts with flounces and cold little patent leather shoes in the rain, then it is quite simply too impractical in a kindergarten. You cannot, you know, climb trees in such flowing robes, or run around outside. In these types of clothes, it is not possible to be a child. (Fieldwork no. 3)

And likewise in another conversation:

Tove: I know I am not supposed to say so, but I do find wet combed hair and little patent leather shoes provocative in children. And the stink of soap! It is like something from the fifties. That way of looking neat is a total turn-off for me. Maybe because of my age. It reminds me of dancing school, but I think children should be children and be able to run around and get dirty.... They should not look nice or be neat. (Fieldwork no. 2)

Or as Stine more generally puts it:

Stine: I don't like it when children just do as they are told. You need to feel that they have their own will. They have to be true to themselves, even in a kindergarten or school. (Fieldwork no. 3)

Much attention is focused on adjusting children's behaviour; yet, as can be seen, some ambivalence can also be traced in this regard. Regular correction exists side by side with enthusiasm for and enjoyment of the young child's imagination, reasoning and fantasy. The children hence encounter somewhat composite reactions. They learn that they must wash their hands, but they are also met with smiles when they come in with hands blackened by bonfire ashes. They are instructed to sit and eat at the table, but they also get credit for their imagination when they, for instance, take their packed lunches and climb a tree 'to play monkeys in a nest'. They are not allowed to play with their food, but they are encouraged to shape the dough into creative shapes when baking, and they are commended when they make figures they can play with once the buns emerge from the oven. It is pointed out on a daily basis in all the observed institutions that the children are not allowed to run inside, and yet you often see children run without being stopped, because the child's expression of physical joy and vitality also inspires indulgence, delight and respect.

The educational project is composite yet also quite distinctive. Through a range of different strategies, the pedagogues seek to inform children of the appropriate behaviour, preferably without telling them directly that they have done anything wrong, and certainly not that *they* (the children) are wrong. Avoiding power struggles, the pedagogues try to smooth out missteps and potential conflicts by ignoring minor breaches of institutional rules, shifting focus, telling jokes, getting the child to participate in group activities, suggesting possible solutions and alternative behaviour and praising children who solve problems themselves. They systematically try to guide children without raising their voices or directly applying discipline. Instead, the pedagogues encourage the children to take social initiatives, engage in activities, find solutions and overcome conflicts without adult intervention. The task of civilising children is thus a demanding one. The pedagogue must regulate the child's behaviour, but loses face if acting too authoritatively (see Elias 1998a). It is necessary to strike a balance between encouraging individual freedom and ensuring social conformity as it is part of the civilising ideal to support children's individual autonomy, yet it gives cause for concern when pedagogues are confronted with children who diverge too greatly from the institutional rhythms and expectations. The challenge of getting everyday institutional life to run smoothly requires a certain standardisation of behaviour, which inevitably becomes a norm against which the individual child is measured. Towards the end of this chapter, I will return to the social implications of the composite nature of the formative project.

Emphasis on Language and Rejection of Violence

On one point, however, reactions are unequivocal. It is not allowed to hit or otherwise hurt others, and any conflicts should be solved through dialogue. The language and the way emotions are expressed play a decisive role in the civilising work in day-care institutions. In the interviews, as well as in the institutional regulations, it is emphasised that the children should: 'learn to express verbally what they feel', 'learn to formulate what they want', 'be included in the planning of activities' and 'consulted in matters that involve them'. They are regularly encouraged to 'tell us what you want', and expressions such as 'no, you are not allowed to hit. Try to explain why you are so angry' occur frequently in the material.

The systematic encouraging of children to explain, tell and express their viewpoints and emotions emphasises the priority given to verbal language. When a child lacks words or expresses himself/herself in more physical ways, the pedagogues often formulate what they perceive to be the child's intentions, thereby showing the children how to verbalise their viewpoints and enter into a dialogue with other children. 'Tell him that you had it first' or 'Say "stop" if you don't want him to do it' are frequently heard prompts which are intended to enable a child to communicate in appropriate ways and take responsibility for the interaction instead of expecting the adult to do so. On a daily basis, children are gathered in small groups where organised conversation takes place. Here the children are asked what they have done or experienced, and they are encouraged to verbalise what they think, like and want to do. They are also instructed in listening to what the other children have to say, and to wait for their turn to speak. Even pre-verbal toddlers are encouraged to articulate their feelings, with the caregiver re-voicing their presumed intentions so the other children can understand. Systematically, children are treated as sensible and reflexive human beings, no matter how young and inarticulate they are (see Rogoff 2003: ch. 8). They are expected to develop a language that enables them to voice opinions and gradually to verbalise their sentiments in balanced and nuanced ways. This emphasis can also be seen in children's internal interactions – in their mutual corrections and, in particular, in their indignation when someone uses violence. 'You have to *say* it'(instead of hitting) is a frequent expression among the children. Moreover, the threat 'I will *tell* on you' (tell the adults) usually has a disarming effect.

In the following excerpt, one of the pedagogues, Søren, clearly states the priority given to language. He has just laughingly chased three 4-year-olds in an attempt to 'punish them' for their 'villainy' (*niddingsdåd*), because they have tickled him:

Eva: Villainy … that is a funny word to use. Do you think the children understand it?

Søren: Of course it is not a common word, and they don't know it. But in the context, the meaning of the word is evident.

Eva: Why do you choose to use a word you know they do not understand?

Søren: Well, then they learn the word. It is of course also because I think it would be fun if they subsequently begin to use the word 'villainy'. I believe that if you have a large vocabulary, you can express yourself in more nuanced ways. In fact, I also believe that you think better and become better at communicating with others if you have more words at your disposal. At any rate, the more you use language, the better you become at communicating.

Eva: Is that something you prioritise in your everyday work?

Søren: In a way you can say that my or our main effort is to teach the children to be nice to each other […] Well, I think […] teach them to communicate nicely with each other, not hit each other, but solve conflicts and, well, be good friends. I don't mean nice in the sense of not swearing. But no verbal mud-slinging. It is not like they should all be good friends, or should not feel anger or irritation … but to learn that, even if we are different, we can talk. And it is just not OK to hit each other. So when I think it is important to know a word, then it is, well, because I see words as a means of communication, a way to curb a kind of primitive brutality – perhaps I am too bombastic … Yes, in a way words are weapons, so to speak. If your language can express subtle differences, then you don't need to use violence. (Fieldwork no. 1)

Although Søren does not use the word, the quotation clearly expresses a civilising ambition – in the situation supported by his playful distance from the act of punishment. Language is described as a defence against barbarism, against 'primitive brutality'; it is a tool to express free thought and respectful communication. This prioritisation of verbal communication is widespread. There is a concerted effort to teach children to express their feelings and to recognise that their expressions have an impact on others. When children express themselves in this way, they are explicitly praised with excitement, strong intonations, lively, positive gestures and phrases like: '*You* are *really good* at explaining yourself'; 'Have you all heard *how well* Simon can explain what Clara feels?'; 'I must say, that was *such a good way* to resolve it [the situation] without the two of you falling out.'

However, not all verbal language receives equal recognition. Some of the pedagogues express concern regarding children's use of language; a concern that is also present in public debate. The worry is that 'children nowadays' are subject to a 'brutalisation of language'; that their language is 'desensitised', that is, derogatory, aggressive or disrespectful when they speak to and about both peers and adults. Even if there is not nearly the same systematic reaction from the personnel as when more violent expressions occur, corrections do take place when the language is perceived as brutal or becomes too vulgar, as in the following conversation among three boys aged 4 and 5:

Anton approaches Janus and Sofus, who are digging in the earth for gold. He grabs a shovel and begins to dig, but is promptly turned away by Janus and Sofus.
Janus: Go away, we are digging here.
Simon: Yes, it is actually us who are finding gold in the ground.
Anton: I am allowed to dig here.
Simon: No, go away. You cannot be here.
Anton: You cocksucker [*pikslikker*] – you are such a bunch of cocksuckers.
The pedagogue Dorte is building a fire a short distance away.
Dorthe: That was an ugly word you used.

Simon: Yes, he says it all the time. Henrik said it first. Isn't that right, Henrik just thinks he is cool.

Janus: Yes, he always thinks he can come here and show off with all the cool words.

Dorthe [in a gentle voice]: We do not want to hear such an ugly word in this kindergarten. Come along, Anton, and help me with these branches. You can look after the fire. (Fieldwork no. 1)

The vulgar is yet another counterpoint to the civilised. As in the example above, there are words that are incompatible with conceptions of childhood and innocence. Even if the personnel are aware that children experiment with the social effects of words, and accept and even support this, they see it as their duty to 'weed out' the children's language and alert them to the fact that words can have meanings that are not suitable or appreciated in all social contexts. Words like 'cocksucker, fuck you, arsehole, shit, nigger, shithead, cunt, I will crush you',[2] systematically engender a response from the personnel. They are, however, not interpreted or explained – contrary to general pedagogical principles when children transgress norms of good behaviour. 'Ugly language', and particularly the vulgar words are, as in the extract above, rejected as unsuitable without further explanation. As pointed out by Elias, one result of the civilising process is that the mere mention of violence and sex in the company of young children has become taboo, an act of violence in itself (Elias 1994 [1939]:149–53) (a situation which is perhaps more apparent today than in the more permissive attitude to sexuality of the 1970).

Corrections and interventions are particularly frequent when children get into a fight as this is perceived as disruptive to the social harmony within the institution.

Ali and Fakhri are each sitting on their bike. They are angry with each other. Ali rides his bike into Fakhri's leg, but Fakhri pulls his legs up out of the way.

Ali: Fuck you!

Ali says it quietly. Fakhri answers him in a similar tone of voice.

Fakhri: Fuck you!

Ali: You little brat!

Fakhri: You baby!

Ali: You little piglet!

Fakhri: You little piglet!

Ali: Fuck you, you dirty swine!

Fakhri begins to raise his voice.

Fakhri: What you say is what you are!

Ali: What you say is what you are!

Both boys are shouting now. Fakhri adds something in Arabic.

Fakhri: You swine!

Ali: You little baby!

Fakhri: What you say is what you are, what you say is what you are.

They scream at each other. Ali again rides his bike into Fakhri's leg. The assistant pedagogue Maria notices and grabs him.

Maria: You know you are not supposed to run into him. You can tell him if you are angry, but you must not run into him. And for that matter, you can both stop screaming. You must speak nicely. Is that understood?!

Ali cycles away. (Fieldwork no. 2)

This example illustrates the ongoing effort to improve children's modes of expression. Teaching children to speak properly, and to negotiate and resolve conflicts verbally is, however, not just a professional priority within the individual day-care institution. As argued in chapter 1, it reflects a general tendency in society where any kind of physical violence or expression of aggression has become increasingly taboo and excluded from socially acceptable conduct (see Elias 1994 [1939]:366–9; Wouters 1992:234; Mennell and Goudsblom 1998:22–3). Reflecting this, children's institutions have been assigned the task of teaching children at an ever earlier age to refrain from any kind of violent means and to use non-aggressive verbal language as their primary mode of communication. The aim is to provide the children with the tools and competences to express themselves in a non-violent manner in order to further their passage into society.

The Ideal of a Well-Balanced Person

Although only vaguely articulated in the formal descriptions of early childhood institutions, the contours of a distinct understanding of the civilised person can be identified through analysis of the ethnographic material stemming from my fieldworks. In this cultural context, a decent person is someone who is able to disregard his or her own impulses and needs when the situation calls for it. It is a socially flexible, inclusive and well-tempered individual who is able to take into account the opinions of others, yet also a person with sufficient clout to express and stand by his or her own opinions. In the pedagogy observed, the civilised human being is interpreted as a well-balanced participant in a social community based on verbal communication and with a categorical rejection of any kind of physical expression of power.

The emphasis on negotiations, interpretations, dialogue and flexibility does, however, have the consequence that moral demands are not expressed with any great clarity. The interaction between children and adults is characterised by composite attitudes in terms of expectations and norms, where any given situation may involve several possible interpretations of what would be the right thing to do. The children encounter encouragement, reprimands and corrections, but they also learn that requests and interpretations can alternate from one situation to the next. Assessments may vary and understandings change. Behavioural norms are not defined by absolute standards, but are shaped through relative social dynamics. The noisy child is reprimanded, but the quiet child may also give cause for concern. Children who are dirty on arrival at the institution may prompt speculation as to the parents' ability to take care of them. On the other hand, too much cleanliness or too nice clothes may also be perceived as a repressive measure against the free will of the child. The child who is good at verbal argumentation will often be listened to, but both the less eloquent and the highly articulate child can be looked upon with concern, interpreted as either insufficiently stimulated at home ('he comes from an environment deprived of language skills') or overstimulated ('they constantly talk to him [...] it gets too cerebral and not physical enough'). A hot temper is worrying, but so is a docile disposition. In short, we are dealing with the maintenance of numerous equilibria and constant assessments and adaptations of the individual child.

As emphasised above, the context-sensitive expectations do not reflect a flaw in professional skills. On the contrary, they are expressions of a specific understanding of the civilised human being as someone who is able to interpret social dynamics and exhibit well-balanced behaviour with a developed sensibility for smooth interactions and fluctuating norms and situations, yet also able to stand up for himself or herself as an autonomous individual. The individual child should understand the variations in other people's reactions, at the same time finding its own bearings, preferably without explicit instructions.

In a professional context, this means a challenging balancing act between supporting and restricting the child; a challenge which is even greater when the childcare professional at the same time needs to get a group of children to function without friction. The balancing act reflects cultural understandings that extend way beyond the institution; for instance, that tensions should not be displayed and conflicts avoided, and that it is a fundamentally democratic concern that the opinions of all present are heard. The pedagogical project is focused on a civil society characterised by closely enmeshed social strata and subtle ways of expressing social distinction. Hierarchies and markers of authority are downplayed, requiring the development of abilities to manoeuvre contextually and interact smoothly in various types of communities. It is this balancing act that the pedagogues face when trying to uphold well-functioning routines and a conflict-free institutional life, while also looking to form children as active participants in civil society. In this sense, the civilising efforts represent an attempt to teach children central cultural values in order for them to be able to behave and interact in socially acknowledged ways, yet also to contribute to a more civilised society (see also the discussion in chapter 5).

The Resistant Child

As stated, the ideal of the civilised person is not presented in very clear terms as it is not described as a concrete programme with well-defined objectives, but an ongoing project intended to ensure a flexible and well-balanced mode of interacting and communicating. However, not all children are equally good at decoding and mastering the implicit expectations and, as I will show in the final section of the chapter, this inequality has distinctive consequences. Some children refer to rules they have encountered in another situation or believe that a certain behaviour is okay as it has not been regulated before, not taking into account that they are dealing with new personnel. These children's behaviour is often corrected. Others are better able to decode messages and adapt their actions to a given situation and tend to encounter much more leeway. This is the case with Jonathan who, in the situation described earlier, gets away with jumping from the bookshelf, which Ahmed and Michael were previously prevented from doing. He doesn't grin mischievously when he is caught doing something against the rules, but apologises or claims ignorance. He includes younger children in his games and seems considerate. He expresses his opinions and feelings with words, and the few times I have seen him strike out in anger, he has always used a pillow, which makes it difficult to see if his action is part of a harmless pillow fight. Of course, I cannot assess how strategic his actions are, but he is evidently less likely to be corrected for the same transgressions as others and his misdeeds are often not perceived as intentional (or 'done on purpose', as the pedagogues say).

To get approval and be given leeway entails the employment of accepted forms of communication and conduct, while also being able to distinguish between requirements which are general and unequivocal, and those that are situation-specific and open for discussion. The child who can decode the often quite implicit requests and improvise according to the situation can use the ambiguity to gain latitude and have new ideas accepted. This child will be commended for his or her independence and personal integrity, even when committing minor transgressions. He or she can strike a balance between, on one hand, the childish, the impulsive and the natural, and, on the other hand, the considerate, the empathic and the controlled. The child who does not master these complex social demands or who cannot find his or her bearings will encounter more explicit regulation. This child will be the focus of negative attention, correction and worry. The pedagogical concern is often not directed at children who lack a certain skill – who cannot sit still, concentrate on a specific task, count or catch a ball. The concern is focused instead on children who do not meet the implicit interactional expectations regarding social interaction in changing situations.

In this way, the inclusive educational practice is not without norms or distinctions. In spite of the apparent latitude given, divisions are noted between those who are familiar with and able to honour the expectations and those who are not. Children who do not live up to the, often implicit, expectations are considered to be lagging behind in their development; stuck in a stage of childishness which, albeit commendable for its qualities of innocence and spontaneity, is a stage that should be abandoned as the child grows older. The concept of the social is normative; it is a pedagogical ideal of civilised interaction, as well as a standard for the assessment of the individual child's normality. The civilising project conforms to civil society's modes of interaction, and any kind of anti-social behaviour – expression of dominance, brutality or selfishness – is perceived as a problematic personal characteristic; not just here and now, but also in terms of the individual's potential to behave in a civilised manner later in life. When such traits are identified, systematic interventions are considered justified.

Civilising interventions, however, can have other consequences than those intended. This is seen in the case of Ali, who on a daily basis engages in conflicts with other children and regularly challenges the staff's admonitions and the rules of the institution. Every day he hits other children and shouts at the personnel, and he is the subject of much concern, frequent reprimands and firm interventions. His way of behaving provokes strong reactions, but it is also evident that he responds negatively to the reprimands he receives, meeting them with defiance. It is also unmistakable that his defiant reactions are admired by some of the other children, and this encourages him to continue transgressing norms. When, for instance, he persuades a small group of boys to throw the other children's shoes onto the institution's flat roof by telling them that if they do it, they will become his best friends, it is clear that his daring is acknowledged and translates into status among the boys. Moreover, when he gets them to continue as soon as the pedagogue who had told them off turns her back, and gets them to shout 'fuck you' at her, it can only be interpreted as a challenge to her power. In this case, social solidarity is created by building opposition to the considerate interaction which the institution prioritise.

Ali is thus able to gather a group and create a momentum focused on breaking the institution's norms. This gives rise to considerable frustration and concern among the staff. They often get into situations where they need to reprimand or physically move or restrain him for a while. However, in such manifestations of power, the pedagogues also experience frustration by not living up to the very standards for social interaction they have established for the children. Or, as Birgitte, the pedagogue in charge of Ali's group, says: 'I hate having to move him or scold him, but I have to get him to stop. It is not nice to see yourself as someone who shouts at children or grabs them and manhandles them physically.' The need to use power is experienced as a pedagogical and civilisational defeat (see the discussion of the same understanding among teachers in chapters 5 and 6, and among parents in chapter 8).

The threat of decivilisation is a latent presence in any civilising project. Civilised interaction implies that the individual accepts it and finds it right, reasonable and worthy of compliance. Where such acceptance and self-regulation is lacking, other, more dominance-based ways of regulating conduct come to the fore. As discussed in chapter 1, several Elias-inspired researchers have pointed out that breaches of the civilising codes – especially in the case of violent behaviour – often lead to increased control, surveillance and explicit regulations of expression, thus underpinning the self-control which functions as the social precondition for the civilising logic (Swaan 2001; Mennell and Goudsblom 1998:20–1; Mennell 2006). The result is that other, more power-oriented rationales begin to dominate. Ryan Powell (2007) stresses that the desire to rectify the social behaviour of groups, who are considered less civilised, involves an expression of dominance. However, such interventions may well have a decivilising impact, although they are not perceived as such as they are legitimised with reference to a civilising mission. Robert van Krieken also addresses this issue when he makes the point that civilising and decivilising processes interpenetrate so that 'societies are barbaric precisely in their movement towards increasing civilization' (van Krieken 1999:297).

It is not my intention here to suggest that the pedagogical interventions in Danish day-care institutions are 'barbaric' or 'uncivilised'. I would like to point out, however, that civilising projects always involve an aspect of dominance which might change into more decivilising expressions of power when expectations and interventions encounter opposition. This is what we, in chapter 1, referred to as the paradox of civilising. In the day-care institutions, I can observe how the pedagogical efforts sometimes encounter resistance and are challenged. As described, such reactions are mostly met with humour, playful interactions, a 'hugging-in' strategy and, in some cases, more explicit interventions. However, when the challenges become increasingly systematic or destructive, the interventions also become more pronounced, much to the chagrin of the pedagogues, who fear their acts may contravene their own standards of civilised behaviour for educators. Often the more interventionist initiatives are justified with reference to the application of dominant modes of interaction being in the child's best interest. This is seen, for example, during a staff meeting when the pedagogue Sofie argues that Ali needs more hard-line discipline:

> If the boy has had no upbringing, it is high time we step in, while he is still young and impressionable. I think it is important that we are very clear on this. It is not good for him if, at a later stage, he doesn't know how to behave. (Fieldwork no. 2)

It is thus possible to observe a process where the soft pedagogy occasionally turns into a more power-wielding, corrective mode. This is particularly the case where children oppose the most salient marks of civilised behaviour, for example by fighting, being brutal towards younger children, animals or inventory, or shouting aggressively at adults and other children. Interestingly, however, it also appears that the firmer interventions by staff lead to further acts of resistance from precisely those children who are the target of the disciplinary measures. My observations and communication with the children in such situations have convinced me that their acts are expressions of protest, and not just signs of maladjusted children. When, for instance, Ali repeatedly steps on the younger Louis' toes during lunch, throws a bun across the room, puts his hand in the soup, and screams into the face of a small child, all the while looking first at the adult, who scolds him, and then at the girl Sidsel, who smiles at him, then it is reasonable to assume that his actions are deliberate challenges to the institutional power structure and an intentional popularity strategy in relation to other children. Similarly, when Mehdi persuades two other boys to crawl over the fence surrounding the kindergarten with him, while they whisper conspiratorially that they are going to 'do a runner', or when Mads, in a fury, throws a chair across the room and shouts 'dirty bitch' at one of the pedagogues who wants him to leave the room, I interpret these acts as deliberate breaches of the civilised ideal with an explicit intention of challenging rules and authorities. This interpretation is reinforced when, for instance, Ali talks about Sofie, the pedagogue who most often adopts a disciplinary approach:

Ali: She is really, really stupid, she is boneheaded. I don't like her.

Eva: You don't like her?

Ali: No. She is so stupid. She always tells me off and takes me by the arm. Real hard.

Eva: What do you do then?

Ali: I just tease her. Sometimes I hit her ... She is so stupid, and so is Sus.

Eva: But you are not supposed to hit?

Ali: I just do it anyway... Sometimes I spit or shout 'fuck you'. Then she gets really pissed off.

Eva: Do you also spit on Birgitte?

Ali: No, only on those who are stupid. (Fieldwork no. 2)

In social dynamics, where actions encounter reactions which, in turn, produce new reactions, protest or resistance modes can develop, targeted against the fundamental norms in the institutional community. The reactions can assume the form of an anti-civilised mode of communication that contests and plays with the norms for use of language, violence, consideration for others and respect. In other words, the protests are directed at precisely 'the social' – the object of the civilising project (Gilliam 2009, 2015; see also discussion in chapter 6).[3]

Reactions of resistance thus testify to the fact that the civilising endeavour also contains the germ of its own antithesis. In fact, it is a project that can include and support individual children, but also generate opposition and resistance among children who feel excluded from the project or are unable to decode the ambiguous messages and demands. The civilising project can, on the one hand, establish egalitarian, respectful ways of interacting, and, on the other, create divisions between the children and anti-civilised reactions of resistance. Any civilising effort includes aspects of dominance and othering which distinguish some forms of interaction as more legitimate than others, thereby generating difference (see discussion in chapters 1, 6 and 9). It is interesting that this divisive dimension can also be observed in these very inclusive environments; that is, the first public institutions in which children operate independently.

The Ambiguous Civilising Ideal

The analysis in this chapter has pointed out how young children in Danish day-care institutions are exposed to more or less tacit information regarding what it means to be a civilised human being on a daily basis. Through explicit instruction and implicit guidance they are taught to interact smoothly, to be inclusive and socially flexible, yet also encouraged to express themselves and be true to their own nature. They learn to control themselves, to listen to other people's intentions and take the expectations of various situations into account, but they are also acknowledged when being disobedient or a bit cheeky. There is an ongoing and systematic effort to teach children legitimate modes of expression; that language is a defence against violence and the civilised human being will reject any use of physical dominance.

These values become evident in many daily interactions, where the pedagogues transform their interpretation of the civilising task into pedagogy in practice. However, this is not an unequivocal interpretation. Many considerations interfere in the daily planning and reactions to incidents. The pedagogues have to strike a balance between attention to the individual child and the children as a group; between, on the one hand, various political requirements in terms of what children should know and learn, and, on the other hand, their own professional assessments of the individual's opportunities and potentials; between central cultural ideals of human interaction and practical considerations with regard to the functionality of daily routines. The professional reputation and legitimacy of the personnel depend on their ability to balance such considerations in acceptable ways.

As demonstrated, this complexity does not mean that norms and requirements are totally arbitrary, but that how these norms and requirements are manifested and the amount of weight they are given in various situations and by different members of staff varies considerably. Some stress the value of childish innocence and expressions of creativity more strongly than others, who tend to place greater emphasis on more regulation and the child's ability to adapt. Some are interested in stimulating the individual child's potentials and developing new goals for learning, while others emphasise the significance of the community. Even if there is an expressed agreement on the value of 'the social', what this value is does not appear in the same way or with the same emphasis to everyone in all situations. Hence a certain ambiguity can be traced, although there seems to be widespread agreement on the cornerstones of the project.

As shown in this chapter, the composite nature and the implicit communication of the civilising project can make it difficult for some children to decode and comply with expectations. For most children, the loose format and anti-authoritarian style of upbringing provide a wide range of opportunities for expression. However, in some cases it seems that the children do not quite understand what is expected of them and some are evidently in the process of developing oppositional reactions to a project they don't master and which defines them as problematic. The civilising project's accentuation of sociality thus provides extended opportunities for self-expression, but it also embodies a marking of differences that can engender an opposition directed precisely at the symbolic cornerstones of civilised interaction.

4

The Not-Yet-Civilised

Negotiating the kindergarten's civilising project[1]

Karen Fog Olwig

> For many people, the memories of houses inhabited in childhood have an extraordinary evocative power. Perhaps this is attributable to the dense and myriad connections that link together what goes on in houses – processes of feeding and nurturance, the emotionally charged social relations of close kinship, and repetitive bodily practice through which many rules of social life are encoded – quite apart from their more practical, material, and aesthetic dimensions. (Carstens 2004:31)

In this quote from *After Kinship*, British social anthropologist Janet Carstens describes the central role of 'houses inhabited in childhood' as family homes where social relations are formed. In modern welfare societies such as the Scandinavian, the majority of children spend most of their waking hours in institutions, beginning with the nursery when they are about 1 year old, followed by the kindergarten when they are 3 years old, and elementary school (as well as various after-school clubs and leisure programmes) when they turn 6. It can therefore be argued that much, if not most, of the feeding, nurturance and 'repetitive bodily practice through which many rules of social life are encoded' takes place in various public institutions and that these, accordingly, constitute important houses of habitation where children may develop 'emotionally charged social relations' of friendship.

In this chapter I will examine the 'house' of the kindergarten as a site where young children experience early forms of sociality that play an important role in their shaping as social beings. A topic of increasing interest in the literature on institutions for children has been the control and disciplining that occurs in these settings as adult pedagogues prepare children to become proper future members of society (Olwig and Gulløv 2003:9–11; James et al. 1998). This institutional socialisation, it has been contended, may constrain the children's social interaction and therefore their freedom to engage in social relations of their own choosing. Such control and disciplining of children, however, can be regarded as a central aspect of the 'civilising' of children that Norbert Elias emphasises as an important part of childhood, and that takes place both in the home and in institutions for children. Elias thus argues that the very notion of childhood involves a designation of children to a category of human beings who need to undergo 'an individual social civilising process' before they can become accepted as full, adult members of society (1998a:190, 1994 [1939]:xi; see chapter 1). This civilising revolves, to a great extent, around teaching children 'correct' ways of behaviour, which in modern Western societies, such as Danish society, entails considerable mastery of feelings and bodily functions. The public institutions' pedagogical efforts, and the self-disciplining and self-control that they promote, therefore, are part of a more general societal project of civilising directed towards children.

The notion of civilising, however, implies not only that disciplining and regulating per definition are key aspects of childhood, but also that children cannot be reared properly through any kind of force. To be civilised is more than being able to behave in a fashion that is regarded as civilised. It also means sharing the social norms and cultural values that are associated with such behaviour. Children, who by definition are regarded as 'not-yet-civilised', therefore must be persuaded to adopt a 'civilised' way of life. Furthermore, they must be convinced in a 'civilised' manner, which means that the civilising adults need to display a great 'degree of caution and restraint, of civilisation' in their relations with the children (Elias 1998a:191). The children, on the other hand, who are 'not-yet-civilised', are able to draw on a register of emotions and bodily expressions not available to the adults as civilised beings (Elias 1998a:191). This chapter will show that the children's position as 'not-yet-civilised' does not just place them in a situation of subjection to adults. It can also be regarded as a resource that presents them with a framework of social interaction and self-assertion that enables them to develop communities of peer relations. This framework, thus, is considerably wider than the formal civilising framework of the institution of the kindergarten may suggest.

On the basis of life story interviews with older children and young adults of Danish middle-class background, I shall here analyse these children's sociality in the kindergarten as it is described in their accounts of their kindergarten life. I will argue that the life stories suggest that the children, during their early childhood, used their 'not-yet-civilised' position to establish common grounds of interaction that played a key role in their development of a sense of sociality, as they negotiated the terms of the civilising process with their educators as well as their peers. Such common grounds, I will show, emerged to a great extent as the children appropriated particular social and physical spaces in the kindergarten for their own purposes, thus turning these adult-constructed places for children into places of their own (cf. Olwig and Gulløv 2003; see also Højlund 2002).

The Kindergarten

According to Eva Gulløv, the kindergarten is surrounded by a great deal of ambiguity reflecting varying views of the place of children in modern society revolving around whether children should be regarded as 'products of nature' or as 'modern individuals, as self-responsible agents or social citizens' (2003:27). Due to this ambiguity, Gulløv states, kindergartens are constructed in such a way that they appear as a home-like or nature-like environment where children can express their creativity as children. She concludes, however, that while 'an important stated goal of day-care practice is to teach children to make decisions for themselves, their choices are restricted by the fact that they cannot place themselves, nor do they have any influence on adult ideas of what is a proper childhood' (2003:24).

This ambivalent view of kindergartens can be related to the tendency to contrast institutions for children with the home, which, according to the Danish anthropologist Susanne Højlund, has resulted in negative depictions of institutions as representing a 'formalization of the children's everyday life' and as characterised by 'mechanical care', 'instrumental contract' and 'surveillance' (2002:19). It can also be linked to more general critical discourse concerning modernity in Western – and not least Scandinavian – societies. In particular, the increasing institution-alisation of modern life has been viewed with scepticism as evidence of the loss of the communities of close, personal social relations believed to formerly frame human lives. Norwegian anthropologist Marianne Gullestad has argued that it is common for Scandinavians to draw a sharp distinction between, on the one hand, the sphere of everyday life in communities of interpersonal relations associated with such positive qualities as 'care, sharing, and togetherness' and, on the other, the sphere of the bureaucracy and market relations linked to the wider society and regarded as cold, impersonal, alienating and dangerous (1991:486–7). This close association between authentic sociality and close, interpersonal relations emerging through everyday life in local communities, however, may represent a nostalgic longing for an imagined society of the past that bears little relation to the kinds of childhoods that children and youths have come to accept as theirs in modern society. This is not least the case in a society such as that of Denmark where, as noted by Susanne Højlund, 'institutional life' has become an entirely 'matter-of-course part of children's everyday experiences' (2009:9).

In a study of young adults' recollections of their kindergarten life during the 1980s, a decade when kindergartens had become an integral part of childhood, the Danish cultural sociologists Kim Rasmussen and Søren Smidt (2001) have shown that the youths did not focus on the problematic aspects of institutional life that many studies have highlighted. Rather, a central theme in their narratives was the various ways in which they, as children, had appropriated and reinterpreted the physical structure of the kindergarten for their own purposes (2001:171). Of particular salience in the accounts of kindergarten life were relationships with other children in the kindergarten and some of the youths still maintained friendships first made in the kindergarten (2001:26, 61–2). This suggests that the kindergarten in many ways figures as a house of positive memories. Central to this experience of the kindergarten, as portrayed in the recollections, is children's feel for 'circumventing, softening, reinterpreting and resisting the established order and the established rules' of the institution (Rasmussen and Smidt 2001:26) as well as their 'symbolic creativity' based on their ability to 'create meaning or add a layer of meaning on top of already given meanings' (2001:65). These independent activities, according to Rasmussen and Smidt, 'comprise one of the constitutive traits of these institutions for children', making children important actors in the daily construction and reconstruction of the institution (2001:85).

Rasmussen and Smidt point to children's basic social and creative capacities as the key to understanding their ability to renegotiate the established order of the kindergarten. Indeed, with reference to American sociologist Erving Goffman's work on institutions, they argue that it is a general human characteristic to test and explore the structure of an institution (2001:170). I will here discuss the social processes through

which children become able to exercise these capacities within the institutional order of the kindergarten. More specifically, I will argue that
children's ability to use their capacity for reinterpretation and creativity
inheres, to a great extent, in their status in the adult-constructed order
of the kindergarten as not-yet-civilised human beings who cannot be
expected to master appropriate forms of emotional and bodily expression.

Key elements in the civilising of children in modern society are the
control of bodily functions, the exercise of emotional self-control and the
mastering of social conventions and manners identified with the middle
class (Frykman and Löfgren 1987 [1979]). Adults are clearly the dominant
party in the civilising project in the sense that they define the social
values and the norms of conduct to be observed by the children. They
are, however, curtailed in their exercise of power in relation to children
by their status as civilised persons. As noted, being civilised they cannot
use noticeable physical force or aggression to make children conform
to the modes of behaviour that they seek to institute (Elias 1998a:191).
The 'not-yet-civilised' children, however, are able to use a wide range
of emotions and bodily expressions that are not available to adults. The
civilisers, furthermore, must accept children's self-expression, at least to a
certain extent, because of the emergence of modern notions of children as
individuals who have the right to 'have their particular identity as children
respected and understood' (Elias 1998a:190; cf. chapters 1, 3 and 5 in this
volume).[2] There is thus a certain tension between the civilising project of
forming children according to dominant social values concerning proper
human beings, and the pedagogic project of encouraging children to
realise their full potential as human beings. This tension is also apparent in
Gulløv's chapter, in which she analyses the ambiguity of the kindergarten
as an institution where children must be treated as both competent
individuals who have the right to determine their own lives, and as people
in the making who need to be trained by pedagogues before they can be
proper members of society.

I propose that this area of ambiguity and contradiction, and the emotions
it evokes and allows, plays a central role in the children's development
of their own forms of sociality and notions of identification within the
kindergarten. My data suggest that, while the kindergarten presents itself
as a well-structured institution, organised to facilitate children's transformation into adult citizens, the children turn it into their own place
by using their prerogative, as not-yet-civilised, to stray into uncivilised
terrain where they can play with, reflect upon and perhaps even challenge

the disciplining and control to which they are subjected. The educators, in turn, respond to the children partly by upholding an overall structure of order in the kindergarten, partly by granting children spaces where their uncivilised expressivity can be played out, yet be contained. The analysis concludes that the micro-processes of civilising that take place in these Danish kindergartens entail an adult–child relationship of interdependence that allows for, even necessitates, a great deal of give-and-take, as both parties negotiate their understanding of the civilising process and the terms under which it can unfold. This ongoing negotiation has important implications for the kind of sociality that the children develop within this institutional context.

The ethnographic study is based on interviews conducted in 2006 with 16 young Danes of middle-class background, ranging from 11 to 22 years of age, who were asked to relate their experiences of growing up in Danish public institutions. These recollections of kindergarten life naturally are not descriptions of these institutions as experienced by the children when they attended them. They are narratives related by youths who reflected on their early childhood in the light of their later life experiences. In their accounts the young narrators contrasted the kindergarten to the school, which several described as boring and demanding with its requirement that they sit quietly in the classroom and listen to the teacher. As will be shown, the narratives give the impression that, by contrast, the young people recalled their kindergarten as a wonderful place where they, as young children, had some of their first experiences of developing social relations with others, both as individuals and as part of a social group. In this way, they also got a feel for 'proper' ways of being with other people.

The narratives must also be seen in the light of the historical and social contexts in which the young people had their first kindergarten experiences. Historically, they refer to the period from the mid 1980s to the late 1990s. This was a time when there was a much stronger focus on child-initiated activities and less emphasis on preparing the children for the formal educational system. The importance attached to social skills through free play is reflected in the youngsters' descriptions of the pedagogues' endeavours to create an egalitarian and inclusive community of children in the kindergarten. As will be seen, in their efforts to form more exclusive groupings and status hierarchies in the kindergarten, children often challenged this pedagogical approach. Socially, the narratives were related by youths with a middle-class background, which means that there was close correspondence between the social norms and cultural values that the family home and the kindergarten sought to instil in the children. They therefore had little difficulty in understanding, and identifying with, the civilising project of the kindergarten. However, since the great majority of the Danish population can be viewed (and views itself) as middle class, broadly speaking, the interviewed youths were not in a particularly privileged position when they attended the kindergarten.

The Well-Ordered Institution

In an analysis of the Danish kindergarten Gulløv and Højlund emphasise that the institution's role as an agent of civilisation is reflected in its overall structure, which presents children with a well-organised daily timetable and separate physical spaces that facilitate the 'disciplining, civilising and cultivating' of children (Gulløv and Højlund 2005:33–4). This structure was quite apparent in the interviews. The youths described how, when they first entered the kindergarten, they were placed in the room with the youngest children under the supervision of a kindergarten pedagogue helped by various assistants. As they became older, they graduated to groups of older children, located in other rooms and supervised by other pedagogues. These different group rooms in the kindergarten were usually identified by a particular colour, animal or other figure to make it easy for the children to remember where they belonged. Finally, after about three years, they left the kindergarten for school and the after-school club.

This clearly demarcated spatio-temporal order set the stage for a well-defined daily structure of activities. As soon as the children entered the kindergarten they took off their overcoat and outdoor shoes, placed them in their own locker in the cloakroom and put on the slippers they were expected to wear whenever they were inside the kindergarten building. Each locker was distinguished by a sign (usually an image of an animal, plant or thing) that would be easily identifiable by the child. Common elements in the daily round of events were circle time in the morning, with singing and various educational pursuits; outdoor activities, for example at a local playground; and collective meals, often called 'fruit', where the children gathered in their particular room to eat together. In between these scheduled activities, children could play on their own.

In their narratives, the youths recalled clearly how the pedagogues impressed on them that it was important to behave properly if they were to be part of the social community of the kindergarten. Every morning at circle time the pedagogues would talk to them about good behaviour, such as being nice to one another, helping each other, including everybody in the games, sharing toys and remembering to tidy up. The collective meals were subject to a number of rules. Thus the children were expected to come as soon as they were called to the meal, and they were not allowed to leave the table before all had finished eating and the pedagogue had announced that the meal was over. One youth even recalled somebody guarding the closed door to make sure that nobody tried to slip away to the outdoor playground during the meal. In this kindergarten, there was also a sign on the door during mealtime with the message: 'Quiet, we are eating fruit.' The youths also remembered that meals were regulated by firm rules, signalling that food had to be consumed under proper material and hygienic conditions. The children had to clear up the 'mess' they made in connection with their play before they could eat, and all had to wash their hands before the meal and brush their teeth afterwards, something that was closely monitored by the teachers. The meals can therefore be described as central events that defined and affirmed the age-based social collectivities of the kindergarten and the need to respect the social norms associated with such collectivities, if one wanted to belong to them.[3]

The Structure of the Kindergarten Reinterpreted

It is easy to detect civilising projects in these accounts of kindergarten life – circle time, with its moral lessons on good behaviour, the ritualised collective meals surrounded by proper etiquette and the general organisation of the kindergarten according to the children's age, presumably corresponding to their competence and degree of civilisation. The kindergarten therefore can be depicted as a rather regimented institution where children were strictly controlled and supervised. Yet, this view of the kindergarten as an adult-constructed place for children does not at all match the accounts of the kindergarten presented in the interviews. The youths rather emphasised that they, as children, saw the kindergarten as a place where they could play and have fun with other children as well as the 'adults' (cf. Olwig and Gulløv 2003:1–2).

The kindergartens, with their abundance of toys and opportunities to play, were described as real places for children. As Anton related, 'I just remember the kindergarten as a paradise, because it had everything that you could dream of.' Charlotte, who attended a kindergarten located on the fourth floor in inner-city Copenhagen, recalled that her kindergarten had:

One big – as I remember it hugely big – play room. And that was where there was a slide. It was really a big slide where you could be both inside – you know, it was like a little fortress where you could climb inside – and on top and then slide down. So you would spend a lot of time there. And inside you could also build another fortress out of wood. And there were also pillows, and dress-up clothes. We used that a lot to make theatre and fun like that. And then there was another room where there were things to make drawings.

Christopher, whose kindergarten was located in suburban Copenhagen, dwelled especially on the big yard at the kindergarten:

I remember clearly how big the yard was at the kindergarten. We even had a giant boat. And we had a lawn with a hill where you could hide down below. There were some willows and bamboo bushes where you could be and hide from the adults. It was simply of giant dimensions. But I have seen it since then and had to realise that it was terribly small. So [it turned out that] the fence of huge proportions I now could just stand there and look over.

In the narratives the spatio-temporal structure of the kindergarten was not described as a constraint, but rather viewed as an important structure of identification and framework of interaction for the children in the kindergarten, as illustrated by these accounts:

We were divided into three categories, I believe, when we were going to eat lunch. You were either magic elf, dragon or fairy. [...] Every group said that they were the best – we are magic elves, and we are the best. But it had no importance. When we played, we did so across the groups. I guess it was mostly for the grown-ups, so that they could manage us better ... (Ditte)

The children apparently realised – at least at a certain level of consciousness – that their imaginative understanding of the kindergarten was just a make-believe play on the kindergarten order. It is apparent from Ditte's statement, for example, that even when the children identified strongly with the 'totem' of their particular group, this group identification as such had little significance for actual social relations in the kindergarten. It was another matter with the age structure that these groupings to a certain extent reflected.

The children themselves seem to have upheld and respected age differences and looked forward to advancing in the age structure when they grew older. Christopher, for example, still vividly remembered the great feeling of being on the right side of the sliding door when it was closed to separate the bigger children from the smaller ones – he had graduated to the room of the bigger kids. The children, however, did not see the age groupings as a way of dividing children according to their age-specific capacities, which presumably was the pedagogues' rationale for instituting this age structure. Rather, as indicated by Christopher, they saw it as reflecting a hierarchy of privileges associated with status differences linked to age. The community of social relations created by the children in the kindergarten, therefore, was not as egalitarian and inclusive as the pedagogues would have liked, judging from their chats with the children during circle time, described in the narratives. The kindergarten community can rather be described as an age grade system, where cohorts of children could advance to a more prestigious higher grade (cf. Fortes 1984). The children appear to have been highly conscious of this status system based on age and therefore attempted to play with children who were older or the same age. Signe explained:

> *Signe*: It was always a little annoying to go downwards [when looking for playmates]. It was something about showing that you didn't play with the small ones.
>
> *Karen*: That was bad?
>
> *Signe*: Well, of course you could [play with the small ones], but you shouldn't do it too often. Because if you had become 'big', it wasn't so good playing with the small ones, because then you showed that you weren't as mature as the others.
>
> *Karen*: There was a certain loss of prestige associated with this?
>
> *Signe*: Yes, a lot.

While the pedagogues probably would have agreed with the children that the ability to keep up with peers is an important sign of proper maturing, the narratives emphasise that they did not approve of the children's social hierarchy, and the exclusionary practices and prestige loss associated with this hierarchy. Thus the children knew that they could resort to pedagogues when they experienced difficulty handling the social hierarchy among their peers. The pedagogues often sat at the main table in the assigned room, where they would make drawings or play games with children. Danish cultural sociologist Charlotte Palludan has called this table the 'architectural basis' of the pedagogical landscape of the kindergarten and characterised it as a place intended to teach the children to sit quietly and to control their urge to constantly move around (2004:155). In the narratives, the pedagogues' table with the organised activities for everybody was rather described as a kind of refuge where they could go if they felt lonely or had had nobody to play with – a situation that, according to Signe, was experienced as embarrassing:

> *Signe*: If you just sat there and had no fun – and the others didn't think it looked like you were having any fun either – then it was a loss of prestige. [...] Then, if you had nobody to play with, you could sit down and draw and pretend that this was what you really wanted to do, and then it didn't matter.
>
> *Karen*: So you learned different techniques that helped you to avoid the loss of prestige?
>
> *Signe*: Yes, to turn it around. And then you sit there and when people come and see – wow she is drawing – then they also begin to draw, and at a certain point in time you can say, do you want to go out and do something or other?

Just as the children reinterpreted the spatial and temporal structure of the kindergarten they developed their own understanding of the pedagogues. In most of the narratives, the pedagogues were not described as trained educators hired to look after the children's development in the best possible way. All who worked in the kindergarten were referred to by the generic term 'adults', but individuals were called by first name, and often further identified by their function in the kindergarten. In one kindergarten, where two teachers were called Christina, they were called yellow Christina and red Christina, because they were in charge of the yellow and the red rooms respectively – and thus were identified by the groups of children associated with these rooms. Another adult was called Kitchen Mary, because she cooked the food in the kindergarten, whereas another one was named Sally Sockie (Grethe Gokke), because she had told the children that one of her best friends had hit her in the head with a hammer when she was a child. These adults were remembered as having particular qualities. Red Christina was good at playing the guitar and very sweet; yellow Christina was a little tougher, but very princess-like with her blonde hair; Kitchen Mary was nice because she taught the children to bake buns, and Sally Sockie was a fun and imaginative person who was good at telling stories.

Not all teachers, however, were loved. The heads of the kindergartens were generally regarded with suspicion by the children, because they sat in their office most of the day and didn't come out to play (cf. Rasmussen and Smidt 2001:105–6). Some of them were actively disliked and described as overly strict, because they tended to give orders, telling the kids what to do and, especially, what not to do: 'She was always the one who said that you were not allowed to do something or other; that you had to play with the others also and stuff like that that you didn't feel like,' as Charlotte noted. Other adults, deemed by the children to be unfriendly, might be imagined to be bad, if not dangerous people, as Signe recalled: 'There was a man who was really fat and always in a bad mood. And then there were rumours that he was evil.' In the children's universe, as depicted in the narratives, the kindergarten therefore was not run by a staff of professionals, but populated by different kinds of adults, judged according to whether or not they were nice and fun to be with. Indeed, some of the youths interviewed noted that, as children, they were not aware that the adults were actually employees in the kindergarten, but thought that they were just there to play with them and help them. As Signe reflected, 'I didn't think about them as private persons, because they were just pedagogues in the kindergarten. I couldn't imagine that they also had children or what they did when they were at home.' She added, 'If somebody had told me – "Lisa [her pedagogue], she makes money taking care of you," I think I would have been quite surprised.'

The Sites of Civilising Reinterpreted

These recollections suggest that the pedagogues to a great extent accepted the children's reinterpretation of the kindergarten as their own place – at least as long as this did not pose a serious challenge to the kindergarten's civilising project and the basic order connected with it. This conclusion is supported by the fact that the pedagogues had organised certain areas of the kindergarten in such a way that children could experience them as special places where they played on their own. The area under the slide in the inner-city kindergarten and the willows and bushes in the end of the yard, described earlier, are examples of such places where adult pedagogues usually did not interfere in the children's play. If they did keep a close check on everything, the children were not aware of this. Thus, the kindergartens were structured in such a way that the children might have the impression that they were on their own, even if they most likely remained under fairly controlled conditions. Such controlled independence was organised formally in the 'cushion room' (*puderummet*), a small room with many cushions where three or four children could spend time together alone. The room was often so popular that the children were only allowed to spend a certain amount of time in it so that all the children would have an opportunity to enjoy it. The great attraction of being in the room apparently was being able to withdraw from the other kids with a small group of friends and do 'secret' things there that others would not know about. Another attraction was being able to keep out unwanted intruders because the room was so small that it could only hold a few children at a time. The room therefore made it possible to avoid the general kindergarten rule that all children had to be included in a game.

The children were not only attracted to places designated by the pedagogues as appropriate for children. The life stories show that, using the emotional and bodily resources available to them as not-yet-civilised, the children developed their own forms of sociality in the central sites of civilising in the kindergarten, such as the collective meal at the central table in their room and the hygienic activities in the washroom. By engaging in alternative, not-yet-entirely-civilised forms of sociality within these key areas of civilising, I suggest, the children became aware of the meaning and limits of proper behaviour and created a place for themselves in the civilised order.

The Meal

In the narratives, the meals were usually described as important highlights in the day. They were not recalled as occasions where the children learned to master proper etiquette at the dinner table and to display their best behaviour, however, but rather as occasions for having a fun time together. Anton recalled:

> when we sat and ate, we had these cups. And whenever you were given a cup, you had to see which number you got and the higher it was, the better you were. And then there were the plates that had

different colours, but if you had the same colour as another one, you said congratulations!

In a study of schools and after-school centres the Danish psychologist Pernille Hviid (1999:14) also notes the custom of the children congratulating each other if they had something in common, such as the same kind of sandwich in their lunch box, or if they happened to say the same thing at the same time. This congratulating, she suggests, was a way for children to express that they somehow belonged together. In this account, however, the number game was also combined with a competition about getting the highest number and thus establishing a hierarchical order. What may have begun as a pedagogical game – the teachers using the numbers on the bottom of the cups and the colours of the plates to teach the children numbers and colours – thus ended in assertions of special relationships, distinctions and higher status based on accidental numbers, a far cry from the order of social inclusion based on proper behaviour that the kindergarten attempted to establish.

The children's eagerness to compete with each other is also apparent in another competition that, according to Maria, often took place when they were making their own open-faced sandwiches in the kindergarten. Thus, the children seem to have used the occasion to compete over who could make the tallest sandwiches. By doing so they were – consciously or not – making a spoof of the Danish festive lunch of *højt belagt smørrebrød* – 'highly piled up open-faced sandwiches':

> *Maria*: We tried to pile it up and make the tallest sandwiches that we couldn't eat at all.
> *Karen*: That you couldn't eat at all?
> *Maria*: Yes, because you had a very little mouth, and you weren't at all able to open your mouth wide enough to eat them. [We laugh.] And it wasn't certain either that you liked them. The important thing was to make a lot of fun things.

Another favourite preoccupation of the children during mealtime, according to Ditte, was toasting and exchanging season's greetings: 'We said cheers [*skålede*] a lot, and we would say Merry Christmas and Happy New Year even if it was May or something like that.' These activities can also be interpreted as a play on etiquette associated with the elaborate Danish lunches celebrated during the Christmas holidays. In Ditte's account, however, the children engaged in such play regardless of the season, and through their rowdy cheers they not only mimicked adult behaviour, but suggested that they were imbibing alcoholic drinks in a rather uncontrolled fashion. They thereby created a sense of sociality on the basis of forbidden behaviour – the consuming of alcohol by children. Unsanctioned behaviour is also apparent in Charlotte's description of the way in which the children ate rice pudding, a favourite family dish especially during the Christmas season:

> I much preferred that we were given food in the kindergarten and that all received the same and so … instead of all that lunch pack stuff. I wasn't so crazy about that. […] It was much more cosy when you sat and ate together. So I remember when we had rice pudding in December, or something like that, and we poured the redcurrant juice in it. It was a fun thing to sit there and do. All of us, right!

Charlotte makes clear that it is not just the pouring of the juice into rice pudding, rather than drinking it properly in the glass, that was fun, but the experience of all the children doing it together as a group.

By introducing such 'uncivilised' behaviour into the meal, and creating a sense of sociality in connection with it, the children were hitting at the very heart of the kindergarten's civilising project. In his work on civilising processes, Elias points out that eating habits are one of the most important gauges whereby a person's social position is measured. A good part of *The Civilising Process* is therefore devoted to describing the development of increasingly refined eating habits as various segments of the population seek to demarcate their superior status vis-à-vis the rest of the population. The significance of the meal as a mark of class status is also emphasised by the Swedish ethnologists Jonas Frykman and Orvar Löfgren (1987 [1979]:116), who characterise meal times as 'lessons in etiquette'. The narratives suggest that the kindergarten meals clearly were intended to be lessons in good middle-class etiquette, but that the teachers at times found it difficult to control the meals. Some teachers apparently resorted to shaming the children, when they did not behave properly. Thus, Christopher recalled that the leader of his kindergarten reproached him when he, in jest, turned his buttered open-faced rye sandwich upside down, so that the cold cuts were hanging down. He found her remark 'Won't you ever be old enough to eat properly?' particularly stinging, because it questioned whether he belonged in the group of older – and more mature – children in the kindergarten. Thus, his sense of shame inhered not so much in his realisation that he had performed an act that was out of order in the kindergarten, as in his embarrassment that he had done something that might put in question whether he belonged among the older children. In her reprimand the teacher was therefore evoking the children's status hierarchy as well as the norms of civilised behaviour she sought to promote.

Most teachers seem to have chosen not to scold the children, but rather played along with the children's games as long as they did not seem to get out of hand. It was quite apparent to the pedagogues that the children did not particularly share the adult idea of civilised sociality at the dinner table based on proper manners and polite conversation. The kindergartens therefore used various games to keep the children quiet, such as the numbers and colour game. It was also common to appoint one of the children to say *værsgo*,[4] the phrase that invites the people around the table to begin eating, and *velbekomme*,[5] the phrase that signals the end of the meal. This table master position was highly desired and given to the children in turn. Other kindergartens went a step further. According to Rasmussen and Smidt (2001:160), one youth recalled that the children were not allowed to begin eating in this particular kindergarten before they were quiet enough to hear a thumbtack drop to the ground. Again the honour of being the one to drop the thumbtack was highly coveted. The children's experiences from different kindergartens indicate that the boundaries for good and bad behaviour varied somewhat. The suburban kindergarten, where Christopher was admonished for eating his open-faced sandwich upside down, appeared to be rather strict about playing with the food, whereas the inner-city kindergarten attended by Charlotte and Maria seemed to accept a good deal of horsing around with the food. This institution, however, was apparently an 'organic' kindergarten with very politically correct parents that cracked down on anything that could be described as unhealthy eating habits. Thus, in this kindergarten the children were scolded if they turned the sandwiches prepared by their parents into *sukkermadder*, sugar-covered slices of bread, by eating the cold cuts first and then putting sugar on the buttered bread. This kindergarten, however, with its emphasis on natural food, went beyond the boundaries of proper behaviour acceptable to all parents on at least one occasion. This was when yellow Christina took the children in her group to her home where she had a chicken pen. When she cut off the head of a chicken and showed the amazed children that it could run around without a head, she received complaints from the vegan parents of two children. In early twenty-first-century Danish society, the definition of correct civilised behaviour and proper manners was not clear-cut, but negotiated in different ways.

Hygiene

The narratives show that the toilets also played a special role in children's development of sociability. Some children liked to go to the toilet in groups of two or three, especially if they would need the help of adults to wipe their bottom afterwards. They did this, Freja explained, to avoid being stuck in the toilet alone for a long time if the adults did not hear them when they shouted they were finished and therefore did not come to wipe them:

> There were always some who sat on the toilets, and then they shouted: 'I am done!' And they could sit there and shout for 100 years, if nobody heard them. [... But] if you sat there three [at a time], it was much more fun sitting there and shouting.

Other studies of children's institutions point to the toilets as popular places of congregation, when the children had to wash their hands or brush their teeth in connection with meals (Rasmussen and Smidt 2001:179). The children, however, did not just perform these cleansing duties according to the adults' directions but saw in the toilets great places to play. According to Rasmussen and Smidt, one of the youths they interviewed recalled that, when they were to wash their hands, they would roll up their sleeves, cover their faces and arms with white soap and spend 'hours in front of the mirror' playing ghosts (2001:168). Another youth related that his friend accidentally had dropped his toothbrush into the toilet. When he helped his friend get the toothbrush out of the toilet, just as the teacher entered the room, she scolded him, thinking that they were playing with the toilet (2001:47). These episodes show that the teachers were experiencing difficulty confining the children's use of the washroom to hygienic activities, in accordance with the way a civilised person would use the washrooms. To the children soap, the toothbrush and the toilet presented fascinating possibilities of play, not just hygienic equipment.

The redefinition of the toilet as a place of play can be viewed as part of a more general tendency, noted by Gulløv and Højlund (2005:35), for children to attribute 'unmarked places', such as hallways or stairwells, with special meanings or to redesignate rooms, such as toilets or entrance halls, as places for play (see also Højlund 2002:266). When the children made the toilet a gathering place where they could engage in play and sociality of their own making, they were creating a place out of what one might call a marked 'non-place' (Augé 1995), in that the toilet was supposed to be used only when necessary to take care of certain bodily functions, and then as discreetly as possible. Because they needed special training in mastering these bodily functions, the children turned this training into a social event that they could enjoy together in a group. Interestingly, this social aspect of toilet activities was facilitated by the fact that toilets for children usually are placed together in a row with fairly flimsy room dividers, or no dividers at all, making it possible for children to talk with each other while they are using the toilet.

The importance of bodily activities as a basis for sociality – rather beyond the boundaries of civilisation – is also apparent in this incident recollected with great fondness by Christopher:

> I can remember [the pedagogue] Christina. [...] She was simply fantastic. [...] And once when there were lice in the kindergarten, we were lice bathed. There was [...] a room where you could go in and paint that had a sink and a footstool where we were deloused. And it was simply so cosy standing there with a couple of friends, and then she deloused us – at least that is how I remember it.

Emotions

Another important basis of sociality was emotional outbursts or the threat of emotional outbursts among the children, who had not yet learned to control their feelings. The children were well aware that they could draw the attention of the pedagogues through emotional outbursts, such as loud crying. The children usually sought the company of teachers, if they had conflicts with each other or somehow had hurt themselves during play. They did this by crying loudly, thus drawing the attention of the teachers. Apparently, crying was ritualised to the extent that it was virtually obligatory if a child received a cut, as Freja explained:

> *Freja*: At that time, we thought that it was really bad to get a cut. When it was bleeding it was very terrible, and then you had to [cry]. [...]

Karen: Did you act up a little?

Freja: Yes, so that the others would notice you. One of the girls, whenever she hurt herself, it was just *vraaa*, so that all could hear it. Then all ran to an adult [says with excited voice]: 'she has hurt herself, she has hurt herself, she has hurt herself!' Every time they heard someone cry, they came. Sometimes it was just because you had been teased, but that is how we are!

By giving their emotions free range, the children forced the adults to pay attention to them, knowing full well that such outbursts had to be brought under control as quickly as possible in the kindergarten. The children had to be careful, however, not to overdo it. Thus, one of the few children described as being really annoying and to be avoided if at all possible was a girl who made a big scene whenever the slightest thing happened to her.

As both a routinised and disruptive event, crying is similar to the phenomenon of 'hugging' that Israeli anthropologist Deborah Golden (2004) has analysed through field data from an Israeli kindergarten. She found that hugging was especially popular among the girls towards the end of circle time. She suggests that, instead of complaining about circle time being too demanding and drawn-out, they would run to the teacher to hug her, in this way disrupting it and putting it to an end. Hugging therefore was not just the children's uninhibited display of affection towards the teacher, but a 'transgression [that] interrogates the boundaries of civilised/uncivilised, educated/uneducated [...] undoing the discursive hierarchies and stratification of bodies and cultures that schooling reinforces' (Golden 2004:402, quoting Anne M. Phelan 1997:92–5). Golden's analysis of hugging thus points to the important point that through the display of strong emotions, whether negative or positive, children can effectively cut off or affirm social relations, in the process changing the daily routines in their institution.

Conclusion

In this chapter I have explored recollections of the kindergarten as a place of emotionally charged social relations developed by children with other children, as well as adults. My aim has not been to produce an ethnographic description of the kindergarten, based on observations of social life as it unfolds within the institution. Rather, by examining youths' memories of their kindergartens, I have explored how this institution has attained importance through time as a house where young children begin a process of engagement in social relations on their own and develop a sense of the meaning and social significance of these relations.

I have argued that the evocative power of memories of the kindergarten derives, to a great extent, from the special role of the 'house' of the kindergarten as a civilising site with long historical roots, where adult civilisers and yet-to-be-civilised children interact in a creative field of relations. Being not-yet-civilised, children, in the words of Elias:

> necessarily encroach again and again on the adult threshold of repugnance, and – since they are not yet adapted – they infringe upon the taboos of society, cross the adult shame frontier, and penetrate emotional danger zones which the adults themselves can only control with difficulty. (1994 [1939]:141)

In the youths' recollections of their kindergarten experiences, such transgressing of the boundaries between civilised and uncivilised behaviour formed an important basis of their experiences of sociality and made it possible to develop through time a sense of the kindergarten as their own place. Thus, the youths described the rowdy cheering and congratulations at the meals, the playing with the food, the collective visits to the toilet and the intimate delousing sessions with the teachers as occasions when the kindergarten became a cosy and fun place where close relations, communities of identification and feelings of belonging could emerge.

From the point of view of the children, it can be argued that the civilising project of the kindergarten succeeded only because the civilising adults acknowledged that emotions and bodily needs, beyond the threshold of the civilised domain, are of central significance to children's creativity and their ability to develop and sustain social relations and a sense of belonging. If the children were not allowed to explore the uncivilised, they would thus not explore their full potential as human beings. The kindergarten accordingly did not attempt to eradicate the children's uncivilised behaviour but rather endeavoured to contain it in time and space, and to teach the children proper ways to control it. I therefore suggest that the complex arena of negotiation between the not-yet-civilised and the civilisers offers an important avenue for further understanding of modern childhoods – and the adult societies that shape, and are shaped by, them.

Such investigations are relevant not only in analyses of the societal civilisation of children that occurs in public institutions. The family home has been regarded as one of the primary places where the civilising of children occurs, and early kindergartens for middle-class children primarily aimed to support the civilising process expected to take place in the home, as detailed by Frykman and Löfgren (1987 [1979]). The childhood home, described by Carsten (2004) as a central site for the development of close social relations, leading to the emergence of a sense of relatedness, therefore has also been a key site in the training of a cultured middle-class layer of society. The regulating and disciplining associated with civilising is thus closely related to the development of close ties of kinship and friendship, as well as strong feelings of belonging. This suggests that strong notions of relatedness and belonging can emerge through children's and adults' mutual negotiation of the civilising project. A precondition for this, however, is that the families' and the educators' perceptions of the civilising project coincide to a great extent. If this is not the case, for example because of experienced or imagined social or ethnic differences, the children can encounter great difficulties in combining their family's and the kindergarten's notions of correct behaviour and good moral values. The result then can be that the children may experience a process of marginalisation and lack of belonging (Gulløv 2009b; see also chapter 3 in this volume).

Since public institutions for children, as well as family homes, constitute significant 'houses inhabited in childhood' it is important to investigate how these different houses are remembered and attributed with meaning as places for the development of social relations and sources of identification. Children are exposed to different houses with somewhat different notions of proper conduct, modes of control and discipline, as well as possibilities of negotiating and bending the rules. This has important consequences for their development as social beings. The significance of the social relations and sense of relatedness that children develop within the family home can be fully understood only if seen within the framework of the broader range of social relations that children develop in other institutions and the houses associated with them.

5

Social Children and Good Classes

Moulding civilised communities during the first year of school

Laura Gilliam

The comprehensive Danish state school, the *folkeskole*, plays a central role in Danish society. In 2015 it catered to 81 per cent of Danish children, and is thus responsible for the basic education of the vast majority of the new generations of Danish children.[1] While a central objective of the school is to uphold the productivity and welfare of Danish society, the *folkeskole* is also considered a key cultural institution in Danish society, contributing to the transmission of Danish culture by teaching, raising and socialising children. In this chapter and the next two chapters, I will look at the school's upbringing ideals and practices and their consequences for children of different ages, genders, and social and ethnic backgrounds. In this chapter I focus on the youngest children in school. I intend to show how the school's objectives to raise future citizens take the form of a civilising project which does not merely aim to create civilised persons, but also has a specific focus on teaching children the social norms and interactional forms perceived as essential to the ideal civilised community. As such, the school does not merely mould individual citizens, but also communities and – importantly – ideals and models of civilised communities.

The chapter also serves another purpose. As mentioned in chapter 1, the norms of civilised conduct emphasised in school are culture specific. While many of the values and recognised forms of conduct will be general and thus also recognised in other societies, I will argue that others are particular to Danish society. By exploring everyday upbringing practices and ideals of school from an Elias-inspired perspective, it is possible to examine both widespread conceptions of the civilised – the cultivated and socially decent – human being and community, and those celebrated and required by the Danish society in particular. As society's primary civilising institution, the school provides us with insight into prevalent and acknowledged norms and interactional forms. However, as we have alluded to in chapter 2, I shall demonstrate that the school is also an institution which, via its own institutional logics and formative work with children, participates in defining which behavioural forms are civilised, good and necessary, and mediates this to the children. In the second half of the chapter, I will discuss the consequences for children of these ideas of civilised behaviour, and how the ideals are reflected in children's evaluations of behaviour and the way children are categorised in school.

More specifically, I will examine this civilising project as it is carried out in two classes of 5–6-year-olds in two different schools. The first class is oB at Nordlund School, which is situated in a northern Zealand suburb and has a pupil segment consisting of ethnic Danish children from an upper middle-class background. The other class is oX at Vesterly School – a school in a western suburb of Copenhagen where the pupils are mostly of a lower class social background and a mixture of ethnic Danish and ethnic minority origins. While there are several differences between these two classes and between the schools' social and ethnic configurations, these issues will not be the primary focus in this chapter.

As part of more extensive fieldwork in the two schools, I spent two months in each of the two classes in 2007 and 2008 respectively. I conducted daily participant observation in the classes and with children and teachers during breaks, and had informal conversations with children, teachers and parents. I also conducted observations in three other classes of grade 0. In oB at Nordlund School I participated in 23 school–home meetings between the teachers and the children's parents. I also carried out semi-structured qualitative interviews with 30 of the children across the two classes, and five of their teachers.

Grade 0 – Transition to School

The school's mission to create good citizens may at first glance seem irrelevant in grade 0. The children are about to begin 10–18 years of education and school attendance,[2] which most likely will bring them into larger society one day, but for this first year of school, school life seems like the goal in itself. To the teachers of grade 0, the objective is first and foremost to mould the children into good school pupils. Yet, as I will argue, it is informative to look at this class, and to take a closer look at the kinds of behaviour that grade 0 children are taught is required in order to go to school, as a correlation can be found between this upbringing project and society's demands on the good citizen.

What used to be called 'kindergarten class' was originally introduced in 1970 as a 'soft' transition from playing in kindergarten to learning at school. However, during the period of increased focus on academic competences in schools, described in chapter 2, it became part of compulsory education and the name was changed to grade 0 in 2009. At the same time, academic content filtered down to grade 0, decreasing the time for play. Yet, grade 0 is still led by teachers trained in kindergarten pedagogy, and is still informally perceived as the class that ensures the children's transition from kindergarten to school. Ideally, inappropriate behaviour and relational dynamics should be rooted out in this class, so the grade 1 teachers can focus on the teaching of academic skills. It is thus here, that the children are to be cleansed of the uncivilised; that is, the more egoistic and undisciplined behaviour which was accepted to some extent in kindergarten from the 'not-yet-civilised' younger child (see chapter 4). In this way, grade 0 can be said to function as a kind of pre-quarantine before children enter the quarantine of the 'real' school, and continue the more refined process of cultivation there (Ariès 1962; cf. chapter 1).

The Social

Tina, the class teacher of 0X at Vesterly School, expresses this when she says that grade 0 is where the children 'should learn how school life works' and be taught the rules of school; that is, to have lessons and breaks, sit still, raise your hand, and participate in communal organised learning activities. As I conducted my fieldwork in both 0B and 0X at the beginning of the school year, I witnessed how the teachers in both classes spent a great deal of energy and time on introducing the children to the behavioural norms and rules of school. In Karin's class at Nordlund School, all the children are able to recite these rules by heart: 'You are not allowed to run around during class, you are not allowed to shout in class, you are only allowed to run outside and during breaks, you must raise your hand, you are not allowed to play all the time', and, as Matilda from 0B points out in an interview: 'You are not allowed to get up on a chair and sing rock songs.'

The children have understood that to be a good pupil you have to abide by these rules of bodily discipline, yet they also know that there is more to it. Here Markus from oB relates: 'You are not allowed to hit, kick, or scratch, or throw apples. And you are not allowed to make anyone feel sad, or to destroy something that someone else is making. And you are not allowed to tease anyone.' These norms are concerned with preventing the children's display of aggression and potential hurtful interaction with others, and reflect an intense focus on the interaction with others; what is referred to as 'the social' in Danish schools, an emic term which, we will argue, is in close accordance with what in Danish society is considered civilised behaviour (see also the discussion in chapter 3). In Danish school rhetoric, 'the academic' (*det faglige*) and 'the social' (*det sociale*) describe the two central dimensions in the school's work with children. As depicted in chapter 2, the child's well-being, its social skills, and the teaching of democracy have been focuses of the school since the ideas of the educational reform movement became part of the schools' doxa. This is partly reflected in the Education Act stipulation that the school should contribute to the pupil's 'all-round development' (LBK no. 747 of 2016). Yet, while teachers often refer to this as a legitimisation of what they call their 'work with the social', 'the social' encompasses more than the child's individual skills, knowledge and progress. As we will see, it also refers to social relations and collective forms that are loaded with interests and meanings related to civilising ideals.

Whereas all teachers experience that they need to consider both 'the academic' and 'the social' dimensions of the classes that they teach, 'the social' dimension is the main responsibility of the assigned 'class teacher'. And, while the interest in the pupils' behaviour and social life is often more intense in the younger classes, the grade o teachers feel that they have a special responsibility for this. The understanding is that it is in grade o that the social foundation of a good class is built, and here that the children learn to interact with others in school. As described by oX's teacher Tina: 'We raise the children to interact with other people in the right way, children as well as adults. Because they enter a new community [at school] where they need to be able to interact.' In accordance with this, a lot of energy is spent in the two grade o classes, working with forms of unacceptable social behaviour, and on teaching the children what is considered good manners towards others. In both classes, each day one morning lesson focuses either on Danish language or maths. Once a week, a visit to the library, a music class and a PE (physical education) class are scheduled. However, the rest of the timetable is reserved for non-academic activities such as a daily 'play hour', where the children play with toys in the class, a daily class assembly, reading aloud, Second Step exercises,[3] relaxation exercises and, after 1 p.m., an after-school programme, where the children play and take part in creative activities.[4] The school day, furthermore, includes many scheduled breaks and physical and creative activities to make the school time attractive for the children and to allow them time-outs from the academic work. However, the non-academic activities are not just recreational but always have a secondary 'social purpose'. Karin, oB's main teacher, thus describes how the aim of the daily 'play hour' is not just to let the children play, but to ensure that the children, through their games, establish social bonds. In both classes, a more organised form of training occurs during the class assembly, where the children gather in a circle on the floor, and in the informal, but teacher-guided, discussions, where the children are seated at their tables. The teachers can focus on practising the alphabet and general knowledge, but time and again there is a subject of a moral nature which the adults – often spontaneously – introduce. In both classes, the occasional distribution of cake among pupils is used to discuss the concept of justice. In class oX, the teacher Tina takes a firm hold of the plate of cakes and asks the circle of children: 'Would it be just if Mette [her assistant teacher] and I just ate all of them?' 'No', several children respond. 'What is it then?' Lasse shouts: 'Cheating!' 'Unfair', says Emily. 'Yes, what if I gave you …', Tina begins to distribute cakes and stops after four children have received a cake. 'What is that?' she asks. 'Unfair', several children join in.

At the class assembly the above-mentioned Second Step exercises are also often used as teaching material to train children to recognise other people's emotions and reactions, and respond with what is considered appropriate behaviour. In the following example, the children from the other grade o class at Vesterly School, oY, are sitting in a circle around their teacher, Sanne. She shows them a photostat of a couple of boys:

Sanne: How do you think this boy is feeling?

Troels: He is a little bored, because the other boy has the toys, so he gets a little sad.

Sanne: Good, that was a lot of information! That brought us much closer. Why is he a little sad?

Troels: Because the boy with the toys said he cannot join in.

Sanne: Can you show me what a sad face looks like?

[A number of the children show drooping mouths, sulk, wrinkle their brows, and pull their chins towards their chests.]

Sanne: Sanja, can you explain with words how somebody would look sad?

[Sanja makes a sad face and points at her own mouth and eyes, tells what they look like, and describes how you lower your head. Sanne asks if any of them occasionally become sad, and the conversation continues.]

Another tool employed by teachers to train the children in empathy and friendliness and to solve conflicts is role play. If there has been an episode among the children and they return from the break in an unhappy mood, Karin often uses role play to show the children how to: 'ask each other in an okay way' and not: 'just interrupt and push the other person away and say "I want to join the game."' In the same role play, the children are also asked to practise 'decent ways' of rejecting other children's requests to join a game. This has to be done 'in a proper way' – and, as Karin suggests, for instance by saying: 'We are just playing a really good game, but you can join us in the next break or you can join us tomorrow.'

Even when something else is on the agenda, the teachers use shared conversations and activities in class to rehearse social interaction. They encourage the children to listen to each other, wait their turn, ask each other questions and discuss a subject in a controlled manner. Likewise, the teachers employ corrective sanctions if anyone interrupts, sneers, makes fun of others or does not participate. If the teachers witness a conflict between the children, they identify the unacceptable behaviour and demonstrate acceptable ways of dealing with the matter at hand. In oX, for instance, Tina takes a firm hold of Hjalmar when, with a big grin on his face, he says 'shit' to Altin, and tells him that she will not tolerate that kind of language: 'Can you apologise?', she asks Hjalmar. When Firat attempts to take a pillow that Lasse is sitting on, and Lasse pushes him away with an angry expression, Tina interrupts and says that he should try to tell Firat what to do instead of pushing. The next time Firat touches the pillow, Lasse says: 'Stop', and Tina commends him: 'Well done, Lasse!' Tina explains the purpose of this instruction as follows: 'We have talked about how you should use your mouth and not fight. And we try to encourage the children to deal with their issues themselves verbally.' In class they have made the children act out small plays about these ways of dealing with conflicts verbally, and Tina and her assistant teacher Mette also act out a role play where they pretend to hit each other and cry and subsequently ask the children what they could have done differently:

> They think it is fun when Mette and I enact this scenario. We tell them, just think if we hit each other every time I was a little cross with Mette, because she said something I did not agree with? What if I hit her? Would you then think it was nice to be in this room with us? Of course they shake their heads.

In a similar vein, the children should learn how to discuss, how to conduct themselves in a public arena, and how to move from one place to another within the school without bothering others. They should learn how to shower together after PE classes without crossing boundaries of decorum, and how to interact in suitable ways in relations with both younger and older children in the playground.

Institutional Requirements or Societal Norms?

What we see here is that the teachers orchestrate the social interaction in class in great detail and do so in accordance with a highly considerate and non-transgressive interactional form. The teachers often explain this focus on the social aspects of school life in terms of the conditions at school. The reason that the children should control their bodies and social behaviour is hence often stated with reference to the number of children in class and the kind of conduct that is necessary in order for a teacher to teach such a group. Here Tina makes this point:

> 23 children milling around at the same time is a no go. You cannot make that much noise when you are so many in the same room. You must be able to put your own needs on hold, because there are many others who have needs. You need to be able to await your turn and to get along well with each other when you have to be together this much and for such a long time.

Moreover, as it is often emphasised by the teachers, it is best for the children's learning if they feel secure and comfortable in class.

These explanations are interesting as they suggest that the teachers train the children in, and endorse certain types of behaviour which are required by the school's institutional practices and conditions. In order to be able to teach, for children to learn and not waste too much time on conflicts, the teachers need a class that functions well socially. This demonstrates that the upbringing project of the school and the conduct it teaches the new Danish citizens is at least partly defined by its institutional requirements. Yet, we will see in the following that the teachers' training of the children's social skills and adaptation to the communal setting are so multifaceted and morally based that it cannot be entirely grounded in functionality, but also reflects strong ideals of civilised interaction and communities. My point is rather to argue that there is an interesting correlation between the norms of interaction that are practically required in school and the dominant norms of acceptable behaviour in broader Danish society, which seems to be caused by a close relationship between school and society. In the following, I will explore these perceptions and ideals, and the dialectic through which they are formed.

Awareness of Boundaries

The described admonitions, correctives, encouragements, exercises and activities are apparently designed to teach the children a specific way to interact. Taking a closer look, what is perceived as 'social' conduct, and what children are trained in and encouraged to express, no matter the context, is the kind, subdued, non-aggressive, empathic, inclusive and cooperative response to other people's verbal or non-verbal communication. In a continuation of the formative work in kindergartens, children are supposed to avoid conflicts, agitation, aggression, noise, pain, emotional turbulence, exclusion of others, selfish behaviour, and types of competition that generate conflict. Even though Tina emphasises in her class that 'it is all right to get angry', she and other teachers will always interrupt when children show anger, attempting to calm them down and getting them to lower their voices.

Looking at the acts that the teachers respond to and avert on a daily basis in the two grade 0 classes, it is noteworthy that such acts are often described in terms of transgression of 'boundaries', whether of others' or one's own. Hence the concept of 'boundaries' often occurs in the teachers' discourse on the learning of social competences; for instance when they say that the children have to learn to 'become aware of each other's boundaries', or that a certain child 'constantly transgresses the other children's boundaries'. However, even when they do not use the word 'boundaries', they use other words such as 'offend', 'hurt', 'violate', 'disturb', 'invade' and 'take up too much space'; words that indicate the perception that individuals are surrounded by invisible borders that should not be transgressed. The children must learn not to offend, hurt, violate and disturb the physical and emotional boundaries around other people, and they should take care not to let their own emotions, body and voice take up more than the physical and psychological space to which they may justifiably lay claim. Yet, they should also take care not to allow other people to transgress the boundaries that are perceived to surround their own self.

This concept of 'boundaries' – and the understanding of a vulnerable, inviolable self which it entails – seems to be a general trait of civilising ideals. It expresses a notion that interaction between people constitutes a symbolic space within which each interacting individual is assigned a certain space surrounded by strict boundaries which must be respected in order to uphold civilised interaction. Thus a certain self-awareness and self-restraint are required in close interactions between mutually inter-dependent people (see chapter 1). The same focus on or indeed 'passion for boundaries' is described in the anthropologist Marianne Gullestad's study of childrearing among Norwegian parents and in Dil Bach's chapter in this book about well-to-do Danish families (Gullestad 1997a:34, see also Bach 2014). In Danish schools, and Danish society more broadly speaking, the general civilising ideal also seems to be based on links between a delimitation of the self, awareness of and respect for other people's boundaries and civilised behaviour. This self-limiting conduct is a central part of the training in 'social behaviour' that is given in schools.

While uncivilised behaviour is generally conduct that transgresses symbolic boundaries between people, the placement of these boundaries alters from society to society, group to group, and also, to some degree, from person to person. In the case of the Danish school, it is nevertheless possible to identify some general aspects from discussions about boundaries. Just as described by Elias (1998b) and Wouters (2011) as a general aspect of the informalisation process (see chapters 1, 2 and 3), requirements in terms of formal politeness have also relaxed in the Danish school, with teachers appreciative of children who are confident and outspoken; however, this does not mean that requirements in terms of self-restraint have also decreased. While physical aggression and vulgarity are still among the most serious types of boundless and thus uncivilised behaviour, notions from psychology about the fragile self and the frail child, who can be damaged, traumatised and humiliated by other people, also seem to have shaped a perception of emotional boundaries as inviolable. It is, to a great extent, the transgression of these boundaries that is emphasised as something that should shame the offender and may cause repudiation and social degradation. Moreover, it is a gentle and conscientious attitude to other people's boundaries and feelings that is required for a child to be considered a 'social' – that is, civilised – being in the eyes of others.

Civilised Upbringing

These civilising norms also require the teachers to show great considera-tion for what they perceive as the children's boundaries. In both grade o classes, scolding and rage on the part of the teachers are relatively rare phenomena. This is partly because the teachers consider the classes 'good classes', and thus rarely find it necessary to tell them off, but it is also because the teachers try to avoid what they see as a stigmatised practice. This seems to reflect a further refinement of the ideal of civilised ways of raising children, which Elias described in relation to the de-legitimising of adult violence against children (Elias 1998a:207). Reflecting widespread ideals of non-authoritarian treatment of children (see chapter 2) and the psychological notion of the vulnerable child described above, a civilised upbringing is now generally perceived to encompass careful consideration of the child's emotions. This avoidance of anger and scolding is contested by some teachers and parents, who find it more appropriate to teach children good manners through negative sanctions and reward, showing them that their actions have consequences. In other classes, I have also experienced another use and legitimation of scolding as a practice inherent to childrearing (see the next chapter). Yet, while there is not complete support for what the grade o teachers describe as 'the positive approach' in the two schools, it is clearly dominant, as displays of anger and scolding generally require an explanation, even among the teachers that practise and defend such an approach.

In both classes, the teachers make explicit demands of and correct the children, but they also strive to find ways to raise children through a 'pedagogy of recognition', and thus emphasise the importance of praising good conduct, and attempt to focus on situations where the children 'get it right'. As they explain to me: the children's boundaries should not be transgressed, they should not be shamed for their actions, and their self-confidence should not be deflated. On the contrary, they should be 'treated positively', made to 'feel appreciated' and allowed 'to be themselves – just the way they are', as Karin puts it. Resembling the pedagogues described in the previous chapters, and the Norwegian teachers and parents in the aforementioned study by Marianne Gullestad, who all share the notion that the child should be allowed to 'be him/herself' (Gullestad 1996, 1997b), these teachers are thus not merely occupied with teaching children proper ways of behaving. They also emphasise that children should be happy, balanced and allowed their individual ways of doing things. They find that their job is to create a 'safe and sound environment', where the pupils feel that 'they are noticed', and where they are not forced to adapt to ready-made templates. While, as we will see, teachers do not always adhere to these ideals, they seem to have a considerable effect on the teachers' treatment of children. The teachers clearly shun displays of negative emotions, such as pronounced anger, and avoid shouting and the use of power in ways they think might subjugate children. They are clearly annoyed when they feel it necessary to scold; they criticise other teachers for being 'authoritarian', 'disciplining' or 'hot-tempered'; and they deny it when the children say they are 'strict'. Vibeke, class teacher for oC, tells me she also avoids sending pupils out of the room, because they should not feel 'outside the community'. In Karin's class, there is a handful of children – all boys – whom Karin feels she needs to keep an eye on because they are 'too forward', 'stick out' or 'bring attention to themselves in inappropriate ways', yet her reaction to their conduct is to pay special attention to them for a period of time. She tells me that she looks for things that merit praise, gives them more hugs than usual or just puts a hand on their shoulder when they are noisy. Seemingly, this approach pays off, as Karin does not have to work on integrating these children into the class for very long before they no longer 'stick out'.

To Fit Into the Inclusive Community

At first glance, it is the individual children and any 'asocial' and 'transgressive' demeanour that are the object of the teachers' upbringing efforts. Yet, importantly, it seems as though, even more than civilised individuals, the desired result is civilised communities. The teachers thus have a two-pronged vision. Even though they are preoccupied with the child's well-being, this well-being is always related to the community of the class and to the child as a part of this community. The ideal is that in the civilised class community, nobody feels excluded and everyone feels at home, and, in order to achieve this, the children should 'behave socially', 'adapt to the group', and 'contribute to the community' of the class. In this way, the teachers' concern with the well-being of the child is united with their focus on the class as a group. Some teachers, however, find that the assimilation to the behavioural norms of the school which they demand from children does not always concur with the ideal described above of the child's right to 'be itself'. Hence Karin remarks: 'I hate the school framework, or the frameworks which [the children] have to fit into. I like that the children can also be themselves, just the way they are!' But even if the teachers occasionally experience these discrepancies, they also express that the respect for the individual child's personality and the attempt not to tamper with his or her self-esteem is part and parcel of the school's civilising project. As such, the ideal of accepting the children 'as they are' and, as the teachers say, 'not violating them' is ideally integral to the concept of the inclusive, civilised community and the inherent respect for other people's boundaries. In the ideal civilised community, everyone is accepted at the same time as everyone adapts, yet no one 'violates' themselves or others in order to fit in. This ideal has consequences for the dynamics of exclusion within the class, which I will return to below. Yet it also means that the only acceptable intention, in terms of changing children's personalities, is that doing so will help the child to adapt. Karin articulates this delicate manoeuvre in the following phrase: 'We try to get them to fit in as much as possible, but without divesting them of their individual finesse.' Yet the result is that the kind of individuality and the 'individual finesse' children are allowed are those that can be combined with the somewhat high and multifaceted demands regarding civilised interaction in class.

Hence, even when nurturing the needs of the individual child, the teachers seem to be particularly concerned with their inclusion in the group and the civilised status of the class. As expressed in the oft-repeated phrases 'nobody should feel excluded in this class' and 'we do not want bullying in our school', exclusion and bullying are not merely unacceptable because they distress the individual children, but also because they challenge the status of the class and the school as civilised collectivities.

The Good Class – the Inclusive and Harmonious Community

The civilising activities and practices I have described are, as such, not just focused on the civilising process of the individual child, but also on the creation of a good community. The teachers attempt to create a harmonious class with a nice, kind, and peaceful discourse and interaction; a tolerant community where there is 'room for everyone' and where children show consideration for each other and for the invisible boundaries of others. It is these, in the teachers' eyes, civilised relations which are the goal of the teachers' work with 'the social' and which they refer to when describing a class as 'a good class'. Thus, as the teachers often emphasise, a good class does not have to be academically strong; a good class is rather the harmonious, 'well-functioning' group.

On the basis of studies of Danish school classes and sports clubs, the anthropologist Sally Anderson has described the sociality required in groups of children who are placed outside the home as a 'civil sociality' – a child-focused type of interaction which is inclusive within the given frameworks (Anderson 2000, 2008). As Anderson emphasises, Danish schools were not always structured into classes and, one presumes, classes originally had a practical rather than a pedagogical function (2000:47–50). Likewise, it is also important to note that the focus on class communities, and the intensive effort to raise children to participate in and contribute to such communities, is a relatively new phenomenon. The educational reform movement's interest in the creation of good spaces for childhood, reinforced by the 1970s focus on community and cohesion (see chapter 2), seems to have led to, perhaps even required, this focus on the class as a social unit. I will argue that teachers' efforts to create 'good classes' are thus an expression of historically and culturally specific, yet now dominant, ideals of civilised behaviour in Danish society, which the school simultaneously bases its civilising project upon and plays a central role in reproducing. I will therefore continue the exploration started by Anderson by taking a closer look at the sociality children are trained in, and that is required in a class, and focus on what this tells us about Danish civilising ideals (see also Jenkins 2011).

The emphasis on the establishment of a civilised community can be seen in the daily play hour and the determination with which the teachers guard this particular lesson. In the school context, where time is in short supply, it is telling that the teachers in both classes spend one of four daily lessons on a play hour, and that this survived the previous year's municipal budget cuts of one lesson per day. Since the children already play during breaks and after-school activities, the fact that one hour each day is allocated to play and observed by adults shows that something important is at stake. At a parent–teacher meeting, Karin emphasises the purpose of the play hour: 'It is not just play,' she says:

the children need it in order to establish good relations to each other. We use the lesson to get a better idea of the children's mutual relations; to talk with the children if there are any problems or if some of them need a chat. We need to consider the children: we should teach them to go to school, and we need to create a good class.

The day after, she tells me that 'the play hour is extremely important because of the focus on the social aspect', and adds that the teachers often use the play hours to observe how the children interact and to see if any of them are not being included in the various groupings within the class. Even if teachers often use the play hour for practical purposes, they find that it gives them an opportunity to 'check up on the community' and the relations between the children, and, if necessary, to adjust these relations by intervening. The play hour thus seems to serve the school's need to supervise what Foucault calls the whole 'social body' of the class (Foucault 1977).

One of the things teachers find in need of adjustment when observing play hours is children who are either 'too quiet' and 'too cautious' or 'too big for their boots' (*'for langt fremme i skoen'* describes someone as too self-assertive or too smart for their own good). Both types of children are mentioned with care and concern, and described as children who need a little help with 'the social'. When the teachers describe the 'quiet children', they usually say that they need to be 'brought forward', that they should 'contribute more', take up 'more space', and so on. On the other hand, the highly expressive children should be 'held down' or even 'sat upon', because they take up 'too much space' or are 'too assertive'. Here the children's ways of acting within the group give the teachers cause to adjust their behaviour and degree of activity. However, as the use of spatial metaphors indicates, what is also regulated is the space the children take up in the group and in its social arena. In effect, the corrections thus come to mark boundaries between the children. This testifies to how the class community is seen as a space where the children should learn to express themselves and negotiate ways of being without taking up too much or too little space or colliding with others. In line with this, Karin almost describes her role as that of a choreographer when she refers to her successful efforts to get Simone to be a bit more vocal in class and among peers: 'Yes, some of them should be moved a little bit forward. Some should move forward and others should move back.' Once again, one of the goals of the teachers' formative work is to create a harmonious, egalitarian community, where each person does not take up more or less than their share of the common space, where activity and sound are controlled, and where nobody dominates others.

At Vesterly School, the focus on the community is also evident in the teachers' postponement of drawing up the new classes until after the autumn break. Instead, they split up the new pupils into a girls' class and a boys' class. They then observe the children's interactions and assess 'who gets along' and 'how they complement each other'. At a parent–teacher meeting, the teachers describe their goal as creating 'homogeneous and well-functioning classes'. In this way, the teachers engage in a kind of social engineering in their attempt to ensure the well-being of the individual pupils, and simultaneously create 'well-functioning classes' by anticipating problematic group constellations. When drawing up the new classes, the teachers are particular attentive to children who may potentially be excluded and attempt to ensure that the classes will be harmonious and inclusive groups where no one is lonely or 'sticks out socially', as it is often termed.

The teachers also often state that 'there should be room for everyone' in already established classes. For example, the teachers do not allow three of the girls in 0B at Nordlund School to perform a dance act without including the other girls, because 'everyone should participate'. Likewise, the pupils in this class are not allowed to turn away anyone who wants to join a game unless, as mentioned above, they promise to include them during the following break. As Anderson argues, egalitarian, universalist appeals, in phrases like 'making room for everybody', are often used in relation to children who are placed in groups outside the family: groups they have not chosen to be with, but towards whom they are told to have an inclusive attitude. The notion of 'everybody' is used as a rhetorical figure that can be adjusted in accordance with the degree of inclusion observed, and hence veil the simultaneous excluding practices (Anderson 2008:165–9; see also Anderson 2000).

In line with Anderson's points, it is evident in both grade 0 classes that when teachers address the notion that there should be room for 'everybody', this refers to the group of classmates only. The obligatory inclusion does not encompass children in other classes, nor are the regular distancing practices performed between girls and boys interpreted as illegitimate or even as exclusion. This emphasises that the understanding of inclusive sociality towards others always involves selective demands and blind spots with regard to whom 'inclusion' does and does not encompass. It is also interesting that children are described as being 'outside' the class, even if they merely prefer to play with children from another class. The children's sociality must be directed towards the class, and it is the class and the 'everybody' it represents which should preferably be whole and inclusive (Anderson 2000:157–60). Anton from 0B at Nordlund School exemplifies this as he prefers to play with a group of boys in the other grade 0 class that he knows from kindergarten. In this case, the teachers attempt to motivate him to build relations within the class by allocating him a seat next to a boy whom they think he should befriend, and by grouping him with other boys during the play hour. While Anton does not seem to be uncomfortable in the class, the teachers' concern shows that he 'sticks out socially', as it is often depicted, that the class is considered his 'natural' social arena, and that his choice of friends is seen as a breach of the inclusive, but also exclusive, community of the class. In order for the group to be a harmonious whole, the children should find their primary friends and relations in the class. As I shall discuss later, this points to the nature of the class as both a 'model of' and a 'model for' the ideal inclusive community (Geertz 1993 [1973]:93–4).

Integration and Acceptance of Differences

The teachers of the grade 0 classes attempt to ensure an inclusive community by strengthening the development of relations across what is, in Eliasian terms, the class figuration. One tool for achieving this is allocating the children new seats, hoping this will make them engage with their new neighbours. Moreover, they try to create a tight-knit community by encouraging, making rules for and engaging parents in social gatherings outside the school. They ask parents, for instance, to co-arrange birthday parties celebrating a group of the children and invite all the children, and argue that this will give the parents an opportunity to get to know each other and cooperate on issues related to the class. Likewise, the teachers attempt to get the children to play together outside school and encourage the parents to invite a broad range of children home for play dates:

> We talk a lot about the fact that it is good to play with each other outside school. It is good to have more than one friend, and at school we attempt to position the pupils in various constellations so they get to play with everyone in order to get to know each other's good traits. (Tina, teacher 0X, Vesterly School)

The ideal class is apparently a class where everyone has good relations across the board, and where everyone is nice to each other in spite of their individual differences. This emphasis on tolerance of differences is expressed by Karin when she describes a class she had the year prior to my fieldwork as 'fantastic':

> It's something about them being able to accommodate each other, in spite of differences. They stuck together and were nice to each other. When I say that a class is fantastic, I do not refer to the academic level, but more to the social aspect. Something about the community in that class. (Karin, teacher oB, Nordlund School)

Another way to create classes that are socially integrated despite individual differences is to arrange so-called 'buddy groups' (also called 'play groups') – an initiative used in many Danish schools. At Vesterly School, the school principal introduces the concept at a parent–teacher meeting. She explains that the school board has embraced this initiative because it has been shown to improve well-being and reduce bullying in schools. She explains that a buddy group consists of four children, a mixture of boys and girls from the same class – and notably not across classes – who do not usually play together. The parents are asked to arrange group play dates for these buddy groups once a month. The idea is that knowledge generates friendship, yet she emphasises that the children do not have to become friends because you don't need to become friends with everybody in your class: 'but you can be buddies with everyone'. This emphasises that the prime goal of these arrangements is not personal friendships, but the creation of the emblematic harmonious community where everybody gets along and nobody is excluded.

The fact that the school principal and school board have taken the initiative to coordinate these play relations shows the efforts brought to bear on the creation of harmonious classes. The strategy is particularly evident in relation to bullying, which has been the subject of numerous school policy initiatives at both local and national level during the past decade. In the two classes, there is an intensive focus on bullying or more indirect exclusion. Again, bullying is primarily regarded as abhorrent because it hurts children and transgresses their emotional boundaries. However, part of the aversion and concern experienced by adults, as well as the national commotion and the many policy interventions, seems to be based on the understanding that spiteful exclusion is considered truly uncivilised behaviour. Children who bully are in acute need of being civilised because they deliberately break the most elementary social rules of civilised conduct. Bullying is seen as an expression of a barbaric nature and a sign of a general decline of social norms, and thus it generates a comprehensive anxiety for the civilised status of the new generation among parents and teachers, as well as among the general public. In the bully lurks the barbaric, uncivilised child, and the class burdened with bullying is perceived as an uncivilised mob of children unaware and unobservant of moral and psychological boundaries. As it testifies to a context in which civilised norms have been abandoned in favour of 'survival of the fittest', the entire class is seen as a disgrace to the school and its civilising endeavour.

Cooperation and Conflict Management

Vibeke, class teacher of 0C, one of the other grade 0 classes at Nordlund School, illustrates another undignified form of interaction: conflict and competition. The teachers generally do not accept these modes in class and feel obliged to intervene. According to Vibeke, she has on several occasions been forced to put her teaching on standby because the children compete as to who can collect the greatest number of milk caps from the quarter litre of milk they are given at lunch time. She explains:

> During the last lesson today, for instance, we were supposed to work on the house of sounds [a teaching method], right? But we had to drop that. Instead we had to have a talk about milk caps, because they were the crux of a major problem in class. The pupils fought over them, hid them and so on. What we have done is to tell them that no milk caps should be passed on to others. If they are to be given away, they must be given to the class. I am trying to find some large cylindrical tube, preferably transparent, and then we will attempt to set a record [...]. You see, my task is to intervene and solve the problem. How do I get them to stop competing for those damn milk caps, exchanging them, hiding them, stealing them from one another and so on? How do I avoid that? [...] I need to find a way to turn this milk cap competition into a shared project. (Vibeke, teacher 0C, Nordlund School)

When a teacher chooses to stop teaching and spend several hours dealing with a conflict about milk caps, this is not a self-evident part of the school's project or a choice which all teachers in all societies would make. It demonstrates the naturalisation of the focus on the harmonious interaction of the class and that the teacher sees it as his or her duty to intervene in cases of conflict or non-cooperative modes of interaction. Vibeke's statement demonstrates that the milk cap feud is problematic because it has generated unacceptable competition, conflicts and factions in class. It is noteworthy that her solution is a shared project – getting the children to cooperate on the task of setting a record; a competition without a defined opponent which is intended to re-establish a sense of harmony and community in the class. This perception of cooperation as integrative is also evident when she discusses the activities she engages in to improve relations in her class. She finds her class 'unintegrated' and composed of children who take up too much space and, as such, she spends a good deal of time on what she calls 'socialisation games':

> In physical education classes, we also spend some of the time practising, you know, that kind of socialisation and cohesion. Today we had an example where we cooperated on a project … we had two teams and the point was to support your team and not just compete, but help the group by clapping and cheering – and you should constantly comment on aspects of the other players' performance, which was really good. (Vibeke, teacher oC, Nordlund School)

At both schools, the PE classes are used in similar ways to train cooperation and avert competition and conflict. While this, yet again, is partly explained by the concern for the well-being of the individual children, I will argue that the teachers' joyful descriptions of classes or projects 'where the children really cooperated' illustrate that cooperation is striven for in this way because it is idealised as an interactional form that expresses exemplary civilised idyll. Civilised forms of engagement with others are also encouraged in what can be seen as implicit exercises of conflict management. In cases of conflict, the children are generally instructed to discuss the issues at hand, and guided in communicating instead of lashing out. However, if the problems become serious, they are always encouraged to 'talk to an adult'. When Karin reads aloud from the children's book *Rubber Tarzan* [*Gummi Tarzan*] to class oB, she asks if the father of the main character is right when he claims that a boy should act like a real man and beat up other boys.

> *Christoffer*: I think he should throw a bucket of water at the big boys.
> *Karin*: Would that be a good idea?

Peter: I think he should make friends with them.

Karin: Now that would be a good idea. How could he make friends with them?

Sara: He could talk to the adults about it.

Karin: Should he tell the adults and then get them to talk to the big boys about making friends with him? I think that would be a really good idea.

As demonstrated by Elias, a significant aspect of the civilising process in Western Europe was the state's monopolisation of violence (Elias 1994 [1939]:369–70). In line with this, it is now considered civilised to refrain from violence and punishment, and to hand over the right to use force to the state authorities. It could be argued that, in school, children are raised to accept this kind of transfer of power when they are told not to deal with conflicts themselves and to allow the assessment of the situation and the determination of sanctions to be conducted by the generic category 'the adults'. The children are hereby implicitly taught that revenge and violence are unacceptable and that the acceptable – and civilised – way of dealing with conflicts they cannot solve is to hand over adjudication and implementation of punishment to the authorities.

A final example of the school's focus on the moulding of civilised communities is the practice of evaluating children as groups. The teachers at Nordlund School use a system of smileys to assess the children's orderliness and behaviour in class. However, these smileys are awarded to the class as a whole rather than to individual children. They primarily explain this group assessment with their concern that individual assessments would 'cause division' and 'hurt' the children. Meanwhile, they also stress that the collective smileys create a shared sense of responsibility and community, since the children are given a red and dissatisfied smiley if they have not helped each other clean up. As Karin relates: 'It creates a sense of community, and in that mode you might as well pick something up from the floor, even if you did not leave it there.' In interviews, the children complain about these smileys as they find it unfair that they are assessed on the basis of other people's actions. However, as suggested by Karin above, the use of collective smileys seems designed precisely to focus on the community and to let the children know that they are not just seen as individuals, but also as part of a collective. Through this, they are given lessons about what characterises a 'community'; that they are obliged to help the group to which they have been allocated and that doing something for others is well regarded. Moreover, they learn that the actions of other pupils within the community also influence how they themselves are perceived. The teachers hope that the social pressure will get the children to assume responsibility for each other and for their communal space, and to consider that other people are involved and affected by their actions. This points to the value of the community, which the teachers like to instil in children, but also to how they consider the class a 'model for' the ideal civilised society; a point to which I shall return.

Consequences for Assessments of Children

The modes of assessing and moulding civilised conduct which I have described above have a range of consequences for the children. The most noticeable consequence is that they influence who the teachers consider good pupils – at least in grade o. As might be expected, significant criteria are academic ability, work ethic, cooperation, calm body language and, not least, due respect for the teacher, combined with desire and motivation to work and learn. However, factors such as being 'social', 'contributing to the community' and being 'integrated in the group' are often highlighted in the teachers' descriptions of 'the good pupils'. Though these factors might also be central in other school systems, I expect that they are not important requirements in the practice of schools in all societies and suggest that they are given particular priority in Danish schools. When I ask the teachers to name the children whom they consider 'good pupils', Vibeke selects a boy from her class and says: 'He is a good pupil in every way. He contributes a lot to the class. He is actually good at explaining, he is good at finding the right words in any given situation, and he is good at making suggestions as to how to solve conflicts.' She selects another boy because 'he has empathy and he is also good at decoding his buddies' signals'. Karin, meanwhile, chooses Veronica, even though she does not find her academically skilled, and describes her as follows: 'She is brilliant! She functions well in a group and in a class, and she makes friends easily.' When mentioning three other girls, she explains her choice by saying: 'She is good to the other children, she is good within the group, and she has a good sense of justice.'

At Vesterly School, Tina emphasises similar aspects. She describes the girl Adelaide as 'social', and, on the basis of observations during the play hour, says:

She is good at organising games and letting everyone find their own place. She is good at pushing for what she wants till she succeeds, but she is also good at listening to other pupils' wishes [...]. She is also good at intervening if some of the others begin to quarrel about toys. When this happens, she is good at mediating between them. She is a good pupil, and good at playing.

Being 'good at playing' is clearly an assessment of the children's social competences (see discussion in chapter 8). These competences include the children's ability to integrate others in games, resolve potential conflicts, and negotiate the games in harmonious ways, meaning without feuds or direct use of power. How this is significant to the evaluation of a child can be seen in Tina's description of Altin:

He is also good at intervening when the boys have a conflict. [*Laura*: make peace?] Create a calm environment, yes, and create a good game. Altin is a quiet boy, and he is not the fighting type. When he joins the other boys in a game, it is as if he puts a damper on them without saying anything. But they kind of know that if they play with him, then it will be on these terms. He cannot be bothered to lie on the floor boxing with the others. He wants to construct a game and the others join his project. (Tina, teacher oX, Vesterly School)

These accounts show that the children considered good pupils are those who are found to contribute to the harmonious and civilised community. They are considered 'good in the group', 'good to have in a class', and they are the children who 'play with a lot of people' and are 'kind to the others', 'calm down the others', 'solve conflicts' and 'stop the others when they quarrel'. The teachers like them because they find them congenial, but apparently also due to their function in the class as regulating and integrating forces who contribute to the teachers' project of creating a well-functioning class. It is the children described as 'social' who contribute to the civilised collective, who are in favour with the teachers and who receive recognition at school. Meanwhile, the children that the teachers define as 'problematic' are those who are experienced as 'unruly' and 'aggressive' children, as transgressing other pupils' boundaries, and as the 'quiet' and 'withdrawn' children. As such, when Karin explains why she finds the aforementioned Anton problematic, she describes him as someone 'who has difficulties joining a group, and problems getting accepted by the other boys. He does not make an effort to join and seems to prefer to stay outside the group.' In Karin's view, five other pupils also fall into this category of less adequate pupils, because they have 'difficulties playing with others and occasionally create conflicts'.

The teachers are also frustrated by the children who are more preoccupied with their peers than with the teaching. This shows that they do not applaud all forms of community in class. When they address children who disrupt the teaching, the teachers often use the threat: 'Do you guys need to be separated?' Likewise, when allocating new seating, the teachers often choose to separate specific children if they joke around too much or are too focused on each other. The teachers also seem to counteract the relations between children if these become too strong and the children disregard the teacher's leadership efforts. The desired collectivity is thus not only the harmonious and inclusive community, but also a unit that can be controlled by the teacher and which accepts him or her as an authority. Hence those who offend against the code of harmonious interaction by generating conflict, bothering the other children or actively challenging the adults' authority are seen as especially problematic. As mentioned above, in oB at Nordlund School the teacher Karin alternately focuses on six of the eleven boys in the class who are the object of her attention and worry. First it is Troels, then Mikkel, Anton, Johan, Peter, and then Markus. In all cases she thinks they are 'too forward for their own good' because they 'joke around', 'speak too loudly', 'take up too much space', 'hit and kick the others', 'tease', 'show no concern for the other children' and 'refuse to take part in communal activities'. In oX at Vesterly School the teachers Tina and Mette are particularly aware of the boy Firat whom they feel 'teases the others, has bad manners, is cheeky' and 'tends to do what he pleases'. For a period of time they therefore monitor him closely and keep an eye on his behaviour and interaction with other children.

Legitimate Exclusions

Apart from keeping an eye on these unruly children, the teachers in grade 0 also have a responsibility to test all the children in order to spot those with special educational needs, including those requiring assistance from speech and hearing therapists, additional motor skills training or consultation with a psychologist. The teachers also keep a vigilant eye out for potential 'repeaters' and 'diagnosis children'. 'Repeaters' are described as 'normal children' who need to retake grade 0, not because of academic problems, which the teachers believe can be addressed in the subsequent grades, but due to a lack of social competences, which is seen as caused by immaturity. According to the teachers, however, children with diagnoses such as ADHD (attention deficit hyperactivity disorder) 'do not belong here', because they are 'not within the normal range' and 'will be better off in another type of institution'. While a policy of 'inclusion' of children with special needs in 'normal' classes has been introduced since the time of my fieldwork (see chapter 2), at the time, these children were often moved to institutions providing special needs education. In both schools, the teachers often discuss the possibility that several of their new pupils 'might have a diagnosis', if they behave unacceptably. While the teachers are not always convinced of the merit of the diagnoses, they sometimes feel that they are obliged to teach pupils who would 'be better off in another type of institution'.[5]

Again it is important to emphasise that the teachers have the child's best interests at heart. However, the previously mentioned two-pronged vision of the teachers entails that they always also focus on group harmony. They often argue that the unruly child, who they believe might 'have a diagnosis', should be moved out of the class as he or she is unable to adapt to the community, 'has problems being in a large group' and 'needs a small group'. The teachers also refer to children whom the parents – based on a joint decision with the teachers – have decided to move to another school, because the children did not make friends within the class, were not included in the community or had conflicts with the other pupils. Regardless of why these children end up leaving the class, it seems to result in a more homogeneous and harmonious class. In her kindergarten studies, Eva Gulløv describes a similar tendency to eject challenging children, and points out that this intervention most probably teaches the children that those who are different and who challenge the foundation of the collective disappear from the institution (Gulløv 2009a:276). She relates this observation to the argument made by Marianne Gullestad that the egalitarian Scandinavian ethos tends to generate difficulties in dealing with difference. According to Gullestad, the egalitarian ideals are maintained by avoiding people who are unlike oneself and thereby evading confrontations with the differences that would challenge the experience of equality (Gullestad 1992:174). As anthropologist Karen Lisa Salamon has shown, the egalitarian ethos may also be the reason why Danish voluntary associations have a tendency to split up and form new associations whenever there is discord (Gullestad 1992, Salamon 1992).

In a similar vein, the Danish school might value the inclusive class and work intensively to ensure it, but children who continuously challenge the good community often end up leaving the class as the result of a variety of modes of implicit ejection, thereby allowing a reinstatement of civilised interaction as well as a sense of harmony and equality within the class. I will argue that these children are not simply a cause for concern because they act unacceptably or are marginalised in class, but because they challenge the harmony and force teachers and other pupils to resort to uncivilised practices, such as anger, extensive scolding, conflict and exclusion. One of the reasons why the children in question become problematic is, as such, because they position the teachers in a state of anomie, where it is socially impossible for them to adhere to the cultural norms of 'the good teacher' (Merton 1957 [1949]; Gilliam 2009). To this end, the more formal exclusion prescribed by psychological experts and the transfer of the pupil to a different institution for his or her own good represents a far more civilised and thus legitimate form of ejection.

Descriptions of Children – Pupils' Plans and School–Home Meetings

Another consequence of the strong focus on 'the social' and on moulding civilised communities is that the teachers at Nordlund School include an assessment of the children's 'social competences' in the pupil plans. The pupil plan is a format for teachers' and pupils' own evaluation of pupils' competences, which was first implemented in 2006 as part of the enhanced focus on academic performance in schools (see chapter 2). In Nordlund School, the plans had just been introduced when I arrived at the school, and I therefore attended the meetings in which the teachers decided the content of the plans. Tellingly, the teachers in the grade 0 classes contend that the children should not only be assessed in terms of their academic performances, but also with regard to 'how social they are': whether they are 'good at cooperating' and whether they are 'good classmates'. In other meetings, I heard identical arguments made by teachers who teach classes at higher levels. In the grade 0 classes, the teachers explain that they stress 'the social' in resistance to the increased focus on academic skills, which they feel places inappropriate pressure on the children. Likewise, they find it appropriate to emphasise the importance of 'how you act socially' to both children and parents in this time of increased academic focus.

What we witness here is how a certain kind of 'social behaviour' in class becomes formalised as an institutional requirement and, via the signed pupil plan, attains the status of a skill which the child – and his or her parents – are formally obliged to perform and develop. The social technology of the pupil plan might mean that some of the hitherto informal demands for civilised behaviour will be standardised as competences which the pupil plan henceforth requires the teacher to evaluate in formalised ways – with grades or smileys. As will be further discussed both below and in chapter 9, this might indicate an emerging trend towards an increased formalisation of the school's civilising work. It is worth noting, however, that this has not decreased the focus on 'the social', and that even before the implementation of the pupil plans, this focus had consequences for children in terms of how the teachers described and assessed them, and constituted a central aspect of the school's relation to parents.

The school–home meetings, which I observed in class oB at Nordlund School, constitute one of the key arenas for this relation between parents and teachers. This was the very first meeting between teachers and parents, and both parents participated in all of these meetings, as well as the teachers Karin and Kia. At the meetings, the parents relate how the children feel about attending school, and the teachers describe whether the children find the academic work 'interesting', 'difficult' or 'easy', and discuss the extent to which they participate in activities. Yet, with a few exceptions, the 23 meetings also focus on whether the children have 'settled in socially', and on who – and how many of the other children – they play with. During these meetings, the teachers tell the respective parents that Emma 'cannot cope with others also needing some of the teachers' time', that they want Anton to 'join the group' and that Matilda is a girl on whom they 'need to keep an eye', because she is 'somewhat forward'. They say that Sofie is 'helping out a lot' and commend other children for their 'many contacts', for being 'a good buddy', 'able to behave themselves', or being someone who 'likes to help make sure everyone is included'. They recommend to several parents that they invite a classmate home once a week. The parents, for their part, talk about their own children. Sofie is described as 'helpful and attentive', Julie Marie as 'having a lot of empathy' and as a girl who 'keeps track of whether anyone needs help' and Emma's parents describe how Emma is 'very empathic' and has had 'a lot of visits' from classmates. According to Peter's father, Peter is 'good at the social' as he 'tries to play with a number of different children'. Several of the parents ask what the class is like. In the case of Mikkel, Karin describes him as someone who 'contributes a lot', but whom she occasionally 'needs to control'. The father assures her that they will attend to this at home, while the mother emphasises that Mikkel 'has empathy'. In the conversation about Selma, Karin describes her as 'somewhat controlling', while the mother emphasises that Selma can be 'proud' and 'keen to ensure justice', but that she is 'not rude' or 'a bully'.

As in the cases of Mikkel and Selma, the observed conversations between school and home often take the form of minor negotiations about the child's personal characteristics. As we see, the topics are often the child's social skills, its empathy and respect for others, and whether he or she adapts and contributes to the group. The parents seem to be competent participants in these conversations and negotiations, and often they spontaneously talk about who their child plays with, emphasising his or her social contacts and competences. It is significant that the parents thus know and seem to agree that a central subject in these conversations should be their child's social skills and contribution to the social integration of the class. This suggests that the parents recognise and approve of the school's civilising efforts, just as their descriptions of the child demonstrate that they share the school's values and are working towards the same goals. The school–home meeting is thus also an arena in which the parents display their civilising ideals and abilities. However, the meetings often involve an implicit negotiation of who has the obligation to bring up the child. 'We will work on that at home', the parents say, and 'We will take care of that, that is not your job.' Or Karin says: 'We will certainly be very supportive of those efforts here', or 'I would like you to deal with this.' At the meetings observed, such negotiations tend to unfold in a friendly, cooperative, and considered tone, which indicates that there is a shared understanding that both parties have a right to the child which the other party needs to respect. The teachers tell me that parents are, of course, the 'primary caregivers and childrearers', but that the teachers also play an important role, because they spend many hours with the children on a daily basis. In the school–home meetings, they also indicate that, by virtue of their profession, they can demand certain things from the parents and have a right to undertake formative work with their children. For their part, the parents seem, at least outwardly, to accept the teachers' right to do so and that the school expects them to prime their children to contribute to the class.

Of course, I do not know if some parents merely put on a show to please the teachers and actually disagree with their approach (that this can be the case can be seen in a series of studies of school–home relations by Dannesboe et al. [2012]). I occasionally heard that some parents wished for more focus on the academic work, such as when Karin describes parents – particularly fathers – who do not understand the importance of the play hour. In this vein, all teachers have stories about parents who disagree with what they do, or who contest the teachers' right to raise their children. Tina, for instance, tells me about a boy who clearly challenged the norms for civilised interaction. He 'lacked respect for the other children, ridiculed them' and:

> He said things like: 'Hell, I just went to the bog.' He had an unfortunate attitude that insulted many people, children as well as adults. I had a talk with his mother about this issue. But she refused to see the problem. She was totally incapable of discussing the facts. She would neither see nor hear the reality of the situation. She felt I was in the wrong. She thought it quite OK that her son reacted the way he did. (Tina, teacher oX, Vesterly School)

These cases exemplify that disagreements about the school's civilising project and the teachers' right to intervene in childrearing may occur. However, the fact that such cases are described as exceptions and extremes emphasises that, in the teachers' general experience, parents accept their right to bring up their children and share the norms this upbringing is based upon. This indicates that many of the children are probably familiar with the norms from home. Even so, the school seems to represent a new context for these young children; a context that requires another adaptation to interactional norms. In the next section, I will take a look at some of the consequences of this adaptation and how they influence the children's understanding of acceptable behaviour, their internal relations, and their categorisations of themselves and each other.

Children's Awareness of the Social Norms

As previously described, the children in both schools are fully aware of what they are allowed and not allowed to do at school, and what it takes to be a good pupil. But they also know precisely which children in class are not merely good at reading and arithmetic, but also at observing the rules of not 'running', 'shouting', 'hitting', 'biting', 'kicking', 'farting', 'teasing', 'speaking all at once', 'being mean to the others' or 'ignoring the teacher'. Describing these unacceptable forms of behaviour, they tend to emphasise conduct that generates physical pain, but behaviour that transgresses psychological boundaries, such as 'teasing' and 'being mean to others', are also stressed. It is interesting to see that when I ask the children what is entailed in *not* being good at going to school, several of them – often boys – get off their chairs and storm round the room, physically illustrating acts of hitting, kicking, jumping on the tables, standing on the chairs, swinging from the curtains, while speaking in loud voices. If they stay put on their chairs, they often gesture wildly with their arms. On the other hand, when the children describe what it is like to be good at going to school, they often raise their shoulders and speak in soft, quiet voices, apparently to illustrate good behaviour. Even if the children here display a certain notion of good manners that the teachers would seldom applaud, because they prefer non-submissive and extrovert children, the pupils demonstrate an understanding of a dichotomy between savagery and a calm, subdued self-restraint which seems related to civilising ideals (see also chapter 6). They also demonstrate an understanding of the fact that good behaviour, at least in school, is defined by your bodily comportment, how much space you take up, how much acoustic territory you claim, and how much you transgress what are considered the boundaries of the other. When Madiha from oX at Vesterly School tugs at my jumper after one of the boys has been scolded for shouting and says: 'I never shout' in such a low and meek voice that I need to ask her three times what she is saying, it is an example of the children's knowledge of the distinction associated with speaking in a subdued voice. The children's awareness of the unacceptability of loudness is also highlighted in a play hour in oB:

Karin has just left the room and some of the boys, who are playing cards, raise their voices and talk enthusiastically. One of the girls, Ellen, shouts at them: 'Small voices!' (an expression often used by Karin as a warning that the sound level is getting too high). When Karin returns a minute later to put on a tidying-up song before leaving again, Ellen climbs up on some stairs and shouts: 'Remember what Karin said: you are not allowed to shout. Small voices!' She stands with arms akimbo and looks down on the other children. Peter gets up from the floor and shouts back: 'Don't just stand there! Come down and help us tidy up!' Now Emma turns away from her chores and shouts just as loudly to them both: 'You are not allowed to shout – small voices!' Troels joins in and shouts: 'Small voices!'

During a break, a couple of the girls show their understanding of conflict and enmity as being unacceptable:

> While skipping, Emma and Sara get into a fight, and Sara assumes a threatening position towards Emma: 'You are cheating, you cheat!' 'I am no cheat', Emma responds, now cross, and pushes Sara away. Sara shouts: 'Don't push.' Three of the other girls from the class who had also been skipping approach them: 'Don't quarrel. You shouldn't quarrel!' One by one, they place themselves between Emma and Sara until all three girls stand between them with Tilde admonishing: 'You should not be angry with each other!'

In both classes, the children often say things to each other like 'don't tease', 'be nice to each other' and 'be a good classmate', and in interviews they express clear knowledge of the kind of attitude towards other children that the teachers approve of. At Vesterly School, Soumaya tells me that you are good at going to school 'when you are kind, when you help each other, and you take a look at another person's face to see if they are happy or sad and ask someone if he or she is sad'. Ellen from Nordlund School expresses the same understanding when she explains to me what kind of conduct will result in an angry smiley from the teachers: 'If you are not very nice all day. If Tilde sat here playing, and I came along and said "you are disgusting" and "you are stupid" and "I don't want to play with you" and "go away" and "I don't want you to be in this school" and "I don't want to sit next to you."'

Likewise, the children demonstrate knowledge of the significance of the inclusive community and of the unity and social exclusiveness of the class when they talk about 'everybody' by way of referring to their classmates and emphasise that 'everybody can join in, the entire class is invited', or argue that 'everyone should have a share'.

A Sense of the Uncivilised: on Shame, Stigma and Social Degradation

As alluded to above, it is difficult to determine whether the school succeeds in its civilising project or merely teaches the children legitimate speech and conduct. Since the children do not use the concept of 'civilising', it is not possible to determine whether they experience various forms of conduct as civilised and uncivilised actions. However, the teachers' descriptions of and reactions to various types of behaviour are loaded with messages as to which kinds of conduct are acceptable and unacceptable, and seem to teach the children that unacceptable behaviour is associated with shame and social degradation. I will argue that this contributes to the children's sense of the uncivilised as they show an awareness that they can behave in ways that they or others would find shameful. In addition, the children seem to have an understanding that, through adopting the social behaviour that is appreciated in school, one becomes morally and socially superior to those who do not behave in this way. Moreover, they express an understanding that those who breach this codex are pupils whom you can dismiss and feel superior to. The children hence express that they perceive certain modes of conduct as distinguished behaviour and others as stigmatising and socially degrading; furthermore, they consider it possible to make a hierarchical distinction between people on the basis of their conduct – thereby displaying an understanding of the inherent notion of the idea of civilised behaviour. This indicates that school teaches them, or at least confirms their previously established conceptions of civilised conduct and civilised ways of being part of a collective.

Taking a look at the ways in which the sense of the uncivilised is developed, scolding or other ways to evoke shame play a central role and can be seen as key civilising practices (see chapters 1 and 6). This does not mean that creating of a feeling of shame is necessarily intentional. Scolding is often caused by the discomfort stirred up by the child's perceived transgression of norms, and its immediate purpose is to urge the child to control itself and to correct the unseemly behaviour (Elias 1994 [1939]:107–9). However, when adults scold children, their action functions as both a demarcation of unacceptable behaviour and an – often public – description of the child, its conduct and motives as undignified measured against the standards of a moral code of conduct and thus as a social degradation (Gilliam 2009, see further discussion on scolding in chapter 6). As mentioned, explicit scolding rarely occurs in the two classes, but now and then the teachers become angry and raise their voices: 'Do you think that you can sit and draw when the others are not allowed to? How do you think he feels when you do that?' Or: 'Take a look around you and see how many have raised their hands, and you just barge in.' Here the scolding is often caused by what is considered the child's transgression of boundaries or inconsiderate behaviour and instructs the child to be ashamed and show more consideration for others. Whereas asocial behaviour in the two grade 0 classes is often dealt with using the afore-mentioned 'positive approach' that draws the norm-breaching child back into the civilised community through recognition, intense attention and inclusion, in other classes this type of conduct sometimes results in social degradation, isolation and temporary exclusion from the community; actions which illustrate the ultimate consequences of asocial behaviour.

Distinctions and Resistance

As noted, the children in both grade 0 classes seem to experience that some pupils are better at going to school than others, and that the former are superior to the latter because they behave in acceptable ways. It is striking that the girls tend to experience that 'the girls', as Matilda says, 'are good at going to school', while the 'boys more often tend to tease', be 'cheeky' and 'tough'. As reflected in the examples above, many of the girls frequently tell each other or the boys how to behave. The teachers often contribute to these narratives on gender differences by asking individual girls to keep an eye on specific boys whom they sit next to or by counting on girls to discipline the boys. When the teachers at Vesterly School abandon their plan about waiting two months to configure the classes, it is because they feel that the class of boys 'needs some girls'. Tina explains it as follows:

> [The boys' class] needed the so-called buffer that the girls say: 'Now let's listen to what Tina has to say,' or 'now we have to ...' or 'come on, stop it' or 'put down that eraser!' In that sense they [the girls] have a very good disciplining function, you could say. They are a great help.

They also often use the girls as examples of good standards. In a PE class, for instance, Karin will say to the children: 'Did you notice that the girls were much better at running around quietly today, whereas the boys shouted and were noisy?' Moreover, as exemplified above, the girls also often spontaneously act as discipliners or as 'assistant teachers', as the teachers sometimes call them in jest. One such instance is when Matilda leans over the table and, in a harsh tone, says to Johan: 'I am keeping an eye on you!'

This points to another effect of the school's civilising project and its focus on 'social' conduct: that adopting socially acceptable and unacceptable behaviour becomes a way for the children to relate to others and create communities at school. It is particularly evident that to adhere to or not to adhere to the school's depiction of acceptable behaviour becomes a central practice of distinction with regard to gender identity and is integral to the children's navigation of the various gender communities in the class (see among others Epstein et al. 1998; Reay 2001; Willis 1977; Ferguson 2000; and chapters 3 and 6 in this volume). What the teachers describe as the girls' 'correctness' thus seems to reflect that some of the girls are very concerned with adapting to the rules and social norms. One example is when Karin in oB has asked the children to collect their lunchboxes first and then their milk. Maya has already picked up her milk, but returns it to the milk crate in order to go to the fridge for her lunchbox before going back to pick up her milk again – apparently because she wants to follow Karin's directives. To a number of the girls, the correctness seems to become a way to elevate themselves above other children; often boys, but also other girls. This can for instance be seen when several girls in interviews say: 'I always sit quietly', when they talk about other children who do not, or when Madiha, as mentioned, whispers in a meek voice: 'I never shout' when someone else is criticised for shouting. Sofie and Julie Marie also express social distance when they describe themselves as 'good at going to school', as opposed to 'all the boys – who beat others up and things like that', but also in contrast to Matilda and Selma, who say 'nasty things' and 'sometimes swear'.

Several of the boys in the grade o classes use a similar adherence to the rules as a school strategy, and pride themselves on being good at going to school. A couple of the girls may also fall out with the teachers because they are 'loud', quarrel with the other children, exclude peers or challenge the teachers. However, in the two classes there are considerably more boys who, either for periods of time or in general, behave in what the teachers consider socially unacceptable ways, thereby rejecting assimilation to the school norms. In class oX at Vesterly School, Firat, among others, talks while someone else is speaking, and wrestles and fights with the boys in the other grade o class. Hjalmar belches and lets off wind unapologetically, much to the teacher's frustration. He is apparently aware of the teacher's aversion to burps and farts, but he clearly gains approval from a number of the other boys for his transgressive behaviour. When he burps, he looks at Hassan with a smirk. Hassan sits opposite him and often responds with a smile, and the two of them are consumed by laughter when Hjalmar farts while I interview them. As we show in many of the chapters in this book, it is often via behaviour perceived as uncivilised, and thus by trans-gression of the boundaries they are trained to respect, that children show courage and resistance, seek recognition and create alliances. Trouble-making and resistance to discipline and regulations of this kind constitute a mode that children have always practised in institutions such as schools (Waller 1961 [1932]; Willis 1977; Gilliam 2009). If you take a closer look at what constitutes 'troublemaking' – being noisy, milling around, teasing others and provoking the teacher – it is often a mirror image of precisely the kind of conduct which the school establishes as its norm (see also chapters 3 and 6). In Karin's class oB we see that it is precisely the request for cooperation and calm interaction which some of the boys take turns in resisting. The tidy-up routine serves as an example: every day, the play hour is concluded with a specific tidying-up song which Karin puts on to indicate that it is time to tidy up the room. When the song is over, all the playthings should be cleared away, and the children ought to be back in their places at the four six-seater tables.

> Towards the end of the song, the children rush around with agitated voices and movements in order to put everything in its right place and get back to their chairs in time. When the song is over, everyone except Johan is in their seats. Agitatedly, the others attempt to calm each other down; they shush and shout at those who talk: 'Be quiet now! We want a big smiley!' They are particularly after Johan: 'Sit up straight Johan! Don't you want a good smiley?' Johan laughs and answers cheerfully: 'No, I want a red smiley!'

It is worth noting that at the start of the school year all the children busily participate in clearing up and getting back to their seats, but as the year goes on, certain children, such as Johan in the passage above, periodically challenge the daily procedure surrounding the award of smileys. After a few weeks, several boys, as well as Emma and Matilda, wait till the very last second before returning to their seats, while glancing at each other with apprehension and joy. One day, a month into the school year, Karin leaves the classroom having just reprimanded the children:

> 'I hope that you will all be back in your seats when I return.' The children busy themselves trying to get those who are not yet sitting down back to their seats. Anton sits down under the table, Johan stands by the teacher's desk, and Matilda stands on her chair and suggests that they dance until Karin returns. Sara asks Anton to take his seat, and some of the girls shout frantically: 'Sit down' to Matilda and Johan. When Karin returns, they are all sitting down.

Alongside episodes where children in the two classes challenge the code of conduct, this shows that practices and communities are forming in the class within the collective which the teacher attempts to build. As Willard Waller stressed (1961 [1932]), the school is not merely an educational institution, but a social world for children in which they are engaged in forming relations with other children. Accordingly, a few months into school life, the children increasingly seek each other's approval and begin to create various groups, based, among other things, on various degrees of adaptation and resistance to the school's educational efforts. Even if, when compared to other classes (see chapter 6 this volume and Gilliam 2009, 2015), this process is not particularly pronounced in the two grade 0 classes I observed, making fun of and challenging the school's rules and norms of civilised behaviour evidently also generates status among the boys. Four of the boys in 0B, and three in 0X, quickly assume roles as those who entertain the others, for example by daring to carry out transgressive acts. This reflects a widespread tendency in which rule-breaking and transgression of norms is part of the mandatory practice to be recognised as a 'real boy' (Epstein et al. 1998; Frosh et al. 2002; Haavind 2003; Gilliam 2009). The result of this, however, is that the category 'boys' is associated with uncivilised behaviour, and that many boys foster this as a part of their masculine identity and community at school.

The cited statements about girls and boys show that the children observe these differences and interpret them as variances in the abilities of girls and boys to act in accordance with the social norms required at school. When some of the girls state that they are better at going to school than the boys, and take it upon themselves to civilise the boys, it indicates that they also see themselves as having better social skills, and therefore as having a higher and more civilised status than the boys. For their part, some of the boys indicate that, for them, it makes sense to resist the school's civilising demands and, moreover, that this behaviour is somehow expected of them. The handling of and adaptation to the school's civilising efforts become modes of doing gender – that is, expressions of various ways of being girl and boy – and ways of positioning oneself in the social world of school.

The Dialectic Between School and Society

Does the civilising project of the Danish school described here serve the well-functioning school by adapting children to the institutional conditions, or does it rather serve the greater society by creating productive and culturally acceptable citizens? Does the school, for example – behind the curtains and even behind the teachers' backs – merely require adaptation to the class communities in schools because Danish society needs compliant citizens? In educational research from the 1960s and 1970s, adaptation to society was often interpreted – as the actual goal of the school's teaching, a 'hidden curriculum' which is learnt subliminally and in parallel to the formal curriculum. The educational researcher Philip Jackson (1986 [1968]) and, in Denmark, the researchers Mette Bauer and Karin Borg (1986 [1976]) described how schoolchildren are thereby socialised to working life – to wait, to disregard their own desires, be passive, submit to often arbitrary rules, be evaluated and subjugated to the power and authority of adults. Along with a range of Marxist-inspired studies, they pointed out that the school is not a great leveller of social differences but instead socialises children to an industrial class society and to their predetermined class position (see for instance Bowles and Gintis 1976; Dale 1977; Gleeson 1977).

In the following two chapters, I will examine the class aspects of the school's civilising efforts, but here I will argue that applying this somewhat functionalist analysis of the relation between school and the labour market to the Danish school is challenged by the fact that what Danish pupils learn at school today is still to be a member of a flock and adapt to the institution's requirement of a restrained temperament and restrained conduct in a group. Nevertheless, in contemporary, post-industrial Danish society there is not the same need as in the industrial society for a segment of obedient 'workers' who function as a group, working on an assembly line supervised by an authoritarian leader. In this perspective, it may seem inexpedient to cultivate the degree of self-discipline required of children, who on a daily basis need to function in groups of 20–30 people in limited physical spaces and, moreover, to coordinate their conduct, wishes and needs with each other and the class as a social community. But does this then indicate that the school is in fact demanding a degree of control of self and body that only serves to support the teaching of large numbers of children and the school's specific institutional conditions? My argument is, rather, that the social training required by the class and the school as an institution is perceived as so highly legitimate because it both serves the well-functioning school and prepares children for 'how you interact with other people', as the teacher Tina puts it, in a highly integrated society. Hence, in many ways, what I have described here as modes of interaction depicted as 'social', and the adaptation to the community expected of the children in the tight-knit class communities, socialise the children to adopt the values and demeanours expected of citizens in the Danish welfare society. That is: to live closely integrated and peaceably together in the kind of mutual interdependence resulting from a differentiated labour market and cooperation across social differences; to take responsibility for the common good and democratic decisions regarding shared societal issues; and to leave violence, punishment and major decisions to the authorities, and relinquish a significant part of your income to the community. My point is not that this is the real hidden curriculum of the school, but that it is a social and moral form developed through a close dialectic between the Danish school as an institution and the Danish welfare society. This correlation is not hidden – it might be implicit and naturalised, but when brought to light, it is well regarded and often celebrated. When I ask the teachers if they primarily educate the children to become good human beings, good pupils or good citizens, they thus all express that these purposes are not mutually exclusive, and that there is a logical connection between them. When explaining the social rules of the school, for instance, they say that the child needs to develop the skills to adapt to these regulations, and that this adaptation prepares the children for life in society. As such, Tina refers to the children's future within a democratic society when she describes why it is useful to learn to raise your hand and vote at school:

> If I were raised to or got used to a situation where I was the only one who needs to be heard, then I could stand at a gathering with 20 other people who feel the same as I do, and we would scream and shout at each other. [...] In order to live in a country like Denmark, there are rules one needs to observe. Whether it is democracy or not, we teach the children that now we raise our hand and vote on this or that issue – there is a purpose to everything we do at school. (Tina, teacher 0X, Vesterly School)

Even if the teachers are not necessarily conscious of such rationales in everyday school life, where the main purpose is to create a well-functioning, teachable class, this effort seems to be legitimised by the fact that they consider the school to be a preliminary stage that introduces them to life 'out in society'.

While obviously this has not been the intention at all times, the school class as a social unit seems to have acquired didactic functions on its own. Taking an Eliasian perspective, we can argue that it has become a microcosm of society: a training ground comprising a closely integrated community of mutual interdependencies instilling a 'fabricated' civilising process that rehearses the civilised interaction required in the closely integrated welfare society. As argued, my point is not that this content of the school's formative work is determined by a mysterious functional relation; rather, it is created by many individual acts (Elias 1994 [1939]:366; cf. chapter 1), over time establishing an imperceptible mutual influence of civilising norms between the Danish school and society.

Part of the explanation is the mediating role of teachers. At school, the children encounter teachers who are carriers of convictions regarding civilised interactions and a project of preparing children to become good citizens in Danish society. Yet they are also institutional actors who need children to adapt to the school institution and its requirements in order to carry through their teaching project. Moulded to some extent by school values and institutional practices, generations of children carry the inherent notions of the good and decent human being and of civilised ways of interacting in groups into their adult life and into society. In this fashion, interactional forms influenced by the institution are disseminated and become 'the way things are done' and 'the way you behave' (Berger and Luckman 1966); the ways children demonstrate their civilised status and engage in groups in contexts outside school are partly modelled on the conduct described as 'social' which the school as an institution partly necessitates and partly cherishes as an ideal. In this way, the school class is both a 'model of' and a 'model for' society (Geertz 1993 [1973]); the school is not merely shaped by and a transmitter of societal norms, the society and its dominant notions of civilised interaction and communities are – via a dialectic relation – also moulded by the school and its institutional conditions.

As some Danish educational researchers have argued, the development towards a greater focus on academic learning and a higher degree of political control of the school might indicate that political pressure is brought to bear on the school to turn children into individual learning projects in order to adapt to the increased global competition (e.g. Pedersen 2011). In a longer-term perspective, this could mean a downscaling of the focus on 'the social' and the community of the school, and perhaps of the ideal of the inclusive and egalitarian class. However, the school's continuing efforts to raise 'social children' and create thriving civilised communities suggest that this tendency, and its implicit challenge to the moral foundations of the Scandinavian welfare society, are counteracted by strong civilising ideals as well as institutional conditions which both reflect and preserve them.

Instead, we see an enhanced focus on 'the social' and, to some extent, as I have argued in the case of the pupil plan, a move towards an increased formalisation of the requirements of civilised behaviour. As we will argue further in chapter 9, this formalisation may indicate what Elias described as a 'decivilising' tendency, yet it also shows the prominence of the school's civilising project (Mennell and Goudsblom 1998a:20). The school seems to have a metonymic relation with society, as it is conceived as a part that represents the whole. Hence it is often treated as a mirror of society, and invested with emotions and dreams of harmonious, inclusive, peaceful and civilised communities. These dreams and emotions are manifested in teachers and parents' attempts to create good class communities. Meanwhile, they are also apparent in the delight which is expressed when a class lives up to these ideals of the optimal civilised community, as well as in the distress in the case of 'polarised' or 'disintegrated' classes, and in the profound anxiety caused by classes with severe bullying.

In conclusion, it is not possible to determine a cause-and-effect relationship between the upbringing norms of school and society in a community where new citizens spend their formative years in institutional contexts. The raising of children in Danish schools reveals dominant cultural notions about civilised conduct and ideal communities in Danish society at the same time as these very notions are influenced by the institutional conditions of the school which, in turn, are shaped by their civilising functions and the school's metonymic relation to society. As the children in oB and oX show, children pick up on the central and normative meaning of this behaviour and of different categories of people, and apply various degrees of civilised and disciplined conduct – behaviour adapted to the school environment – to position themselves socially and create communities and identities at school. Thereby, the school not only plays a formative role in turning children into civilised citizens; it is also a setting for the production of alternative practices and communities which children identify with and are identified in relation to, and which, over time, may prove significant to their participation and position in the broader society.

6

The Impossible Bilingual Boys

Civilising efforts and oppositional forms in a multi-ethnic class

Laura Gilliam

These kids, they're kids who need special treatment. You can't just come in and teach, and you must have found that too? You can't just come in and teach, and say: And here's what we're going to do today! You have to keep on top of them at all times, you have to constantly keep an eye on them, you constantly have to perform therapy on them, you have to tell them off. (Dorthe, class teacher 4A/6A, Sønder School)

Most Danish teachers describe teaching children about social interaction as an important part of their work, while stressing that what they term 'the social' should not take too much time from 'the academic' (see previous chapter). Yet as their class teacher Dorthe describes above, 4A/6A at Sønder School is one of those classes which frustrate teachers because they find they need to expend a disproportionate amount of energy dealing with the children's behaviour and interactions. Taking a closer look at this class will provide insight into which types of behaviour require a special civilising intervention – thereby illustrating the civilising ideals. At the same time it shows how certain children challenge the norms to negotiate status among their peers and challenge the teachers – thereby providing insight into unintended consequences of the civilising project of the school. Finally, this class also tells us something about another key aspect of the civilising process, namely the link between civilising and distinction, as outlined in chapter 1. Class 4A/6A's teachers describe a strong correlation between the children's behaviour and their social and ethnic backgrounds. As such, Dorthe explains the behaviour of pupils in 4A/6A in terms of what she refers to as their 'resource-weak' and 'bilingual' parents, and of their childhood spent in a poor, ethnically diverse neighbourhood. These views reflect a common explanation of children's problematic behaviour among teachers and shows how social categories – in the case of 4A/6A, gender, class and ethnicity – are called upon in school in order to explain children's conduct. In the next chapter, I will examine the same topic at a school in a more affluent area with children from what are broadly referred to as 'resource-strong' homes. As such, these two chapters will extend the analysis presented in the previous chapter and explore the consequences of the school's civilising project for the construction of social categories, relations between social groups, and children's ways of understanding themselves and their position in social and moral hierarchies in broader society. In the previous chapter we saw how this applied to gender in the two grade 0 classes. In this and the following chapter we will see that the older children, ostensibly because of their multispectral self-image and new social horizons, place their school experiences in the context of a larger social cosmology.

The chapter is based on fieldwork conducted in the aforementioned class at Sønder School, located in a formerly working-class area of central Copenhagen which is now an ethnically and socially mixed area comprised of families and students. I refer to the class as 4A/6A as I conducted the fieldwork during two periods: first at the grade 4 stage, and later at the grade 6 stage. While 40 per cent have an ethnically Danish background, 60 per cent of the 10–12-year-old pupils in the class are first- or second-generation immigrants or refugees and describe themselves as Moroccan, Palestinian, Turkish, Kurdish, Albanian, Pakistani, Peruvian and Romanian. My fieldwork in the class took place over a period of seven months in total during 2002–3. For comparison, at the end of the chapter I will briefly refer to class 9X from Vesterly School (one of the schools described in chapter 5), located in a western suburb of Copenhagen. Fifty-five per cent of the children in this class have an ethnic minority background while the remaining 45 per cent have an ethnic Danish background. The fieldwork in this class was conducted as part of more extensive fieldwork conducted at the school in 2009. In both classes, the fieldwork consisted of participant observation of teaching, interaction and dialogue during both lessons and breaks, in classrooms and in the staffroom. At Sønder School, I also observed parent–teacher meetings and staff meetings. In addition, I conducted informal conversations and a total of 51 semi-structured qualitative interviews with pupils, teachers and the principals from the two schools.

The Impossible 4A

Sønder School is located in an old brick building in an urban residential area. Corridors and classrooms are run-down. The children's jackets and forgotten shirts hang from rows of coat hooks, while their bags lie sprawled on the floor or leant against grouped two-person tables, which have been pushed askew by children running past, mucking about, or simply being restless. Class 4A is usually a lively place and not in a way that the teachers approve of. Some of the children sit quietly in their seats, but others shout and argue, and there is often someone pulling, pushing or trying to escape the grasp of a classmate. The teachers frequently have to spend 5–10 minutes calming things down, trying to solve conflicts which started during the break, and getting the lesson under way. Sometimes, it is not possible and the teachers trudge frustratedly back to the staffroom and complains about the class – or about 'the impossible 4A', as the class is commonly known. When I tell the middle-aged PE teacher Preben that I am conducting fieldwork in the class, he replies:

> Oh, you're in that impossible class. It's the worst class in the whole school. There's plenty to study there – they're impossible the lot of them! You can meet them in front of the gym after I've thrown them out. They don't know how to behave properly; they have no manners. (Preben, teacher 4A, Sønder School)

In the staffroom the teachers often despair of the children's behaviour. They are concerned about what they describe as the children's 'lack of social competences' and talk about how they should learn to show consideration for one another and to see how their actions affect others. As the class teacher Dorthe indicates in the passage quoted above, she is worried that she spends so much time dealing with 'the social' that she does not have enough time for 'the academic'; that is, the teaching which she emphasises that the children sorely need. But it is not only the academic level that concerns the teachers. It is apparent from their discussions in the staffroom that they also find the class problematic as it goes against their ideals regarding good harmonious communities and does not constitute a positive environment for the individual child's development. The teachers consider it morally unacceptable that there are children who are hit or violated in other ways in the class, or that children are bullied and excluded from the group. They are also annoyed that the children swear and curse, as well as sneering at and mocking others. As such, the class does not constitute the inclusive and friendly – civilised – community which a good class ideally should be; that is, as described in the previous chapter, a class that is characterised by empathy, respect for classmates and inclusiveness, where everyone plays with everyone else, and where conflicts are dealt with amicably through democratic processes. The teachers do not refer to such behaviour as 'civilised', but, through their demands and criticisms, they indicate that what they feel is lacking, and what they wish to encourage, is considerate social and self-aware interaction with others which they, as the teachers described in the previous chapter, find is required in a tight-knit community. That this is perceived among the teachers as civilised, in the sense of elevated above other behaviour in terms of decency and morality, is reflected, for example, in Dorthe's response when asked what she considers the most important role as a teacher in relation to a class:

> That they become decent people, plain and simple. I think that is the most important role. The fact that they have to become decent people. And decent people, that's people who are able to properly relate to their fellow human beings. (Dorthe, class teacher 6A, Sønder School)

The Impossible Bilingual Boys

Although 4A/6A as a whole class is referred to as 'impossible' in the staffroom, you do not have to listen for very long to the teachers' talk before it becomes apparent that it is usually the seven ethnic minority boys who are mentioned in a negative context – Hamid, Kamal, Merdzan, Yosef, Üzlan, Enrico and Deniz (the latter is replaced by Mohammed in grade 6). Together, they represent seven of the ten boys in the class. Although teachers sometimes mention a couple of the girls and two of the three boys with ethnically Danish backgrounds when complaining about the class, it is the names of the boys with ethnic minority backgrounds, or the term 'the bilingual boys', which are mentioned time and again when discussion turns to trouble, teasing and conflicts with the children. As one of their teachers, Bent, says: 'as I see it, it's the bilinguals who cause problems'. The teachers stress to me that they do not care about the children's ethnicity and they evidently use the term 'bilingual' in reference to the ethnic minority children to avoid terms directly referring to their ethnicity and to emphasise that it is the children's language which is important at school.

Yet it is clear from the way it is used in opposition to the term 'Danish children' that it refers to the children's non-Danish ethnicity. As such, despite their intention to be blind to ethnicity, the teachers' talk of 'the bilingual boys' behavioural problems' shows that they relate this behaviour to ethnicity.

Much field research in Danish schools has highlighted how boys of immigrant background are treated as a problem (Kofoed 2003; Staunæs 2004; Gitz-Johansen 2006; Gilliam 2009). Here I will argue that there is a clear civilising dimension in this problematisation. It can be heard when the teachers refer to the 'bilingual boys' as 'violent, aggressive and inconsiderate', but also as 'lacking social competences' and 'inner control'. 'Social competences', like the notion of civilised behaviour, suggest certain skills which are required to interact with others in appropriate ways, while the concept of 'inner control' points directly towards the ideal and requirement of internalising social norms which Foucault describes as 'self-discipline' and Elias as 'civilising' (see chapter 1). It is also seen in the teachers' statements that the boys behave the way they do because they 'are not capable of looking at themselves from an outside perspective', and therefore have to be 'externally regulated' by the teachers. They are regarded as not having learned the required forms of social interaction or the introspective gaze which results in a sense of shame regarding inappropriate behaviour:

> I believe that the task with the bilinguals is all about addressing their values, to change their sense of responsibility and get them to reflect on how they act and how they come across to others. And one of the most important tasks in doing that is to get them to think about themselves and adjust their sense of responsibility. (Dorthe, teacher 4A, Sønder School)

Thus the teachers feel that the boys lack the self-awareness and appreciation of other people's boundaries, which we have seen are a central aspect of the school's notion of civilised behaviour (see chapter 5).

An Ethnic Divide in Civilised Behaviour

In 4A/6A, the children themselves are aware of the reputation their class has and often tell me: 'We are totally impossible!' But even though being an 'impossible class' is described as their shared identity, the children are well aware that the reputation mostly relates to the boys in the class, and, in particular, to the seven boys they themselves refer to as 'immigrants', 'foreigners' or 'Muslims'. 'It's mostly the boys who are Muslim that cause so much trouble, and then get the others involved', as Nada – who herself identifies as 'Muslim' – puts it. Interestingly, both the ethnic minority children and the ethnic Danish children talk about how 'immigrants', 'foreigners' and 'Muslims' cause more trouble and are more aggressive than 'Danes', who they say are 'quieter', 'calmer' and 'nicer' to each other. In order to explore this further, I asked Merdzan, who describes himself as a 'foreigner', what he thought it would be like to attend a class consisting only of 'foreigners' (purposefully using the term he had used himself in the interview):

> *Merdzan*: It would be nothing but trouble, I reckon.
> *Laura*: But why, why is that?
> *Merdzan*: I don't know, there are a lot of foreigners who like causing trouble.
> [...]
> *Laura*: What about the Danes, they don't like causing trouble?
> *Merdzan*: No, not like Casper and Frederik, for example, they don't like to.
> (Merdzan 4A, Sønder School)

Later in the interview, Merdzan refers to 4B, the other grade 4 class, which has a reputation as being quieter and calmer than 4A. He attributes this difference to there being fewer 'Muslims' in the class: 'There's maybe three Muslims, or something like that. Here we're like seven or something.' Enrico describes the same experience of the group he identifies with – 'the foreigners' – as causing more trouble when I ask him how it would be with a class consisting entirely of 'foreigners':

> Well ... then I think there would be too much trouble, and I reckon we would never do any homework and what have you, because we're all like: 'blah, blah', and there wouldn't be anyone saying: 'Stop that' and things like that, and no-one who, like, would tell the teacher.

Meanwhile, he describes a class only containing 'Danish children' as 'boring, because most Danes never cause trouble'. Nada makes the same point: 'The Danes are ... like ... if no-one ... if no-one persuades them to do it, then they're always little angels.'

In the children's eyes, the difference is also about being 'peaceful' or 'violent'. When I talk to Hamid about a class with only 'Danes', he explains: 'Then there wouldn't be so much fighting and stuff. Because it is always the Arabs who start the fight [...]. They're, like, more violent', before correcting himself that it is mostly the boys. As such, the children express an understanding of differences in term of civilised behaviour between 'Danes' and 'foreigners/Muslims', or in this case 'Arabs'. While this can be ascribed to their internalisation of stereotypes from media or the public debate, and while other factors outside the school, such as experiences in the local neighbourhood, are surely influential, the children often refer to the school context when making these comparisons between ethnic groups. This suggests that this understanding, to a large extent, also refers to their experiences with concrete individuals at school. Another thing worth noticing is that they tend to generalise on the basis of specific children's behaviour at school and do not take into account examples which do not fit this generalisation. As such, Hamid is the only one who mentions that the 'Muslim girls' do not cause trouble. Moreover, they tend to explain these instances in ways that uphold the generalisation, as Nada does in the quote above, when she explains some of the 'Danes' participation in troublemaking, by saying that the 'Muslim boys' have persuaded them.

As we will see, some of the ethnic minority boys themselves attribute a certain positive value to aggressive behaviour. But quite a few of the boys also describe 'the Danes' as 'good' or 'better people', who 'communicate' and 'cooperate', while they describe 'foreigners' as 'more aggressive' and 'violent'. When I ask Hamid in grade 4 what he thinks of 'Danes', for example, he responds: 'They are good people and very fond of each other, and if there is a problem, then they try to sort it. They talk to each other. Not like other countries; they fight, and the problem becomes much bigger.' In grade 6, Hamid and Merdzan relate a similar experience, when I ask them about a distinction between 'Danish boys' and 'foreign boys', which they have just made:

Laura: Is there any difference between Danish boys and foreign boys?
Merdzan: Yes, I think so. Foreign boys cause more trouble.
Hamid: And the Danes, they're, like, more calm.
Laura: Why's that?

Merdzan: They've had a better upbringing. [...]

Laura: Do you think ... Have you not been brought up well?

Merdzan: Well yeah, but ... I think Danes are more, like ...

Hamid: [interrupting] ... calm

Merdzan: They listen to what their dad and mum say.

(Merdzan and Hamid 6A, Sønder School)

The ethnic Danish children also express that 'foreigners', 'immigrants' and 'Muslims' behave inappropriately and aggressively in school. Kira talks about how it would be 'kind of a bit difficult' at a school consisting entirely of 'new Danes' (as she calls them) 'if they were noisy and sat and talked to each other in lessons and stuff like that'. Like Merzdan above, another of the ethnic Danish girls, Mette, uses the parallel class 6B as an example of her experience of 'immigrants' as troublemakers and 'Danes' as more calm.

Mette: For example, in the other grade 6 class, there's like a lot of Danes; they're a lot different. Much more friendship ... have always been calm, and all that stuff ... can learn a lot more. They're way ahead of us in terms of learning.

Laura: Okay, why is that? What can the reason be?

Mette: Don't know. I mean, it's hard to say that it is because there are more Danes, but I don't know. But I actually think that is why a little bit. There aren't so many to cause trouble.

(Mette 6A, Sønder School)

Harmonious Integration as a Civilising Ideal

These understandings stand in stark contrast to the experience that the teachers and the principal want the children to have from attending a multi-ethnic school. They not only hope, but also expect that the encounter between 'Danish' and 'bilingual children' in school will make the children tolerant of one another, and that the bilingual children, by attending a Danish *folkeskole*, will be socially and culturally integrated into Danish society. As is evident in the strong political impetus towards enrolling ethnic minority children in the Danish public schools and day-care institutions, this integration is a central element in the contemporary civilising project in Danish institutions (see chapter 2). Similarly evident in the way both politicians and teachers discuss this theme is that the civilising ideals also encompass harmonious inter-ethnic relations. As the school is generally viewed as a microcosm of society (as discussed in the previous chapter), the multi-ethnic school, and particularly the individual multi-ethnic class, seems to be expected to represent the ideal well-integrated multi-ethnic society. Here children with different backgrounds should meet on equal terms, play and make friends with one another without regard for ethnic and religious divides, accept and learn from each other's differences, socialise in a civilised manner, submit to the common good by following common rules and participate in democratic decisions regarding life in the classroom.

In 4A/6A, this ideal of successful integration is challenged. Although friendships exist in the class across ethnic divides and a number of the ethnic Danish children state that it is a good thing to be in a class with 'kids from other countries', the children have an experience of an everyday characterised by strife and a divide between the ethnic Danish and ethnic minority children in terms of civilised conduct which runs counter to the ideal of an atmosphere of tolerance, equality and friendship in the multi-ethnic class.

Explanations for Uncivilised Behaviour

The teachers generally explain what they perceive as the 'bilingual boys' behavioural problems' with reference to their cultural and social backgrounds. As such, even though most teachers profess they do not want to pay attention to ethnicity, a number of them explain the behaviour of 'the bilingual boys' as culture-dependent on 'Muslim childrearing'. Here the teacher Niels explains:

> The Muslim families have an inverted pyramid [compared to] us, when it comes to childrearing. Danish childrearing is very intensive at the beginning but becomes less and less so as children become increasingly independent. Muslims, they treat young children like kings, especially the boys, and the older they get, the more intensive the childrearing, and then, when they reach puberty, then they have to abide by all the rules. They find that extremely difficult to deal with. (Niels, teacher, Sønder School)

This 'inverted pyramid' explanation is criticised by researchers for an essentialist and reductive approach to the variations and changes in childrearing among Muslims, as well as for its restricted notion of freedom and responsibility (Tireli 2003:24). Nevertheless, it is a dominant model of explanation among Danish teachers when explaining the differences between Danish and Muslim childrearing and the troublesome behaviour of ethnic minority boys at school. 'The Arab boys have big egos', says the principal of Sønder School, while the teacher, Peter, likewise feels 'the Muslim boys are cocky':

> But I think a lot of it has to do with young Muslim boys not having chores to do at home and not yet having a sense of community. They develop that the day they get a family. Then it is them who ... yes, maybe, hopefully before, I mean, that's [a sense of community] bloody well the thing that we're supposed to give them, but it's [...] very much me, me, me. The Danes are also like that, but not to the same degree. (Peter, teacher 6A, Sønder School)

In the disapproval of 'egos', 'cockiness' and 'me, me, me', we once again see that it is the regard for others which marks out the civilised – what is referred to as 'being social' in Danish day-care institutions and schools (see chapters 3 and 5). From the perspective of many teachers, the problematic attitude to others arises from a lack of socialisation and over-indulgence of boys within Muslim homes. The perception that the boys become 'small kings' and have 'big egos' stresses how, as discussed in chapter 5, it is regarded as unacceptable to take up too much space within the class community. The teachers find, however, that this behaviour is only characteristic of the boys because the girls, in their eyes, learn a different sense of responsibility. They may criticise the way that the girls are not given enough freedom and have too much responsibility, but they generally experience the girls as being far more 'harmonious and social'. One explanation for this is that the girls are kept at home, unlike the boys, who the teachers think spend too much time on the street with other boys, elder brothers and cousins. This reflects how places and physical spaces are considered more or less appropriate for children, as well as a cultural understanding that children's upbringing, experiences and interactions should be supervised by adults, whether at home or in institutions for children (Olwig and Gulløv 2003). At the same time, it reflects another type of explanation for the boys' behaviour which does not focus on over-indulgence but, on the contrary, on neglect and a lack of proper upbringing, understanding and care for the boys within the home. Along similar lines, explanations as to why the ethnic minority boys in the class fight or hit others are often based on an assumption that they themselves are hit at home. When some of the boys have been in a fight, Dorthe thus says that she 'wants them to find out that it is wrong to hit, for it to give them a "no" feeling, but they can't do that because of their upbringing, because they have learned it at home, because the adults at home hit them or do not care about them'.

Compiling the various assumptions regarding how boys are raised in ethnic minority or Muslim homes, it is evident that they stand in clear contrast to the teachers' ideas about civilised upbringing. The latter seems to be defined according to a Danish middle-class norm of 'good upbringing' taking place in the 'good family' and forming the basis of the 'good childhood'. Such an upbringing offers children a correct and timely dose of care, responsibility and freedom; they learn to take responsibility, encounter egalitarian gender roles, are listened to and acknowledged. In contrast, it is assumed that 'the bilingual boy' does not receive the upbringing and understanding under tender adult supervision which the civilised upbringing entails, but is instead beaten, suppressed and ignored. At the same time, it is assumed that he is given too much leeway, is allowed to take up too much space, is mainly socialised by other children, and does not learn the social norms for civilised interaction or respect for others, meaning that he has not internalised the shame associated with violation of civilising norms (see chapters 1 and 5). Thus portrayed, 'the bilingual boy's' upbringing epitomises a lack of civilising and uncivilised childrearers.

In spite of this, the teachers describe the parents as generally supportive of their efforts in relation to the boys. As such, the parents admonish their sons not to cause trouble and tell them off when a teacher phones to inform them of their latest antics. However, the teachers often report that the parents do not understand the importance of community in the class and, for example, do not invite the other children home or respond to invitations to birthday parties. In the teachers' eyes, this shows that ethnic minority parents do not share the view that the school should nurture this social community (see chapter 5); nor do they feel the necessary sense of responsibility to encourage social relations between pupils and an inclusive class community. According to the teachers, this is a serious problem and underlines that 'the bilingual children', here both girls and boys, do not learn the necessary social competences at home.

A Matter of Resources – the Danish Class Discourse

Although the teachers use cultural explanations for the socially inappropriate behaviour of 'the bilingual boys', they often immediately emphasise that this is not grounded in ethnicity, as the same problems exist among what they term 'weak Danish children'. Like Dorthe, they underline that it is 'the children's situations at home that cause them problems, regardless of whether they are bilingual or not', or, as the principal says: 'Essentially, I think it [a child's behavioural problems] is a question of resource-strong and resource-weak families, and it goes in all directions, plain and simple.'

This view that behavioural problems at school or in kindergarten among ethnic minority children are caused by social factors has been described in a number of studies (e.g. Gitz-Johansen 2003; Bundgaard and Gulløv 2007). It reflects the most legitimate explanation of children's behaviour in Danish schools; namely, that it is related to what teachers refer to as the amount of 'resources' within the home. It is noteworthy that the teachers stress that the concepts 'resource-strong' and 'resource-weak' do not only allude to economic resources, but also to the families' social, emotional and time-related resources. As such, Dorthe, like several other teachers, underlines that families of lower social background can have other important types of resources, such as time and energy to spend with their children, and that a middle-class or upper-class status is by no means enough to ensure a good upbringing if parents do not also have time and emotional space for the child. For instance, she criticises some of the ethnic Danish middle-class mothers for being too busy with their own things and not having time for their children. Here we see a focus on time which is also evident among the affluent families described in chapter 8. Although the teachers thus deny that class status determines parenting abilities, the concept of resources is nonetheless a statement about capital – economic and cultural capital and that these possessions – that is in Bourdieusian terms, the family's position in the social space – explain the child's behaviour and social competences (Bourdieu 1986).

Whereas social class is often treated as irrelevant due to the relative equality of Danish society and mentioning someone's class seems to be a taboo in Denmark (Gilliam 2009), the concepts regarding 'resource-strong' and 'resource-weak' families appear to be a legitimate way to refer to class. As in the anthropologist Sherry Ortner's description of a similar avoidance of talk about class in America, this taboo does not mean that class is without cultural relevance. Instead, class distinctions are expressed using other, more legitimate categories (Ortner 1992:169). In the Danish context, the concepts 'resource-strong' and 'resource-weak' seem legitimate because they are able to refer indirectly to the class distinctions that people do in fact experience, and because they communicate a social awareness that the resources necessary for living the good life are not equally distributed. At the same time, as stressed above, 'resource-strong' and 'resource-weak families' cannot be directly equated with higher and lower class. Instead, the concepts make explicit the widespread notion in Danish society that economic resources alone are not enough to make a good family and can even be morally questionable if not accompanied by a prioritisation of time and space for the child (see chapters 7 and 8). The reference to 'resource-weak families' is therefore able to communicate sympathy with and an unwillingness to condemn families facing social and economic adversity, while at the same time alluding to their lower class and lack of parenting skills.

Likewise, as educational researcher Thomas Gitz-Johansen stresses, Danish teachers' focus on ethnic minority parents' social impoverishment involves an effort to avoid prejudice and stereotyping of ethnic minority groups (Gitz-Johansen 2003). Despite the good intentions, however, it has a severe stigmatising effect. In line with what I described above, Gitz-Johansen reports that the teachers in his study tend to imagine that the ethnic minority children have childhoods marked by a tough environment and a lack of stimulation and care within the family (2003:70–1). Studies of Afro-Caribbean boys in England and of African American and Latino boys in the United States show the same tendency: that teachers, often based on limited personal knowledge regarding the boys' families, expect a lack of resources, care and upbringing in the homes of these boys (see for example Connolly 1998; Ferguson 2001; Lewis 2003). In my material from the three schools, and across the five classes where I have conducted fieldwork, the same pattern emerges. The teachers also talk of 'resource-strong' families among the ethnic minority families, but there is a clear link between their perception of a child as being a 'good pupil' and their perception of the family as 'resource-strong'. This pattern is most striking in 4A/6A. When I ask the class teacher Dorthe to tell me which children's families are 'resource-strong', she mentions most of the girls; that is, the pupils in the class who behave in accordance with the school's social norms. With the boys, it is less clear-cut; she mentions the two ethnic Danish boys, Rasmus and Casper, and two of the ethnic minority boys, Enrico and Yosef, explaining her choice of the latter by the fact that their parents 'cooperate' with her. In contrast are the rest of the ethnic minority boys, all of whose families she perceived to be 'resource-weak' – economically as well as socially and psychologically, as she stresses. Here it is interesting to note the clearly gendered and ethnic pattern regarding which children's families are perceived as 'resource-weak' families, and to bear in mind the statistical unlikelihood of an over-representation of parents of boys among socially impoverished families. This suggests a kind of backwards reasoning, whereby the boys' misbehaviour at school stigmatises their families as 'resource-weak', and the teachers then expect them to be lacking in terms of the time, attention and care the parents devote to their children.

It is to be expected that cultural differences exist with regard to approaches to childrearing among parents with different ethnic and social backgrounds, that these are guided by different civilising ideals, that girls and boys are brought up differently across cultural traditions, and that all these factors have an impact on the children's demeanour and interactions with other people. Here, however, the difference is also presented as a difference in the level of care provided, and in the degree of civilised conduct, whereas the cultural and individual differences in terms of family life and upbringing between different ethnic minority families are not considered. In addition, the boys' behaviour at school is explained entirely on the basis of their lives outside school and their upbringing at home. Below, I will consider the social dynamics in schools which can help to explain how children come to perceive that there is an ethnic and gendered divide in their own and other children's behaviour.

The Quiet Ones and the Wild Ones – Social Categories in Schools

As mentioned in the previous chapter, the sociologist Willard Waller describes the school as a social world comprised of the people who live in it and the web of relationships which they weave between them (Waller 1961 [1932]). According to the philosopher Nelson Goodman, social worlds can be distinguished from one another through 'the relevant kinds they comprise' (Goodman 1978:10). In other words, the categories that people use to divide a social space can tell us something important about the differences and valuations that are attributed importance, and thereby about what is 'at stake' in this social field (Bourdieu and Wacquant 1992:98–9). In 4A/6A, I sought insight into these categorisations at school by asking the children to sort a pile of cards with their classmates names in terms of who they saw as similar and who as different in the class, and who they themselves were most and least similar to. Although there were individual ways of naming the categories, the children's criteria for 'likeness' generally related to gender, ethnicity, religion, friendship, who was 'clever' or 'dumb', and who was 'quiet' or 'wild' (Gilliam 2009). The categories regarding gender, ethnicity and religion are examples of objectified social categories made relevant within the school context. The latter categories, on the other hand, point to the key role played by social relations, social and bodily adaptation and acknowledgement of skills and intelligence in children's experience at school.

When the children sorted the cards in terms of who was 'quiet' and who was 'wild', they consistently divided their classmates according to gender – not 'the quiet girls' and 'the wild boys', but rather 'quiet girls' and 'wild girls', 'quiet boys' and 'wild boys', with the latter also referred to as 'the ones that cause trouble'. This suggests that the 'quiet' and 'wild' categories are simultaneously categories of gender and categories of ways of being a pupil, and thus demonstrate how different ways of 'doing gender' and 'doing pupil' are internally connected. While I cannot describe the children's categorisation in detail here, I will point out that, when categorising themselves, the girls were clearly drawn to a category of 'quiet and calm', but 'fun', while most of the boys aspired to the 'wild' category, either in a form they defined as 'fun but not mean' or a 'troublemaking' form.

It is noteworthy that the children thus distinguish between themselves and others at school using categories that refer to various degrees of physical activity and social behaviour – and thus categories that can be used to differentiate degrees of civilised conduct. The teachers also often used the words 'quiet' and 'wild' to categorise different children. As such, in the institutional context, both children and teachers partly assess and categorise children on the basis of their bodily demeanour: their sounds, their bodily activity, how much space they take up, and how they use it (see related understanding in chapters 3 and 5). As mentioned, the categories 'quiet' and 'wild' also refer to the children's social interactions with one another. The children explain that 'quiet and calm' also means being 'well-behaved' and 'doing as the teachers say', and maybe being happy and lively, but 'calm' and 'friendly' in social interactions with other children, while being 'wild' implies 'causing trouble', being 'mean', 'wanting to decide', 'hitting' and 'teasing'. Being 'quiet and calm' thereby does not only refer to bodily control, but to the pupils' general self-restraint. Likewise, being 'wild' and causing 'trouble' also refer to opposing the school's demands to be a cooperative and considerate – civilised – classmate.

The different statuses attached to the various gendered pupils' categories of 'quiet' and 'wild' suggests that the children do not just arrive at school 'quiet' or 'wild' based on their upbringing. This does not mean that bodily and social behaviour are not and cannot also be internalised as habitual practice. But it is clear that the children in 4A/6A, like the younger children in chapter 5, can position themselves in relation to different gender and pupil positions in the school space by acting either 'quiet and calm' or 'wild' and thereby gain social acceptance and prestige within their peer group and among different groups of friends. The girls are very conscious of the fact that they gain recognition from the teachers, but also from the other girls, by being quiet in lessons, lively and fun during breaks, and 'inclusive' and 'social' in their interactions with each other. As such, several of the ethnic Danish and ethnic minority girls talk in disparaging terms about the ethnic Danish girl Kira, who they find too 'wild' and 'mean' to the others, just as they stress that 'it's important to be nice to each other'.

Among the group of boys, the positioning manoeuvres are even more intense. From the boys' ways of categorising themselves and distancing themselves from other boys as being 'least like me' when sorting the cards, it is clear that a norm prevails among them to be 'wild', 'cause trouble' and avoid doing schoolwork. The same social demands can be heard in the boys' derisive comments to the other boys when they do not participate in the troublemaking, conform to the teachers' demands to their behaviour and engage in lessons. These boys are singled out as 'little professors', 'mummy's boys' or 'girly', and are excluded from the boys' play and friendship. In the following quote, Enrico has been sorting the name cards and describes his manoeuvre to stay good friends with the popular boys, Merdzan, Kamal, Yosef and Hamid, while avoiding being associated with the two unpopular boys Mohammed and Üzlan:

Laura: So, what do you have to do to be able to hang out with the four of them?

Enrico: Sometimes we just, like, do some stuff, and then I hang out with those guys [Merdzan, Kamal, Yosef and Hamid], and then after three days or so, then if I haven't done anything for a long time [...] and haven't played with them, and so on, then I slowly start lagging behind. And then when I see that I'm falling a bit too far behind, that they almost don't care to [play with me], then I hurry up and do something so I get a little higher up, because I don't want to go all the way down to them.

Laura: [interrupting] You mean Mohammed and Üzlan?

> *Enrico:* ... then I begin to, yeah, then they come [Mohammed and Üzlan] and want to talk to me [...]. Then I try to get back up there again [points to the cards with the names of Merdzan, Kamal, Yosef and Hamid].
>
> *Laura:* Yes. What is it then that you ... if you can sense that you are about to be excluded, and you're close to joining Mohammed and Üzlan, what can you do then? What do you need to do in order to get in?
>
> *Enrico:* Yeah, sometimes I make trouble and stuff and try to, like, try to do like they do.
>
> *Laura:* 'Like they do'? I don't understand what you mean?
>
> *Enrico:* I mean, if they [Merdzan, Kamal, Yosef and Hamid] are making trouble and stuff [...] I try to play with them again. It's like, if they go down and do all kinds of stuff, then ... let's say they go down and smash up a bike, then I'll go with them and smash it up and stuff.
>
> *Laura:* Yes. What happens then? Do you get in then, or ... ?
>
> *Enrico:* Yeah, then I'm ... and then I also have to say something tough and stuff like that. Then you also have to say something. That's what they [Mohammed and Üzlan] can't figure out. They can't figure out for themselves what to say.
>
> (Enrico 6A, Sønder School)

Enrico illustrates here how troublemaking is a type of performance among the boys which must be practised in order to remain part of the community and at the top of the hierarchy, among the dominant boys. Alluding to this performative character, the boys also state in interviews that they 'act cool' and that 'it's like a show we put on'. It is also apparent in the way the boys keep an eye on each other when they're causing trouble in a lesson and attract each other's attention: 'Did you see what I did?' Several of the boys tell me that they would like to 'quit' the troublemaking, and that their parents admonish them to 'behave properly'. They themselves also talk about people who are 'good people'; they tell me that you have to be 'well-behaved' and 'good' to others in order to be a 'good Muslim'; and they show in other ways that they are well aware of common social norms for interaction. In addition, four of the seven ethnic minority boys feel themselves that the trouble they cause is not 'mean', just 'fun', and dissociate themselves from the 'mean' type of trouble they feel others are making. However, the boys' internal behavioural norms require something else of them. When Enrico tells me that you have to 'say something tough', he refers to making disparaging comments to others. In the same way, swearing, using vulgar words, teasing, pushing and hitting others all earn respect among these 10–12-year-old boys.

Patterns in Praise and Scolding

Troublemaking and a tough tone are not practices particular to the ethnic minority boys in 4A/6A, but practices that many ethnic Danish children in Danish schools, albeit usually boys, also perform. It is moreover important to stress that ethnic minority boys can also have a different reputation. In 9X at Vesterly School, the seven 14–15-year-old ethnic minority boys in the class are, for example, known in the staffroom for being 'sweet', 'nice, well-mannered' and 'polite' boys. At school they are very courteous, polite to teachers, and friendly towards the other pupils. The boys themselves tell me that they have a reputation for being 'tough' among their friends in the neighbourhood, and a few of them are involved in petty crime. While one of them tells me that the harsh tone and boastful attitude are required on the street, one can conclude that they are not required in the same way between the boys at school. Though it is difficult to determine the reason for this difference between them and the boys in 4A/6A, it is noteworthy that these boys' teachers express a fondness for them and have positive expectations of them, and that several of the boys, including the dominant boys, find that they are well-liked by teachers and do relatively well in class. This points to the difference made by the school and class context, and by relations between teachers and pupils. Nevertheless, both older and more recent studies have described the same challenge to the norms of social conduct that we see in 4A/6A among groups of boys with entirely different ethnic backgrounds in English and American schools (Willis 1977; Ogbu 1987; Frosh et al. 2002; Ferguson 2001). The interesting thing is that, although it is more often groups of boys who bond over troublemaking, aggression and crude language, it is often groups of socially and culturally marginalised boys – white working-class and Afro-Caribbean boys in England, African American boys in the United States and boys with migrant backgrounds in Denmark – that come to define their communities around such behaviour.

In order to understand this, it is illustrative to look at the experiences of the pupils in 4A/6A. When I asked the children to place the cards according to who did academically well in class, what emerged was a clear ethnic and gendered pattern in the categorisations. The ethnic Danish

children were generally to be found at the top of the children's categorisations, the ethnic minority girls in the middle, and the ethnic minority boys
at the bottom as those who the children, including the boys themselves,
described as 'the stupid ones' or 'the morons' (Gilliam 2009). If I asked
who the teachers liked, the same pattern emerged – the ethnic minority
boys placed themselves at the bottom and described how the teachers
preferred 'the Danes' and 'the girls', and did not like 'immigrants' like
them. During the seven months I was present in the class, I also observed
an ethnic and gendered pattern in that the pupils who participated most in
lessons and were praised and highlighted as good examples, as well as 'good
classmates', were first and foremost ethnic Danish pupils, and, to a lesser
extent, the ethnic minority girls. On the other hand, six out of the seven
pupils who received extra lessons were ethnic minority children, just as it
was usually ethnic minority children – and mostly the boys – who did not
participate in class discussions, could not provide the right answers to the
teachers' questions, and were corrected and criticised. Likewise, it was the
ethnic minority boys who were told off and ordered to leave the classroom.
Even though the boys' troublemaking certainly contributed to this pattern,
it amounted to a pronounced ethnic and gendered pattern in terms of the
recognition from teachers which the children experienced on a daily basis.
It is important to underline that the teachers did not want to discriminate,
but felt that this pattern emerged behind their backs and was rooted in
the children's different competences and behaviour. However, the themes
of the teaching and class discussions, and the teachers' assessment of
pupils' competences are based on the Danish school's privileging of the
Danish language, and particular forms of cultural knowledge and modes
of interaction. As such, it is no coincidence that it is the ethnic minority
children who do not have the cultural knowledge and do not speak
the standard Danish required and rewarded by the school, who more
frequently appear less clever, and who lose their motivation for taking an
active part in lessons and find other ways to assert themselves.

It is clear that this is a case of a vicious circle where the troublemaking of the ethnic minority boys is both the cause of and caused by their
experiences of being 'stupid' and 'bad pupils'. It is impossible to determine
where this circle begins, and what we see in chapter 3 is that it might start
spinning through experiences in kindergarten, but it seems evident that
the experience of not feeling competent and of teachers not liking 'people
like me', is a key factor in the construction of alternative norms among
children at school (see further discussion in chapter 9). Thus adjusting

to the school's demand for civilised behaviour seems to be woven into a negotiation about gender and pupil positions, but also about ethnic and religious identities at school.

The Schooling of Gender Norms

As we have seen, among the girls in the class, it is considered most proper to be 'quiet and calm', but 'fun'. This is consistent with a general norm regarding what a proper girl is like, but also with the school's norms for the good pupil. As we saw in the last chapter, the good pupil shows self-restraint and does not overstep other people's boundaries, but, on the other hand, is not subdued either. Although many girls do not match up to this or choose other paths, girls can often live up to the norms for girls among their peers and the norms for pupils at school at the same time. What I am suggesting is that social conformity, courtesy and discipline are not just essential characteristics of some children or girls, but also, as we saw in the last chapter, part of a strategy for a number of children, and girls in particular, as a path to recognition and support from adults at school. The correlation between the norms for girls and the civilising norms of the school nevertheless means that, in many classes and schools, girls – as a category – come to 'monopolise' being 'a good pupil' and, vice versa, that being 'a good pupil' comes to connote 'girliness'. Although this takes on a multitude of local forms, it generally seems to occur in an ongoing dialectic with the construction of the category of boys at school, in a process where the social norm for boys is defined in opposition to the social norm for girls, and thereby implicitly to the social norm for pupils (Mac an Ghaill 1994; Connell 2000; Gilliam 2009). There are multitudes of ways of being boys and girls, and the genders can only appear as opposites through the mutual exclusion of what they have in common. Yet the social construction of gender is dominated by an oppositional logic, which means that when certain properties are ascribed to one gender, the other gender must be characterised by the opposite properties (Rattansi and Phoenix 1997:128; Thorne 1993). In particular, the norm of tough masculinity is marked by this opposition to the feminine category. As shown in studies of boys and masculinity, this is a norm which all boys must relate to, but which they find different ways of dealing with (e.g. Epstein et al. 1998; Frosh et al. 2002). The same studies stress that especially marginalised boys with low cultural capital are engaged in this particular masculinity form as it offers them an alternative power to cultural capital and academic success. As stated by Raewyn Connell:

> Masculinity is organized, on the large scale, around social power. Social power in terms of access to higher education, entry to professions, command of communication, is being delivered by the school system to boys who are academic 'successes'. The reaction of the 'failed' is likely to be a claim to other sources of power, even other definitions of masculinity. Sporting prowess, physical aggression, or sexual conquest may do. (Connell 2000:137)

The boys acting tough at school thus have power to position the otherwise privileged boys as improper: as 'girly', 'mummy's boys', 'nerds' and 'swots'. And in this context, it is the courage to stand up to adult authority and transgress the boundaries of what they allow and demand, and thereby of civilised behaviour, which bestows status (Ferguson 2001:169). In 4A/6A, it is clear that 'behaving properly', as the teachers are constantly admonishing the boys to – by being empathic, friendly and considerate, that is behaving in what is considered a civilised manner towards others – has become synonymous with behaving 'like a girl', and thus avoided. Both the ethnic Danish and ethnic minority boys are subject to this norm. However, it is clear that two of the three ethnic Danish boys, Rasmus and Casper (the last, Frederik, is considered 'quiet' and just like a 'girl'), attempt to strike a balance between doing a bit of schoolwork and a bit of troublemaking. And although Rasmus is one of the cheekiest of the boys, they both tend to stop when the teachers' limit has been reached. These two boys find that they do relatively well in class and that the teachers like them, and they thereby seem to have something to lose, thus making them less motivated to participate in the oppositional acts. The reverse is true for most of the ethnic minority boys whose experience is that the teachers do not like them, that they are 'stupid', and, as such, that they can never achieve the position as the good pupil anyway.

The Bad Boys: the Foreigners, the Immigrants and the Muslims

The experiences of these two groups of boys at school and their reactions create a pattern that 'Danes' do not cause trouble – 'Casper and Frederik don't want to', as Merdzan says – and that 'the immigrants' and 'Muslims' do. This conclusion has a self-reinforcing effect because the community

which the boys have established around troublemaking also becomes
defined as an ethnic and religious community. When Merdzan, Kamal,
Yosef, Hamid and Deniz sorted the cards, they generally placed the cards
with their names on together and explained their similarity by them all
being 'Muslims', 'foreigners' and 'making trouble'. In an interview with
Yosef and Kamal, they explain their grouping of the five ethnic minority
boys like this: 'We are the most aggressive. We hang out together. We are
the same, because … it's religion', and give as an example that 'we pray
together'. On other occasions the same boys tell me that a 'good Muslim' is
a 'good person', and conclude that they themselves are not 'good Muslims'
because of their troublemaking. Nevertheless, their experiences at school
lead them to see a link between 'troublemaking' and being a 'Muslim'. To
them, their oppositional community and their rebellion against the 'quiet
and calm' and 'social' behaviour required in school is a part of belonging to
their 'immigrant' and 'Muslim' community.

Consequently, causing trouble also becomes a way of demonstrating
their ethnicity, whereas 'behaving properly' – and thereby in a civilised
manner – not only puts them at risk of being perceived as 'girlish' and
as 'mummy's boys' in the eyes of the other boys; they are also in danger
of being excluded from the boys' ethnic and religious community. Significantly, several of the ethnic Danish children tell me in a similar vein
that they consider an ethnic minority boy who makes trouble is 'more
Muslim', while behaving properly makes him 'more Danish'. When I
ask them which of the children who they describe as 'Muslims' are the
'most Danish', they point to one or more of the ethnic minority girls and
explain that it is because they 'behave properly'. Rasmus makes the same
connection between behaving well and being Danish. In an interview, he
has divided the cards with the names of the children into 'the Muslims'
and 'the Danes', which leads me to ask him if the children he describes as
'the Muslims' are not 'Danish' in any way:

Rasmus: You mean their behaviour?

Laura: I don't know. It depends on what you mean by being Danish?

Rasmus: I mean behaviour, definitely, and then, of course, where you,
what […] your background is.

Laura: But then, what is 'Danish' behaviour?

Rasmus: I would say fairly good behaviour. I don't know why. I don't
think they cause as much trouble as Muslims.

Laura: But then aren't there, are there not any of the Muslims who don't cause trouble?

Rasmus: Well yeah, of the girls, there's all of them, they don't cause trouble, and the boys, there's … Mohammed, he doesn't cause as much as the others, but he does too.

(Rasmus 6A, Sønder School)

While the children of Muslim background argue for another view of being Muslim in interviews, describing a good Muslim as a good and respectful person, what we have also seen above, is that they make the same connection between being Muslim and making trouble. It is worth noticing, that when explaining this they often relate their experiences in school with depictions of Muslims as terrorists and wars in the Arab world that they know from the media and public discourse (Gilliam 2009, 2015).

Stigmatising Modes of Discipline

In the above, I have focused on the social dynamics which contribute to the construction of the ethnic categories at school. The teachers' approach to bringing up the boys does, however, also contribute to this. The teachers generally feel that they must compensate for the failure of the boys' parents to provide a proper, civilised upbringing for their children. As quoted earlier, Dorthe finds that she must 'address […] their values in order to change their sense of responsibility and get them to reflect on how they act and how they come across to others'. The principal puts it as follows:

> [The] big task is trying to teach them … to give them certain norms and certain tools to navigate society, to react appropriately. And there are different ways of reacting in different cultures, there certainly are … but I think we can give them some norms and teach them how to navigate various situations, social situations, but also give them some competences and some self-confidence. (The principal of Sønder School)

As the class teacher, it is primarily Dorthe who is obliged to teach 'the bilinguals' these social norms and appropriate ways of reacting. In her eyes, the majority of the children in the class are 'care-intensive' and 'insecure', and they are therefore 'dependent on routine', and need 'stable' and 'straight talking' adults in their lives. She finds that she needs to keep the pupils on a 'tight leash' in order to be able to teach, but also so that the children, and especially the boys, can learn what she calls 'inner control'. In order to teach them this, she feels that she has to keep a constant eye on them, reprimanding and directing them when they overstep other people's boundaries. The teachers are frustrated that they 'have to put them under surveillance, be the bogeyman, have to control them' and 'have to tell them off', and often express that this kind of pedagogical approach is far from their ideal of a positive relationship with pupils. However, they feel compelled to do this as the children need 'external control'.

Echoing central civilising themes, the problem in the eyes of the teachers is that the boys have not internalised the rules and the regulating sense of shame required for decent and proper interaction with others. The teachers encourage this internalisation by stressing the rules and proper ways of interaction, and trying to instil a sense of shame in the boys. In order to do so, they have agreed to come down hard on any missteps the boys make by reprimanding them, telling them off and throwing them out of the classroom. Dorthe often chooses to sit in on other teachers' lessons to keep an eye on the boys and writes down in a notepad if they do something wrong. But she also spends a lot of time resolving conflicts, training the children in what appear to be social norms of civilised conduct. Here she often tells them in an angry and frustrated tone that they should 'say things quietly and calmly', 'not annoy people', 'be kind to others', 'show compassion', 'not interfere in how others live', 'not order others around' and 'speak giraffe language', the latter being a non-violent communication form that she has attempted to teach the children.[1] She often asks the boys whether something they have done or witnessed gave them a 'yes- or a no-feeling'. The intention is that this reflection on whether one has done something good or overstepped someone else's moral boundary should help them develop awareness of these boundaries, a sense of shame and 'inner control' (see discussion on boundaries in chapters 5, 8 and 9).

Yet, every so often, the teachers end up scolding the boys, much to their frustration. Some of the teachers are ashamed of this, as the ideal teacher is not supposed to scold and be angry (as discussed in the previous chapter), but it is clearly also a practice with a civilising objective. Scolding is used as a way of dismantling the power which the children have temporarily manifested through their troublemaking, thereby re-establishing what the teacher finds to be the proper power balance between teacher and pupil. However, it also serves to instil shame in the child by describing the child's behaviour as immoral, degrading or transgressing social norms. This is most obvious in that adults often stop telling children off when they show signs of shame by apologising or crying. The frequently public dressing down also contributes to stigmatising the child or the group to which it belongs. Through criticism, reprimands and scolding, the ethnic minority boys in 4A/6A hear, for instance, that they 'don't know how to behave properly', 'have not thought things through' and 'do not contribute to the class community'. Whether this is justified criticism or not, it informs the boys and the rest of the class of how the teachers regard boys like them. Teachers talk about and apportion blame to the boys as a group: 'You lot are always disturbing the others', or 'You lot don't know how to conduct yourselves'. The boys also refer to being told off when they explain to me why they believe that the teachers do not like 'immigrants' like them. Statements such as 'when you lot are given responsibility, you abuse it', and 'it concerns me that you don't learn how to behave properly at home' become descriptions of the children's collective identity which they may be able to reject as unfair, but which clearly become part of their self-understanding. The same applies when the boys are thrown out of the classroom. Over time, they and the rest of the class have noticed that it is usually boys like them – 'the immigrants' or 'the Muslims' – who receive this punishment and, from this, learn something about this category. As Ann A. Ferguson describes it: 'Moments of public punishment are powerful learning experiences about social location and worthiness' (2001:94). The punishment contributes to the boys' experience of belonging to the same category, characterised by the same inappropriate behaviour.

Monopolisation and Inversions of the Civilised Ideal

What the scolding also communicates is the characteristics of the decent and civilised person. If one compiles the behavioural norms that are communicated through scolding, admonitions and praise of the children, a picture emerges of this person as: someone who does not swear or shout, speaks nicely, eats nicely, does not annoy people, can work with others, does not cause trouble, contributes to the community, is a good friend who understands other people's feelings, offers constructive criticism, resolves conflicts in a fair way, shows compassion, does not interfere in how other people live their lives, does not tell others what to do, is tolerant of diversity, is not sexist, is not selfish, admits his or her mistakes, thinks things through, pays attention, is self-analytical and self-critical, helps others, and feels empathy for those who are old, weak or different from the norm. Since these characteristics are often used to describe or praise the girls and the ethnic Danish children, the pupils at the same time witness that they characterise some categories of children better than others. Everyday experiences of teachers' praise and criticism seem to contribute to the children's understanding that 'the Danes' and 'the girls' are 'good people', and better – that is more civilised – than the 'Muslim' and 'immigrant' boys.

This is also true of the teachers' references to 'Denmark' and 'Danish society' in their teaching. The teachers often refer to 'Danish society' when discussing forms of behaviour and society held in high esteem. As the principal stressed in the quote above, the teachers generally believe that the task of integration entails, among other things, teaching the boys how to behave in Danish society. In line with this, and following the enhanced focus on Danish nationality in Danish schools since the turn of the century (see chapter 2), the teachers use a considerable amount of time talking to the children about 'Danish society', its structure and rules. In Dorthe's lessons, she often refers to the Danish constitution, Danish democracy, rules and traditions for gender equality, and other ways in which the Danish state and legislation support rights and the maintenance of a fair, just and indeed civilised society. She also refers to the Universal Declaration of Human Rights in order to show that there are universal rules about such things, but for the most part, she and the other teachers refer to 'this society' and 'the Danish constitution' as something good, tolerant and civilised. While this often happens in the context of criticism of the boys' behaviour, it seems to contribute to the children's experience that 'Danes' behave better and are morally superior, at the same time as underlining an apparent contrast to the character of the ethnic minority boys. Even though it is not their intention, the teachers thereby, and through their failure to mention positive aspects of other societies, take out a sort of Danish patent on civilised behaviour and establish a monopoly in terms of the civilised person.

What we thus witness in 4A/6A is the tendency of civilising projects to counteract themselves. As we described in chapter 1, this seems to be caused by the inherent paradox that exists between civilising as integration and civilising as distinction. According to Elias, dominant groups within society want to civilise other, 'uncivilised' strata of society, while simultaneously maintaining their own higher status (Elias 1994 [1939]:382–5). As such, the Danish school is intended to integrate ethnic minority children and mould them in its image of the decent human being, but at the same time excludes these children from the civilised category by giving them a sense that it is monopolised by the 'Danes'. The response of those excluded is that they distance themselves from the civilising demands and find strength in the position of the uncivilised that is afforded to them.

It is worth noting that the boys' troublemaking and cultivation of a harsh tone takes the form of an inversion of the civilised ideal. The boys have turned the norms of civilised behaviour upside down in order to pointedly reject the demands they encounter from their surroundings and from an institution which they find hostile and restrictive. As such, the harsh tone and aggressiveness are best understood as what Paul Willis (1977) described as a 'counterculture', precisely modelled on the demands for civilised interaction that prevail at school (Gilliam 2009). Internally among the boys, there are social rules and demands for unity and solidarity. But the friendliness and empathy the boys show me during interviews seem to be actively avoided in their interaction with the other boys because it is associated with girliness and with conforming to the demands from school and Danish society. Thus, nice and polite behaviour in school is associated with being 'integrated' – a term the boys use derogatorily for someone who adapts, just as 'acting white' was used among the black students in Signithia Fordham's famous study (Fordham and Ogbu 1986).

This reflects the exclusionary tendency inherent in the civilising process mentioned in chapter 1, whereby those treated as 'uncivilised' gradually learn to identify with an alternative ideal outside the civilised category and with forms of behaviour that are considered uncivilised. The class of 4A/6A illustrates the nuances which have to be taken into account in order to understand the relationship between civilising, social norms of conduct, social categories and distinctions. As such, it can show us a social dynamic between the school's apportionment of recognition; its civilising project; teachers who, despite their good intentions, end up stigmatising groups of children; and children from marginalised groups who are trying to understand their experiences at school and position themselves favourably in this social world. As we have seen, included in this process is a construction of and attribution of civilised and uncivilised traits to different broad social categories – in this case gender, class, ethnicity and religion. The school's civilising project and, importantly, the children's reactions to it, thus have implications for how children understand and 'do' gender, ethnicity and religion at school – and, in a longer term perspective, for which forms of behaviour the genders and different social, ethnic and religious communities will be identified with.

7

The Decent Citizens

Lessons on moral superiority and the immorality of wealth in a class of privileged youth

Laura Gilliam

They are ... and I will use the expression 'good children' again – because they *are* good children. [...] They are in fact good in *all* respects. They even have positive attitudes [...] and the atmosphere, the positive atmosphere you find in this place and in the classroom is quite simply precious. Of course some days are better than others, but they have, like, a thoroughly kind and positive attitude to each other. And the purpose of being here is partly to learn and partly to have a nice time together. (Lise, class teacher 9B)

Lise is the class teacher of class 9B at Nordlund School in North Zealand, just north of Copenhagen, Denmark. Nordlund school is located close to a scenic area in a residential neighbourhood with large villas, single-family detached houses and terraced houses owned by what the teachers describe as 'resource-strong' families. Like the class at Sønder School, described in the previous chapter, class 9B also has a special reputation and common identity, yet while the former has a reputation of being 'the impossible class', 9B is known as 'the good class'. The teachers refer to them as 'sweet' and 'sociable' children, and, comparing themselves with the school's two other ninth grade classes, the pupils call themselves 'the nice class' or 'the angel class'. The pupil Christian describes the class as follows: 'We have always been considered the teachers' pet class. The nice class. We are always on top of our homework [...] we are clearly the ... you know, the leading class in the school.' As seen in the initial quote, the class teacher thinks that the pupils have 'a thoroughly kind and positive attitude to each other' and, in a similar vein, the teachers often describe the pupils as 'well-behaved' and marvel at how 'all the pupils get on well with each other'. Yet as indicated by Christian above, this positive reputation of the class also refers to the pupils' academic level and work ethic, and to the experience expressed by teachers that the majority of the young people are 'ambitious', 'serious', 'hard-working', 'skilled' and 'intelligent'.

In this chapter I will look at Nordlund School and 9B as an example of the ways in which the meaning of being civilised is constructed and negotiated in what is considered a 'well-functioning' class, in a 'privileged' school with 'resource-strong' families. The aim is to illuminate the connection established between class, civilised conduct, resources and behaviour in schools. At this point the pupils in 9B are approaching the end of their school life, and, according to the teachers, they do not require much further regulation of their behaviour. However, this does not mean that the civilising lessons of the school have come to an end. A closer look at 9B's daily lessons can illustrate how, through the teaching and conversations with teachers, pupils learn about appropriate forms of behaviour and civilised forms of societies, and not least about a social hierarchy of civilisation in which they themselves are placed vis-à-vis other social groups and categories. In 9B, the pupils come to understand that they are placed near the top of this hierarchy. This is interesting in relation to the previous chapter's description of a problematic class involving children who are faced with a completely different set of expectations. However, this neither means that the two classes are representative of the ways in which all children with a lower-class ethnic minority background and affluent ethnic Danish youth, respectively, behave at school, nor does it typify what these groups of children experience there. At Sønder School some classes are described as 'well-functioning', and at the more affluent Nordlund School there are classes in which groups of pupils make trouble and end up in conflict with teachers. Yet being at opposite ends of the socio-economic spectrum, the two classes demonstrate the internal variation in the Danish folkeskole and the very different lessons it can potentially give different children regarding identity and civilised demeanour via its educational practices.

With the exception of three pupils who have one or two parents of ethnic minority background, 9B consists of pupils with an ethnic Danish background. As part of my extended fieldwork at Nordlund School in 2008, I followed this particular class for approximately two months. The fieldwork consisted of participant observation in the classroom, during breaks, and in the staff room, as well as informal conversations and qualitative semi-structured interviews with the pupils in the class, the teachers, and the school principal. Moreover, I participated in a parent–teacher meeting, several staff meetings, as well as in 25 school–home meetings in the class.

The Good School

As described, 9B has a particularly positive reputation. This reputation influences the pupils in the class – they know they are part of a good community of high standing. Nordlund School has a similarly positive reputation. Teachers, parents and children alike participate in a strong collective we-narrative in which Nordlund School figures as a particularly good school. It is often mentioned that the school has, for a number of years, been placed in the top 20 in the Danish think tank CEPOS's ranking of the average grades achieved by pupils at Danish schools. Moreover, teachers proudly inform me that figures indicate that 97 per cent of the school's pupils learn to read within the first six months of the first grade, whereas the national average is 75 per cent. It is also a well-known fact that a majority of the school's pupils go directly on to academic studies.

Another aspect mentioned with pride is that Nordlund School defines itself as a no-bullying zone – 'where you need not be afraid of being harassed'. The teachers report that many pupils have moved to Nordlund School because they were bullied at their previous school, and they have been welcomed with open arms. A teacher describes it as follows: 'In fact, the children always succeed in being integrated into the classes at Nordlund School, mainly because we have this inclusive culture where there is room for everybody.' According to 9B's class teacher, Lise, the reason is that the children are what she herself terms as 'civilised':

> They know how to … live their life, and how to behave towards other people and things like that. None of them are in doubt about that. […] This goes for all the children. It is one of their core values. Even though they are in puberty and occasionally have turbulent issues, they do not doubt as they say 'what is okay' and how to behave; that is, what is acceptable and what is not. (Lise, class teacher 9B)

The school generally has a strong social profile and is described by adults and children alike as a 'nice' and 'safe place' to be. Many credit the school's success to the principal and several of the young pupils in 9B explain the good reputation of their class by referring to how they have been 'brought up' by their well-liked class teacher Lise. Yet interestingly, when adults and children talk about the many qualities of the school, they tend to say in the same breath that this is related to the school being 'very privileged', pointing in particular to 'the privileged area' or the school's 'affluent, well-educated, ambitious and supportive parents'. While the school is a regular Danish *folkeskole*, the catchment area, as well as the school's image, seems to endow it with an attractive group of parents. Even if some children in 9B have less affluent parents, most of the parents are highly educated, and a large number of them – especially the fathers – work in prestigious professions, for example as lawyers and professors, have good positions in major companies or within the public sector, or they are independent entrepreneurs. I often hear teachers describing the parents in terms such as: 'Well, this is the Nordlund neighbourhood after all … and well, they are good citizens.' This social position is associated with parental skills: 'Our pupils have good parents who, in most cases, take care of their children. We agree on most issues and the parents are extremely supportive of our efforts.' The school's location and clientele seem to imply that the parent group have certain characteristics; for instance, a particular relationship between parents and children, and between parents and the school. The teachers tend to voice these aspects in comparisons with other areas, as Lise does here:

> I am also extremely privileged that I work in this municipality. The first 13 years, I worked at [she names another school in the neighbourhood], and since then I have worked here, where we are just so privileged! Anyway … we have often discussed the fact that […] those neighbour-hoods, for instance in central Copenhagen, the areas with many ethnic children, how extremely difficult it must be for the teachers to get things to work. First they need to create a space in which to work, and then they need to get the parents to cooperate. It must be a challenge. The parents of our pupils are such a homogeneous group. […] They agree on all counts. (Lise, class teacher 9B)

Thus, similar to the teachers at Sønder School described in the previous chapter, the teachers tend to attribute their pupils' behaviour and academic potential to their parents' resources and to express a social awareness of the unequal distribution of such resources. However, among the teachers of Nordlund School, the description of the privileged area and equally privileged parents, as well as the contrasting images of other areas and schools which teachers often evoke at the same time, is part of the positive we-narrative of Nordlund School. This obviously contributes to the feeling of present and future success, status and security which the teachers, parents and children get from their association with the school. In 9B, the teachers, as well as the pupils themselves, often express expectations that they will do well, complete long educations, and have prestigious jobs, or what they term 'a high position' in society. The teachers refer, for instance, to 'when you move on to high school and higher education' or say, as Lise does to the class: 'Already in first grade, some of you were very ambitious. I remember reminding you that you would not be going to high school just yet.' At the school–home conversations, the teachers also have serious conversations with the majority of the pupils and their parents about their ambitious plans for the future. Having spoken to a careers adviser, the young people report that they have enquired about how to become a doctor or a lawyer, and make jokes about asking the adviser how to become a refuse collector, thereby demonstrating their awareness of their expected trajectory towards prestigious jobs.

Alongside interviews with the pupils, such episodes show that they are conscious of their social standing and feel that they are among the Danish elite. However, they also express that they and their parents have an expectation that the school will provide an important foundation for the reproduction of their privileged social position. The school thus seems to be part of a harmonious unit of competent teachers, well-behaved and academically gifted children, and resourceful, ambitious parents who support the school and reinforce each other's status and self-esteem internally in the group. As described by Connell et al. in relation to an American 'ruling class school', Nordlund School offers 'the reproduction of class position by access to meritocratic careers', but also 'exclusiveness and a sense of social superiority' (Connell et al. 2000 [1981]:301–2). However, my experience was that the feeling of being a member of an exclusive and socially superior club did not just involve an experience of being particularly privileged, but also of being a more civilised human being. This feeling of superiority does not apply to all of the young people in the same way. Moreover, as described in the following, it is constantly held in check by parallel negative understandings of 'privileged' and 'rich people', and by a cultural appreciation of the 'ordinary people', as well as ideals about avoidance of expressions of superiority.

Decent Citizens

As in other schools (see chapters 5 and 6), the principal and teachers at Nordlund School stress that the objective of the school is not merely to train the pupils' academic skills, but also to bring them up to become socially responsible and well-behaved. Class 9B's teachers relate how, through the years, they have made an effort to teach the pupils to 'respect the rules of the community', to tell each other what upsets them in a conciliatory tone, to apologise to each other, and to solve everyday conflicts through dialogue and meetings with those involved. During my fieldwork, most of the lessons I observed included teachers' descriptions of 'empathy', 'common decency' and 'social rules'. The principal reports that he often admonishes the pupils to remember that 'everybody should feel comfortable here, and that this will only be possible if we consider our interaction carefully'. Echoing the grade 0 teachers described in chapter 5, he explains this by referring to the conditions of the school institution: 'We are a large number of people interacting within a small area.'

Likewise, the pupils of whom the teachers speak particularly well are those who have 'the ability to sense if someone is not feeling well', who are 'inclusive' and 'self-aware', and who 'have a social conscience'. The values expressed by the teachers refer to the same civilising ideals of verbalisation, inclusion, and awareness and respect for other people's boundaries in a shared space that we have seen teachers and pedagogues express in the other chapters. Yet, in spite of this prioritisation of the task of upbringing and making children 'social', the teachers also emphasise that this is not as demanding a task at their school as at other schools, particularly when it comes to the older classes. It is indeed striking how little time is spent regulating behaviour in class 9B. As we shall see, the teachers influence the young people's opinions and conceptions of good behaviour, but their general attitude is that teaching good manners is not necessary in this class. Instead, they spent their energy on what they term 'the academic' and on other formative practices, such as promoting what are considered good attitudes to society and work. When I ask the principal what his mission is in terms of the upbringing of pupils, he answers:

> Well, our objective is to turn the pupils into good citizens who are prepared to stand up for each other in altruistic ways. For instance, by going into politics. Not just going into politics for the sake of achieving one's own goals. But to sacrifice oneself for others and to do one's bit for

the greater good of the community. We would like to educate our pupils to participate actively in a democratic society. [...] The objective is to make decent citizens of our pupils. (The principal, Nordlund School)

I often hear this narrative, that the children must be turned into 'decent citizens', and that this entails taking an interest in other people, developing a critical stance and contributing to society. The school nurtures this concept of being a decent citizen in various ways: the teachers often talk about democracy with the class, they set up mock elections, and there is great emphasis on creating a free and open environment for discussions in the class. In this way, all teachers prioritise time for discussion, and the pupils are obviously used to discussing and accommodating a wide variety of opinions in class. This leads to occasional disagreements and clashes between different opinions, some of them of a political nature, between pupils and teachers. During the time I spent in the class, I witnessed a couple of instances where the teachers' critique of individual pupils' attitudes or ways of life generated lively debates, and the pupils chastised the teachers for not giving them space to do and think as they please. The youngsters seem to be used to being listened to and respected, and often they are the ones emphasising democracy, egalitarianism, and tolerance in class. While the teachers often get annoyed in such situations, they appreciate the young people's attitude as yet another example of the school's excellent work, and the particularly decent nature of the pupils.

Another tendency is the focus on optimising the pupils' academic competences. Due to the pupils' good behaviour and high academic level, the teachers feel that the only thing the school can do is, in the teacher Søren's words, 'to motivate them to do even more'. The teachers find that, for the majority of the pupils, this only implies a fine-tuning, focused primarily on improving their attitude to work. This is expressed in the school–home conversations, where pupils are lauded for being or encouraged to be 'focused', 'ambitious', 'serious', to 'have their things in order' and 'work hard'.

When the teachers talk about the 'good pupils' in class, they focus not just on those who do well academically, but also on those who are 'committed', 'participating', 'enjoying school' and 'ambitious'. Nevertheless, the teachers also send out other signals. Discussing the pupils' plans for the future during the school–home conversations, the teachers encourage the students to choose to study the subjects that interest them, take their time, or spend a year at a so-called 'continuation school'[1] before they enter high school. This advice is, however, mostly given to pupils who are unresolved about their future plans or to those whose parents express higher ambitions than their children. The teachers' ideal is evidently that the motivation for education should come from the pupils themselves and not be forced upon them by their parents. One can argue that this appreciation of enthusiasm and motivation facilitates the school's educational efforts and later the youngsters' approach to work. However, it also expresses an ideal that a civilised society does not discipline its citizens to strive and toil, but is founded on people's free will and enterprise. We also see that the ideal of enthusiastic motivation ('*lyst*' in Danish) tends to become a yardstick for the good student and thus part and parcel of the normative requirements facing the individual pupils at school. As a result, it is not enough to do your work; it is problematic if you do not have an enthusiastic attitude towards school.

The Nice Boys

In contrast to the pupils, and especially the boys, in 4A/6A at Sønder School described in the previous chapter, the young people in 9B attempt to observe these requirements of school and assess each other according to how diligent and active they are in class and 'how interested they are in school things'. Furthermore, comparing the class to 4A/6A, in 9B 'the good pupil' is not only associated with the female gender, and there is another behavioural norm for boys, acknowledging their commitment and high performance in relation to schoolwork. Even though a handful of the boys are not preoccupied with schoolwork, they all discuss their assignments and academic subjects. Internal competition for high marks among the boys also demonstrates that competence and diligence translate to high social esteem. It is also worth noting that the teachers do not experience the boys as potentially problematic or as troublemakers as they do in 4A/6A. The teacher Lise talks about several of them as 'nice' or 'good boys' who 'do their homework', 'like the school', 'are positive, pleasant, and well-mannered'. These boys may also be challenged by the tough masculinity norm presented in the media and in various social contexts, if not by their family and circle of friends. However, most of them obviously feel above this norm, and do not need it to compensate for a lack of cultural capital, which is what it offers to more deprived children (Gilliam 2015). By virtue of their academic success and future prospects, they are on course to achieve what Connell calls 'social power', and they are clearly aware that they are able to distinguish themselves on the basis of their privileged backgrounds (Connell 2000; see also chapter 6). When I ask 15-year-old Thomas why they generally adapt to their teachers' demands, his response is characterised by the understanding that he and other young people in this neighbourhood are morally superior to youngsters in other areas:

Thomas: But it's probably also the environment. I think it also has to do with us coming from out here. We don't spend ... our everyday life, surrounded by troublemakers. At least very few of us do.

Laura: What is so special about your environment?

Thomas: It is a very law-abiding environment – not, you know, a troublemaker environment. I don't think so. Of course, during the weekends, where we meet up with people from [he mentions a school closer to Copenhagen] and things like that, in those situations we really feel the difference. For instance, Camille and I, as well as Asger, Benjamin, Mads and Peter, have often gone out to meet them. You really feel a huge difference. Because they are just the kind that fights ... And it is not just for fun – it is for real ...

Laura: And how do you guys differ from them then?

Thomas: We try to stay very neutral [...]. We would never begin to hit each other. You know, for real, with fistfights, aiming at the head so that you really feel the blows. I don't think we would ever do that. I find that inconceivable, so ...

Laura: Why don't you do that? What do you think is the difference?

Thomas: The way we are brought up. Our surroundings and ... the amount of respect we have for our parents and the school.

(Thomas 9B)

As seen here, the boys distance themselves from aggressiveness and perceive it as something that characterises pupils from other schools and areas. In line with this, when pupils in 9B are considered difficult by teachers, it is not because of tough masculinity. A consequence of the school's high level and demands in terms of academic ability and commitment seems to be that the pupils criticised by teachers are those who are not sufficiently committed to school; such pupils are perceived as 'apathetic' and 'not serious'. However, a specific group of pupils are described by teachers as 'the weak group'. These four boys and one girl are seen as 'academically challenged' and as lacking motivation. The teachers explain this in terms of them facing challenges at home due to parents' divorce or illness, yet they also draw on the explanation of 'low resources' referred to in the previous chapter. While the other pupils live in large villas and the coveted terraced houses in the area, three of the boys do not live in the neighbourhood, and two of them live, respectively, in an apartment in the local council housing project and in inner Copenhagen. Anna's mother is from Eastern Europe and her father is English, while Jakob's Muslim father is known by the class for deserting his family and returning to his homeland. The way these relatively ordinary youngsters are problematised indicates that the privileges of the parents and pupils at Nordlund School become a standard against which other families and children are assessed and found wanting.

Teaching Distinctions – the Bad, the Humane and the Free

Even if the absence of uncivilised behaviour in the class seems to make regulation of conduct redundant, there is still quite a lot of communication about suitable behaviour and conceptions of what is (un)civilised in the teaching and in class discussions. Besides the focus on academic skills and knowledge, quite a large part of the teaching concerns subjects which have a normative dimension, and which explicitly or implicitly tell the young pupils about civilised and uncivilised ways of being in the world. This ranges from ways of interacting with other people to ways of interacting with the environment and one's own body, such as in biology classes, when a certain type of lifestyle and of climate consciousness are described as socially distinguished and more civilised than a less considerate approach to the environment and the body. These normative descriptions seem to constitute a significant part of the teaching and upbringing in the school. A characteristic aspect of these descriptions is that, in almost all cases, some 'Others' are defined who are critiqued and indirectly described as uncivilised in various ways. In this way, certain types of conduct or agents are presented across the various disciplines as appropriate or morally superior, or conversely as criticisable or backward. It must be emphasised that 9B is not special in this respect, even if it can seem glaring when I, in the following, bring together the examples. The use of contrasts between civilised and uncivilised people and forms of conduct seems to be a widespread mode of inculcating social norms and constructing distinction between human beings, and it is an intrinsic part of the upbringing practices of school institutions (see discussion in chapter 9).

One example of this practice comes from lessons in Knowledge of Christianity (called 'Christianity'). Here, a group of pupils do a presentation on a Buddhist demonstration against the government in Burma, where people were shot down in the street. In the subsequent discussion, the teacher Lise critiques partly the Burmese government's suppression of religion and the shooting of demonstrators, and partly the fact that an astrologist has decided where the capital of Burma should be located. She exclaims: 'We do not understand such a country at all; it is so very different from the West.' Another example is from a Social Studies class, where the teacher Tom shows a documentary on Danish entrepreneurs working in China. In the programme, the Danish entrepreneurs point out that you have to keep the Chinese workers on their toes, and that 'they look you in the eye while deceiving you'. The class denounces this statement as racist, but the fact that the Chinese work '24/7 for low wages' is commended as the expression of a laudable 'work ethic', while low wages are seen as a sign of appalling working conditions in China. The teacher and pupils also touch upon 'the low standard of working conditions for labourers', how some workers 'do not get paid for the first week' and that 'slums and pollution are common in China'.

Both conversations are typical of the normative dimension in teaching, which I have also observed in other schools. During discussions of the subjects in question, contrasting images of Others are constructed (cf. Hall 1996) – in this case other countries or parts of the world – where people engage in or are subject to negative or unworthy practices and conditions. As a result, these 'Others' are presented as morally inferior in relation to more humane and thus civilised societies, which have civilised conditions and forms of behaviour. Moreover, as in the examples depicted above, the normative conversations tend to be brief, and are often characterised by a few exchanges which merely establish a consensus on what to reject. Nevertheless, more or less implicitly, a 'we-identity' is constructed (Elias 1996 [1989]); a group which dissociates itself from a given conduct and acts differently and in a morally superior way. The 'we' mentioned by Lise above is synonymous with the 'West', but as we shall see below, the 'we' changes in size and nature. It is scaled up and down from being the pupils' residential neighbourhood, their social class, religious group, nation, all the way up to encompassing Europe or the West.

The identity of the uncivilised 'Others' also varies. In geography classes, countries like China, USA, and India are described as disgraceful environmental polluters, which do not comply with the international environmental agreements. In one lesson, the debate turns to a general discussion of China and how this country not only prioritises the industry over environmental concerns, but also demolishes private houses in order to make room for factories, prohibits parents from having more than one child and is perceived by both the teacher Søren and the pupils as having 'irresponsible and inhuman authorities'. In history lessons, one topic is the former Soviet Union. Following a presentation by a group of pupils on 'the absence of freedom of religion' and how people were influenced by 'the freedom they saw in the West', the teacher Jens Ole reports how 'respectable patriarchs in Russia come home every night dead drunk because of the tradition for vodka consumption'. He tells the class how vodka production has been state subsidised for years and asks the rhetorical question: 'Because a population that is drunk does what?' Trine answers: 'Does not notice what goes on in society!' Jens Ole nods and describes how something similar happened in Pakistan, where the British rulers taught the local population to smoke opium. In all three cases, either a people or a government is thus described as immoral and backward in relation to an undefined shared norm.

Another history lesson focuses on the end of the Second World War. Here the same teacher, Jens Ole, spends part of the lesson discussing what would be recognised as clear-cut civilising themes. The class has watched a documentary about the relationship between the Russians and the Germans after the war and, with great dedication, Jens Ole talks about the German approach to the Russians during the war, their murders of children, and how the Germans amused themselves with 'sinister games'. According to him, this is the explanation as to why the Germans did not dare surrender to the Russians. 'They were afraid of the Russians' revenge. The Germans preferred to surrender to the British or to the Americans.' He goes on to tell the class how Russia did not take part in the Nuremberg Process, but chose instead to conduct their own process. He relates:

> The SS soldiers were shot without a trial, and the Russians used empty concentration camps to detain German minorities in the Eastern countries. This discussion inevitably raises the question: Should evil be repelled with evil or should we try to transform evil by means of good examples?

The lesson continues with an account of the division of Germany, and Jens Ole describes how Russia was hell-bent on revenge because of its experiences with the Germans. Conversely, he argues, Britain and the USA were more interested in rebuilding the country and generating wealth. He then shows a contemporary American propaganda movie, where Germany, Italy and Japan are portrayed as countries that eliminated freedom of speech, cultural activities, the judicial system and unions, and forced their populations to live with various prohibitions, compulsory labour and enforced patriotism. Subsequently Jens Ole points out that the film attempts to represent the world as divided into 'a free world and an enslaved world', while a number of the pupils address the fact that Germany, Italy and Japan are represented by stereotypes and compare this representation to George Bush's description of 'the axis of evil'.

In spite of these meta-perspectives on the film's messages, the lesson includes a number of positive descriptions and assessments of free will, the gracious winner, and the humane sanctions ascribed to certain nations – the UK and the USA. In the same manner, certain types of action and certain nations, such as Germany and Russia, are represented as barbaric, vengeful, despotic, morally deficient and thereby uncivilised.

One might say that these civilising lessons are integral to the subject of war itself. But the point is precisely that the Second World War – just like other much discussed issues such as slavery, witch-hunts, genocide and political regimes like Nazism, Stalinism and Apartheid – is a central element in the school's efforts to teach children how to recognise, comprehend and relate to the uncivilised in its purest forms. In this way, the civilising anxiety and moral lessons drawn from the world wars that we describe in chapter 2 are reactivated in Danish classrooms over and over again. Moreover, these narratives also contribute to the ascription of various degrees of civilisation to certain nations or categories of people. Two central aspects in this assessment of civilised status, which surface in the discussion of war and appear frequently in the representations of the morally superior, are, on the one hand, the free-spirited rational individual who, of his or her own free will, adapts to the rules of social interaction, and, on the other hand, the democratic form of government and ordered society that support this individual. The teachers and pupils often dissociate themselves from oppressive governments, inhuman or unjust treatment of members of a society, as well as from irrational behaviour and authoritarian people. Even though Denmark may not be explicitly mentioned in these discussions, they often imply Denmark's association with countries or regions, such as the West, Europe or Scandinavia, which are referenced in opposition to the oppressive, inhuman, unjust, irrational and authoritarian countries and regions; that is, as a contrast to what is presented as uncivilised.

The We-Identity of 'The Danes'

When 9B's class teacher, Lise, hears the pupils' descriptions of the SS officers' misdeeds, she shakes her head and responds that 'in a society like ours, such acts would result in a bad conscience'. This exemplifies how the young people, even when the teaching concerns subjects unrelated to Danish society, are more or less explicitly invited to identify with a civilised 'we'. As mentioned, this is a typical characteristic of discussions of moral issues in class. This does not mean that there are no negative we-representations, but the representations of 'we', 'us', 'our community' and 'our society' which teachers and textbooks mediate are generally positive and come across as civilised when compared with others. The 'we' – or what Elias (1996 [1989]) terms the 'we-identity'– that is presented is often defined in terms of nationality. 'Denmark' and 'Danes' tend to be presented as the natural shared category of the class, and as the normal category, in the frequent situations where a 'normal' is defined in contrast to something which is rejected. The young people in 9B clearly already identify as 'Danes', yet the school's focus on Danish culture, evident in the school's curriculum, traditions and teaching (Kryger 2007; Gilliam 2009; Jenkins 2011), most probably contributes to their identification as Danes and their positive national sentiment.

During lessons in all subjects, Denmark, Danes, Danishness, Danish history, the Danish welfare system, and democracy are mentioned and addressed in positive ways. However, in 9B, this reinforcement of a civilised 'we' is manifested most comprehensively in a class project entitled 'Denmark and the Danes'. On the first day, the pupils each bring an item which, for them, illustrates Danishness. Among other things, they bring rye bread, liquorice, an effigy of the fictional Danish hero Ogier the Dane (*Holger Danske*), a book on Danish memorials, a football, a CD with the singer songwriter Kim Larsen, tealight candles symbolising Danish *hygge* (a friendly, cosy atmosphere broadly identified as an epitome of Danish culture), and a political pamphlet which the pupil in question sees as a symbol of democracy. Apart from these material symbols, the pupils and their teacher Lise also mention association activities, the royal family, Danish nature and Danish childhood.

Fifteen-year-old Niels has brought a printout of the national anthem to class. This prompts Lise to relate how she once heard it performed on an outdoor stage, where all 6,000 members of the audience stood up and joined in the singing: 'I tell you, it sent a shiver down my spine. It does not get more Danish than that!', she relates to the responsive group of youngsters. Lea and Mikkel have brought a comic strip by the well-known Danish cartoonists Wulff and Morgenthaler as an example of 'Danish culture', particularly 'sarcasm', 'irony' and 'freedom of speech'. Lise responds: 'I almost choke on my coffee when I read this comic strip over breakfast' (in her newspaper). 'We are very liberal indeed here in Denmark. The Danish libertarianism ...', she says, writing the term on the blackboard before continuing: 'There is almost nothing you cannot do or say in Denmark!' The girl Synne is dressed all in black in a punk style and states that she has brought herself as an example of Danish youth culture. This develops into a discussion of 'tolerance' and 'freedom of speech', terms which are then written on the board. Several pupils have brought Christian crosses and Bibles along as symbols of the Christian faith. Jesper is one of them: 'The Christian Lutheran church is the official faith in Denmark – it is very Danish.' Aske joins in: 'Danish society is to a great extent founded on Christian values; loving one's neighbour is also associated with the welfare state – taking care of each other.'

Even if this was not the purpose of the activity, it turns into a small celebration of Danish national icons, and of Danish culture in general as it is perceived by the pupils and the teacher; that is, *hygge*, liberalism, tolerance, freedom of speech, 'neighbourly love', democracy and Christianity. Among the daily routines at the school, there are several examples of what Michael Billig terms 'banal nationalism', where, in everyday events, the nation 'is indicated, or "flagged" in the lives of its citizenry', without ritualisation or ceremony (Billig 1995:6). However, this session, which is not untypical of the way Danish teachers often address Danishness as a theme for reflection and teaching, is in fact more explicitly constitutive of nationality than banal. In part it gives the pupils a lesson in national identity, and in part a positive experience of the Danish national community's virtues – and not least its civilised characteristics. Although this cannot be compared to the growth of the national we-identity among Germans before and during the Second World War, which Elias described, it shows the schools' role in evoking an image of the nation within the young people's 'individual self-image' and thus in stimulating an 'identification with the nation' which in ordinary life often remains mute. (Elias 1996 [1989])

Christianity as the Civilised Religion

As discussed above, the teacher and several of the pupils associate Danishness with Christianity and ascribe neighbourly love to the Danes because of their Christian faith. This is another example of a civilised 'we' constructed in class; a Christian 'we'. The teachers and a number of the pupils talk about the 'we' of the class and the school as 'Christian', juxtaposing this with other religions or denominations other than Protestantism, which are presented as less civilised. Catholicism, for instance, is described as based on a 'faith in authorities', and Islam is implicitly depicted as authoritarian and morally offensive in comparison with what is perceived as the Protestant faith's focus on the ethics of the individual and the relationship between God and the individual human being. This is supported by the textbooks used in class. In a Christianity lesson, the pupils are reading a chapter describing the difference between Christianity and Islam. The text states that the most important message of Christianity 'is to love your neighbour like yourself', while the central tenet of Islam is described as 'to observe the rules of the Qu'ran'. The class teacher Lise, who also teaches Christianity, uses the comparison in a class debate:

Lise: What do you think? I mean, their strict rules go against the commandment to love your neighbour.

She goes on to talk about a school in Aarhus that she has heard of where the children had not had anything to eat because of Ramadan. The school had provided food for the children because they were tired and were 'literally falling off their chairs from exhaustion'.

Lise: Here we have two opposing perceptions. Should we observe the rules of the Qu'ran or should we make sure that our children are well nourished and comfortable?

She turns to the only pupil in the class who has a Muslim parent.

Lise: Jakob, do you celebrate Ramadan in your household?

Jakob shakes his head. Lise turns to the class.

Lise: What do you think [of the observance of Ramadan]?

Benjamin: I think it is ridiculous!

Lise: But is it ridiculous, really?

Benjamin: There was this footballer who could not complete the second half of a match because he had not eaten during Ramadan and was exhausted.

Lise: [Sighs] Yes, we can conclude that Ramadan has an effect on all levels of society.

Helene: At my father's school [her father is a teacher], some parents think that their children should be just as religious as themselves and observe Ramadan. It was appalling during Ramadan – the teachers had to make sure that the children were not too exhausted.

Lise: Is that right? But this applies to a large population here, so we cannot ignore it.

Jesper: There was a boy in my previous class by the name of Ali. His mother was very religious. He ate nothing, or just something like an apple, during the day.

Lise: Yes, did that influence his schoolwork?

Jesper: No.

Lise: I suppose they learn to live with it.

Aske: We talk about Ramadan, but we do not know why they observe it!

Lise: I don't know, do you?

Aske: No.

Lise makes a note on a piece of paper.

Lise: I have made a note that you will give a presentation on that subject [turns to the class]. It must be a very literal reading of the Qu'ran.

Helene: I have heard that they have to try to live like those who have nothing in order to better understand their plight. In a sense, that is also about loving one's neighbour.

Lise: Yes, there is nothing negative about that, is there?

Benjamin: We could actually learn from that.[2]

(Christianity lesson, 9B)

A week later, Lise again addresses the issue in class. She has found some material on Ramadan and asks the pupils to take turns reading sections aloud. After the first part, she says:

Lise: Last time we discussed a school in Aarhus where the children were so exhausted from hunger that they fell off their chairs. However, on the radio I heard an imam who said that children should not observe the fast. I feel such pity for them – imagine if Ramadan falls during the summer. To us that is a completely foreign way to live.

[The next bit of text describes how menstruating women need not observe Ramadan.]

Lise: Yes, that is probably because they are considered unclean.

Selma: [Ironically] Yes, ugh!

According to the next part of the text, Muslims eat after sundown during Ramadan.

Lise: Yes, by that point they must be starving! From a rational Christian perspective, it is neglect. You prevent small children from consuming food and water all day – that is neglect.

Thomas: What about the young babies?

Lise: They are probably taken care of.

A girl: That is horrible. Just think if you are a staunch believer, then you would observe Ramadan and not give your children food.

[The text explains that after sundown the Muslims gorge themselves with food.]

Lise: It is quite healthy to fast, but if they eat plenty at night, then what is the point? In one of the municipalities there was a big party at city hall with lots of delicious food when Ramadan was over. But naturally some were against that, because it is not a Danish tradition.

Helene: Yes, Pia Kjærsgaard [former leader of the Danish People's Party], probably!

(Christianity lesson, 9B)

In the two discussions outlined above, the difference between Christianity and Islam is constructed as a difference between, on the one hand, Christians' love for their neighbour and rational approach, and on the other hand, Muslims' unquestioning adherence to religious rules. Ramadan is described as a cause of child neglect, and hence as a morally reprehensible tradition. The implication is that Muslims, particularly the staunch believers, are more irrational and less humane than Christians because they unthinkingly abide by their religion's commandments, even the inhumane ones. As we see, the teacher does not know why Ramadan is observed, nor does she know that children and pregnant or breastfeeding women need not observe it, and she is pleasantly surprised by what she perceives as legitimate causes and sensible exceptions. However, the discussion quickly turns to an exchange of critique, indignation and mutual reassurance that 'our' Christian culture is morally superior. In this situation, the teachers and several of the young people often take it for granted that the 'we' of the class and the school is Christian. This is sometimes challenged by the atheist pupils, and quite a few discussions focus on the legitimacy of Christianity. It is worth noting that the critical approach towards Ramadan is also criticised by some pupils in the class.

As is the case in the passage above, pupils often distance themselves from 'xenophobic' Danes – here with reference to Pia Kjærsgaard, then leader of the right-wing Danish People's Party. As will be further illustrated by examples in this chapter and in chapters 8 and 9, this seems to establish a civilised, moderate position midway between two inappropriate extremes: fundamentalist Muslims and intolerant Danes.

Class Consciousness

The establishment of a civilised intermediate position also applies to the construction of social classes. Where the civilised 'we' mentioned above refers to Christians, it is clearly a class 'we' which emerges during an English lesson, as illustrated in the following. The question of social class arises during a conversation about two photographs in an English language schoolbook, designed to generate a discussion on social inequality in Britain. The first image portrays a large family sitting on a sofa in a living room; the second image is of a young man positioned in front of two sports cars. The English teacher Dorit asks the pupils to take a look at the first image of the family:

Dorit: What do you see?

Aske: There is a family. The woman is smoking.

Thomas: [Interrupts] Even though there is a baby in the room!

Dorit: That is not important in those circles. What is the room like, Kristine?

Kristine: The room is rather messy; it's not expensive things, it's not like design [furniture] or such.

Dorit: What about the floor, what does that look like?

Trine: It's a carpet; it's cheaper than a wooden floor.

Mads: I think that maybe the father has abandoned them, because there is no man in the picture and they look pissed off. The dog seems hungry, as though it hasn't been fed; it looks like it found something to eat under the sofa.

Dorit: Can you tell me any other signs which tell us what kind of family this is? What about the baby? Isn't it in a strange position? It seems like it's just a bag of bones. The legs are stretched out in different directions; it doesn't look comfortable. What does it tell you? [nobody answers] I think it looks like they are not paying attention to the baby.

Normally you would put a baby in a cot when it is sleeping; this one is just sleeping in the middle of the living room.

Asger: I think the girl is maybe a teenage mother, because there are a lot of them in Britain.

Dorit: Yes, you may be right, but we don't know. What do you think of the family?

Peter: They look like losers.

Dorit: Ah, Peter, losers? I don't like that word. But they're maybe lower middle class. What do you think of the mother? What does she look like?

Iben: Her clothes look cheap.

Dorit: What kind of food do you think she eats?

Mads: She probably eats fast food – a lot of sweets and cakes.

Dorit: What kind of people eat that? ... [provides the answer with emphasis on each syllable] The low-er mid-dle class!

Simon: I think they look very British, as if they are going to the pub?

Dorit: Ah, but don't Danish people go to the pub?

Simon: Yes.

Dorit: But what kind of people go to the pub in Denmark?

Simon: Young people and ...

Dorit: [Interrupts] Yes, but your father doesn't go to the pub, does he?

Simon: No.

Dorit: It's not all kind of people that go there. What kind of people go to the pub? – It's the low-er mid-dle class. And it's the same with smoking. The mother here smokes, even though it's very expensive. In Denmark, a lot of people have stopped smoking, because they know it is unhealthy for them. Here at our school, almost nobody smokes any more. But what kind of people still smoke?

Asger: The lower middle class?

(English lesson, 9B)

In the passage below, taken from the next English lesson, the class listens to an audio clip where the young girl in the family described above talks about her school. Dorit follows up with a discussion:

Dorit: What does it say about the school? I think it was horrible!

Camille: There was a lot of kicking and fighting.

Dorit: What about the teachers?

Camille: They were making fun of her?

Dorit: Yes, they were making fun of her! A lot of people drop out of school in those circles.

Iben: It's rough and tough.

Dorit: Yes, they don't have so many opportunities.

Asger: There are not so many jobs to get, so it doesn't matter if they go to school or not.

Helene: A lot of people give up.

Dorit: There should be some adults to tell them what to do, but they don't. Why don't they?

Helene: Her mother is not a good role model; there are no role models.

Dorit: What do you think her life will be like?

Sune: I think it will be awful!

Dorit: Oh, do you think so?

Mads: I don't think she will be rich, but she will be happy. She wants a job as a social worker, and she will be good at that, because she has the experience.

Dorit: Yes, and she has a goal. She will probably be married and have five children [Dorit smiles].

Jakob: I think she will be married to some moron who will get drunk and what have you.

Dorit: So you think she is a 'loser' [sighs]?

Jakob: Yes [laughs].

Helene: I think she could go either way.

Dorit: Do you think she will leave Bootle [the town in which the family lives]?

Thomas: No.

Dorit: Once in Bootle, always in Bootle ...

(English lesson, 9B)

In the audio clip, the girl states that she is happy about her life and is looking forward to going to high school. Dorit points out that the pupils can learn from this that one's prejudices are not always accurate and that one 'might well be a happy person and have a good life in spite of living in poverty'. She tells me later that her intention was to get the pupils to face up to their prejudices. However, in class she activates the social class categories by repeatedly referring to 'the lower middle class', and actively participates in portraying this 'lower middle class' as amoral and uncivilised. This episode is only atypical because teachers rarely participate this explicitly in the discursive construction of social class and in the negative description of the 'lower middle class'. Yet this kind of construction often occurs, just in shorter interludes and with more implicit references. The entire conversation is quoted here in order to show the large number of subjects of civilising import which constitute markers of distinction related to social class of which the pupils are competent users. On the basis of a single photo and a brief conversation recorded on tape, the pupils and their teacher are able to construct a complete image of the unfortunate, but also uncivilised, lower class. During the conversation they address everything from poor taste in clothes and design, unhealthy and uncontrolled eating habits, smoking, drinking, neglect of and indifference to children, excessive sexuality, teenage pregnancies, aggression, punitive teachers, tough environments, lack of enterprise and poor social mobility. Dorit states that she encourages the pupils to compare the girl's situation with their own in order to remind them of their own privileges. However, the lesson and dialogue show that the description of the lifestyle of the lower classes functions as a mirror reflecting the pupils' civilised class position.

Thus both the textbook and the conversation Dorit initiates invite the young pupils to participate in the discursive construction of the Others, and thereby themselves, as members of distinct classes. According to the sociologist Beverly Skeggs, the middle-class construction of the working class consists primarily in the consolidation of the middle-class self-narrative: 'Class is a discursive, historically specific construction, a product of middle-class political consolidation, which includes elements of fantasy and projection' (Skeggs 1997:5). The discussion in class thus appears to be a distillation of these fantasies and projections of other social classes. It defines for the pupils the multiplicity of relations, whereby, on the basis of their economic and cultural class position, they can claim distinction in terms of better taste and moral superiority.

The Amoral Rich

The discussion in the English class described above is unique with regard to the explicit deploring of a 'lower middle-class' life. I will argue that it can only take place because it happens in a context of – imagined – social equals; but even here it is an exception. As we have seen, feelings of superiority are aired and established in relation to many themes in this school context. But the inferiority of people with a lower-class background is something that is most often merely hinted at or implied in conversations, or articulated in combination with an awareness of the social problems of people of lower social standing. As such the young people most often comply with the norm of a keen observance of the illegitimacy of expressions of class superiority (Wouters 2011). This is supported by their teachers, who explicitly show their dislike of such expressions.

In line with this, while the school contributes significantly to the consolidation of the pupils' privileged class position, it also modifies their positive self-understanding with a counter-narrative regarding 'the amoral rich'. As mentioned, the second photo in the English textbook is of a young man surrounded by sports cars. The class listens to an audio clip where the young man talks about himself, and here it becomes evident that the cars belong to his father, with whom he lives following his parents' divorce. Dorit asks how the pupils can hear that he is rich. Peter refers to the fact that he attends a private school. Dorit points out that he perhaps does not live with his mother 'because she might be busy at work or she might have a new husband'. She also thinks that he sounds 'spoilt'. The pupils change the subject to the 'boarding school' he attends, and express that it could be 'snobbish' and only for 'rich people' who have problems with their children, who might be 'unhappy at school'. Helene thinks that he has not seen 'how the other half lives' and continues: 'He is probably rich, but also selfish.' Dorit adds: 'Perhaps his life is empty? He wants to be in advertising, and he will not use his education to help other people, like being a doctor or something – he's selfish.'

This description of the young man is typical of a widespread discourse about those termed 'rich people' at this and other schools. Besides the narrative describing them as good, 'resource-strong' parents, many of the school's parents are also referred to as 'busy, rich' parents. The teachers feel sorry for the children because they find that, due to their workloads, their parents tend to neglect them. This, they find, leads to a bad conscience, and the parents consequently do not restrict their children's behaviour by setting boundaries, instead compensating for their lack of time with material indulgence, while leaving the upbringing to au-pair girls (often from the Philippines). The result is badly behaved, spoilt and anti-social children. Parallel to Bach's discussion in chapter 8, this group is thus described as parents who might have economic and material resources, but are unable to offer the time and the care required for a good upbringing of children. Here it is the teacher, Tom, who thinks that most of the children in his class have had a 'good upbringing', but that there are some, including the approximately 25 per cent he assumes to be 'raised by au-pairs', 'who have a difficult time':

The parents spend a lot of time away from the home. I have pupils who can be emotionally unstable and suddenly feel sad. Often it is because their parents only arrive home at 7 p.m. and until then the au-pair looks after them. The children can have difficulties with this sometimes. You could say that they are a bit neglected in this way. (Tom, teacher 9B)

While Karin, the teacher responsible for class 0B, which was described in chapter 5, experiences that many of the children are 'little projects', she finds that others are neglected:

Over the years I have had the experience that some kind of neglect occurs. I believe that the parents have had to juggle large workloads. Many of them have big jobs in order to maintain the big houses in this prestigious suburb. Evidently, you feel that some of the children have a tough time. They arrive before 8 a.m. and are picked up late. Mum and Dad travel a lot – there may be an au-pair at home who collects them, and she might not speak Danish. (Karin, teacher 0B)

Interestingly, the narrative of the 'busy, rich parents' and their neglected children is just as widespread an explanation of problematic children in Nordlund School as the story of the 'resource-weak parents' and their neglected children at Sønder School, as described in chapter 6. The narratives share the depiction of behavioural problems as caused by neglect – or rather the wrong dose of care in terms of parental time, attention and material resources since, in the case of Nordlund, parents' excessive or misjudged care can also result in spoiling and 'little project children'. In Nordlund School, as in Sønder School (described in chapter 6), the right dose is assessed in terms of the child's behaviour in such ways that the child becomes a benchmark of the parents' ability to balance and appropriately dose resources (see discussion in chapter 8); however, it is also assessed on the basis of the parents' wealth. Extreme wealth and children's excess of material possessions are seen as indications of empty materialism. This is associated with the wrong values and priorities if the wealth is not understated or carefully combined with precisely the socially approved parental qualities.

The young people are clearly aware of the understanding of the amoral aspect of extreme wealth and how it can be associated with immoral and uncivilised lifestyles. I hear this in many of my interviews, where the pupils distinguish their own group from 'the rich' and talk about the latter

as 'more refined' (the Danish word is '*finere*') than them, but 'spoilt' and
'egotistical'. This scenario is also described in a small play which some girls
from the parallel class, 9C, perform in the context of their project work.
They have given the play the title 'Rich Young People and Neglect'. In the
play a girl tells a psychologist and a counsellor that her parents are too
busy to talk to her and just hand her an American Express card and suggest
she sleeps over at a friend's place. She relates how she feels neglected,
takes drugs, has sex with men she doesn't care for, and uses other means
in an attempt to get her parents' attention. As here, a recurring theme in
classroom debates is the relation between, on the one hand, parents' busy
lives and material excess, and, on the other, young people's extreme use of
drugs, alcohol and sex; that is, their excessive and amoral behaviour.

Superficiality and True Values

The English lesson's portrayal of the rich young man and the teachers'
depictions of rich parents are examples of representations of wealth as
morally reprehensible within the school context. Further examples
can be found in the classical Danish fairy tales and short stories which
9B, like many other Danish pupils, study in their Danish lessons. With
commitment and enthusiasm, Lise gets the young people to analyse and
discuss these texts and the characters they portray, and she often uses
them to emphasise values and norms in the ways people treat each other.
Here the interesting issue is how the moral point of the classical Danish
texts in the curriculum tends to be that true values are found among those
of limited means who lead an ordinary life. Moreover, these fictional texts
often describe striving for material wealth, social status and power as
reprehensible, superficial, and a course that will ultimately lead to a fall.
An example of the latter is found in the widely read fairy tales of Hans
Christian Andersen. When reading 'The Shepherdess and the Chimney
Sweep', the class engage in critical discussion of the princess in the story
who, according to the pupils, is 'spoilt', 'weak-willed' and 'a curling child'
(a term referring to a child whose parents sweep all obstacles out of its
way). Furthermore, Lise describes the story's character of 'the Chinese' as
a 'power seeker' who topples to the ground and breaks into pieces. When
the class discusses Andersen's 'The Gardener and the Noble Family', the
point is made that the noble family is 'false' and 'artificial' and feel they
are 'high above' the gardener. The class agrees that, in actual fact, the
noble family depend on him, because they cannot maintain their image

without his gardening skills. It is pointed out by Lise that the greenhouse represents 'the privileged layers of society', whereas the vegetable garden symbolises 'the poor: and where does Andersen think you find the most beautiful flower? In the vegetable garden!'

In this and similar descriptions, the pupils are introduced to a story about form versus content, which Norbert Elias describes as central to the understanding of civilised behaviour among other groups of limited means. As demonstrated by Elias, this is also a central aspect of the bour-geoisie's way of distinguishing themselves from the nobility – that is, that the court nobility might feel superior, but their way of life is decadent and their status hollow (Elias 1994[1939]:433). As a contrast, the fairy tales and classical Danish short stories introduce 'the true values' of ordinary people, and even if the pupils do not identify with this social class, their participa-tion in discussions about snobbery, the superficial rich and the artificiality of the noble family demonstrates their knowledge and application of this moral evaluation of social differences. This again illustrates the under-standing that the Danish school conveys to its pupils – that privilege and material resources are not unambiguously prestigious. Even if 'poor people' are celebrated in these classical texts for their true values, other narratives circulate which instead establish the intermediate position – here the middle class – as morally superior and the most civilised position. This is accomplished by distancing the middle class from, on the one side, the 'resource-weak' (see chapter 6), who have social problems that make them unable to act appropriately, and, on the other side, 'the rich', who are too busy and selfish, give priority to economic and material rather than emotional and temporal resources.

That the pupils themselves are aware of these issues is apparent in interviews. Several of them express a self-critical attitude to their own privileges, but also make an effort to relate examples of more extreme cases. A case in point is Thomas, who talks about 'children of rich parents' whom he contrasts with 'us', that is 'people of normal wealth'. He explains that 'the middle class' must be those who live in Copenhagen City, and the 'lower middle class must be those whose mothers are, like, assistant nurses and, well, single mothers':

> *Thomas*: And then there's us who – we just don't know how lucky we
> are. And we're like constantly on about ... oh, why can't we have that,
> and now he has ... Even if we are already spoilt rotten, we complain

and complain and complain. So in some ways, we are the upper middle class.

Laura: Upper middle?

Thomas: Upper middle. And then there must be those who are ... high, what could you call ... rich ... the rich class, can you call them that? They must be the ones who really are those we know as the snobs, the spoilt little devils. The children of Strandvejen [the name of the road, lined by huge mansions, along the coastline north of Copenhagen] and yes, people like that, right?

(Thomas 9B)

Like Thomas, many of the pupils locate themselves in a contestable, but still morally superior, position between lower and higher classes. Thomas exemplifies how the pupils rarely use the word 'class', but still recognise class and hierarchical terms such as 'low' and 'high', 'upper' and 'under' as concepts that can describe their experiences of social distinction and differences in behaviour and lifestyle. Emphasising Sherry Ortner's point that class positions are often expressed through other categories (Ortner 1998:9–10), they also often indicate social differences by referring to locations – typically 'in the city' and 'in Brøndby and Ishøj' (two poorer Western suburbs), as opposed to the richer suburbs of 'North Zealand'.

Even if the narrative of the amoral rich challenges the self-perceptions of the young pupils, they are thus still able to find a morally advantageous middle ground as young people who are neither deprived and badly brought up nor too rich and too spoilt. Instead they can present themselves as suitably privileged and well-raised to be decent and civilised citizens. Nevertheless, the narrative of superficiality, spoiling, inappropriate excess and neglect of children seems to have a normative function as it demarcates their privileges as well as describing how they can stay on the right side of this boundary. It is interesting that the understanding of parents who neglect and/or spoil their children is an image that is constructed of both 'rich', and 'resource-weak' and 'Muslim' families (cf. the previous chapter). At Nordlund School, the depictions of class evidently keep the privileged youngsters' positive we-narrative in check. Furthermore, it teaches the pupils important lessons about the connection between social class and civilised conduct, the indecency of material excess and spoilt behaviour, the appropriate understatement of privileges, the ideal equality between classes, and the appreciation of content as opposed to form.

In this context it is significant that the upper-class status – of being among 'the rich' – which applies to some of the pupils at Nordlund School, is a category which the teachers do *not* share with their pupils. The teachers can place themselves within the categories of Danes, Christians, Westerners and middle class, yet they do not identify with the upper class. Comparing this with the relationships between the children at Sønder School and their teachers, the same goes for the 'resource-weak' and the 'Muslim' categories: these were categories the teachers did not share with the pupils. This could indicate that the teachers' own backgrounds and the extent to which they identify with the school's pupils and their parents are significant in terms of what the school teaches its pupils about identity and civilised categories. The material from Sønder School and Nordlund School thus demonstrates that it is crucial whether the children and their parents are included or not included in the 'we' of the school and the teachers, as this will often be the category which the teachers more or less consciously represent as civilised.

This demonstrates the significance of the local social context, and especially the significance of the school's social and ethnic constellation of children and teachers, and the school's experience with various groups of children. Schools with other constellations can thus provide children with rather different lessons on identity and on the civilised status of various social categories. Most children are presented with categories of more or less civilised people and societies in school, yet Nordlund School's teachers' understanding of the children and the school as members of their own civilised category seems to translate into a more unimpeded construction of 'we' – here 'the (upper) middle-class, Christian, Danish, European or Western category' – as the morally decent and civilised people. Even though there are young people in 9B who do not always feel included in this 'we' – Jacob's father is Muslim, several are not Christians, and others define themselves as 'of a lower social class' – it seems as if the teachers are not restrained in their presentation of the civilised and uncivilised categories in the same way as they are in socially and ethnically more diverse schools. As is evident in several of the examples presented here, children and young people participate in the construction of these categories, whether by reinforcing them through their own ways of acting or through discourse and debate. Even so, the example of 9B shows that challenges and criticisms of the understanding they encounter via their teachers also occur and, moreover, the teachers contest the pupils' conceptions of various points. Thus the school's civilising approach and its consequences are often changed and challenged by the pupils as well as the adults.

The School's Civilising Lessons

In 9B at Nordlund School, we have observed how, via teaching and conversations between teachers and pupils, the school teaches these privileged pupils about their own civilised status and the moral claims related to this status. Moreover, it presents them with a narrative about various social categories in Denmark and the wider world, and with a more extensive social cosmology that contains a comprehensive hierarchy of more or less civilised actions and categories of people and societies. This does not seem to be the explicit intention of the school, but it is a consequence of the way the pupils are taught about civilised behaviour and societal forms, which always involves a singling out of the amoral, the inappropriate, and the uncivilised. When comparing these civilising lessons in 9B with those of the two grade 0 classes (chapter 5), as well as of 4A/6A (chapter 6) and the children's experiences here, you see that, in 9B, the class as a social space is no longer in focus, and that gender and ethnicity are not the only elements addressed. In the ninth grade, the gaze is directed towards the world, and a much larger spectrum of categories is defined and positioned in a hierarchy of 'more or less civilised'. Here the teaching describes several ways of being civilised and uncivilised and various contexts of distinction. Hence a much more refined civilising ideal is developed, as well as a more complex moral map of the world. In 4A/6A, as well as in 9B, it is 'the Danes' and 'the resourceful' – the middle class – and in the ninth grade even 'the Christians' and 'Westerners', who are presented, more or less implicitly, as the civilised norm – that is, as the considerate, the philanthropic, the compromising, the rational, the democratic, the egalitarian, the healthy, the tasteful people who are kind to children and the environment and who work for the common good. At Nordlund School, this seems to contribute to the pupils' experience that 'people like us' are better than others. In principle, this is not because of their ethnicity or class, but by virtue of their mastery of a civilised code of conduct – which, in turn, refers to their class and ethnicity. In this way, civilising lessons at school tend to obscure and thereby legitimise and naturalise the construction of correlations between, on one hand, social and ethnic categories, and on the other hand, degrees of civilised conduct.

8

The Civilised Family Life
Childrearing in affluent families

Dil Bach

Kirsten: There are some really good kids … There are some really good families. They are smart, they know a lot, and they are used to being in a family where you behave properly. They are polite, they are fantastic sports. Someone like Cathrine's Philip, he is just a really lovely young man.

Dil: What do you mean when you say he's a good kid?

Kirsten: He's a good kid because children shouldn't just behave themselves. He's cheeky too … They have to be, otherwise something's not right … I like families where you can sense that they make time for their children, when they take an interest in them … I almost only encounter families like that out here. They are also a bit more privileged … They are well-educated, and they have enough money that they don't have to work so much … (Kirsten, pedagogue)

I think the problems north of Copenhagen have to do with parents having lots of ambitions on their children's behalf … They don't have much time and energy for their children because they need to earn money to pay for the big house and three cars … (Ditte, teacher)

This chapter is an analysis of childrearing in affluent families. The quotes above, from my fieldwork conducted in a high-income area north of Copenhagen exemplify two dominant narratives regarding such families. The first is about 'good, well-resourced families'. The second is about 'bad families' who, in their pursuit of money and prestige, neglect their children. These narratives stake out the boundaries of a moral landscape for parenthood in Denmark. The narratives are shared by educators and families, and the childrearing strategies of the affluent families relate to this moral universe. In addition to the expectation that parents spend time with their children, the narratives imply a composite civilising ideal for children, where 'good' children must be courteous, smart and social but also cheeky. The families in my study have taken responsibility for this task and invest considerable time and resources in their children. Their childrearing strategy is characterised by establishing boundaries while at the same time creating openings towards the outside world. Parents try to regulate their children's conduct, but also to be attentive, provide stimulation and make room for play. It is this civilising strategy that I will present in this chapter. I will argue that, although much of the childrearing task has been outsourced to schools and day care, individual parents are held accountable for their children's behaviour, well-being and so on. Despite the many hours spent outside the home, the child's behaviour is seen as determined by parental endeavour. Children and childrearing are therefore key elements in how families relate to one another and how their identities and social and moral status are defined.

This chapter concerns 15 families who are capital-rich, in the sense of sociologist Pierre Bourdieu (1986). Their economic capital is particularly evident, but most of the families also have an abundance of social and cultural capital, that is, they are highly educated and have extensive social networks (1986:243). In addition to owning large houses, several of the families also have holiday homes in attractive locations. Furthermore, they have expensive cars and go on holiday several times a year. The fathers typically earn enough that their families can live comfortably without additional sources of income. Several of them are managing directors or partners in law firms. I have chosen to study capital-rich families because a large volume of capital is a prerequisite for what Bourdieu (1979) calls the ruling classes' 'taste for freedom', that is, the opportunity to choose and prioritise rather than doing things out of necessity. Capital-rich families in particular are therefore expected to do 'the right thing', which may make society's civilising ideals particularly apparent. The criticism is correspondingly fierce if such families fail to live up to society's expectations.

In the affluent families I have studied, it was the women who had taken responsibility for the children's upbringing, and it was primarily the women who had the time to be interviewed. As a result, this study mostly concerns mothers. I interviewed the mothers in their homes, joining the families for meals and participating in various events. I also had the opportunity to conduct more formalised participant observation in two of the families, visiting each of them ten times, when I observed everything from the family waking up to the children being put to bed. In addition, one of the mothers kept a diary for me. All things considered, I have seized every possible opportunity to produce a broad range of empirical material. Besides these affluent families, I also interviewed some of their less well-to-do neighbours, as well as speaking to a number of child professionals. My fieldwork was conducted between the end of 2005 and the end of 2008. Consequently, the age of the individual children, as indicated in parentheses after the child's name, will vary between different examples.

Respectability

The childrearing strategies and interpretations of what it means to be civilised, which are in play among the parents in my study, can be illuminated using the concept of 'respectability'. Sociologist Beverly Skeggs (1997) addresses this concept in her book *Formations of Class and Gender – Becoming Respectable*. Skeggs' study is about the relationship between the middle and working class in England, but several of her findings are relevant to the Danish context and concern more general identification processes. I will demonstrate how some of her points regarding the lower echelons of society also apply to its upper strata. Skeggs provides a historical account of how, in order to be able to define themselves as respectable, moral and civilised, the middle class constructed the working class as uncivilised and vulgar. As such, respectability implies moral authority (1997:1–4). It is organised according to that 'which defines appropriate and acceptable forms of behaviour' (Palludan 2005:103).

Skeggs points out that being working class still connotes a lack of respectability, while the behaviour of the middle class has been historically encoded with respectability. She describes it as the privilege of the middle class to take respectability for granted and not care what others think about them. While the working class can never be sure of the right thing to do, this is among the primary characteristics of the middle class. As such, the respectable and the non-respectable are associated with particular positions in social space, which, in turn, are associated with the presence or absence of recognition. Skeggs thus views respectability as a fundamental signifier of class and a way of 'othering' certain groups. However, at the same time she shows that these processes also occur horizontally, whereby a struggle takes place within the working class between the respectable and 'the problematic'. She points out that, whatever the circumstances, respectability is always relational (1997:74–95). It is precisely this aspect that I will underline by showing that the affluent families can only define themselves as respectable by defining someone else as non-respectable.

Skeggs' concept of 'the respectable' has many similarities with 'the civilised' as described by sociologist Norbert Elias (1994 [1939]; see also chapter 1). However, although the respectable and the civilised are almost automatically associated with the upper echelons of society, both Elias and Skeggs demonstrate that it is not necessarily the upper class that are regarded as the most proper. In fact, they both show how, in a historical perspective, the middle class has not only contrasted itself 'downwards' to the working class, but also 'upwards' to the nobility, which was characterised by its own type of vulgarity in the form of exaggerated displays of power and excess (Elias 1994 [1939]:421–35; Skeggs 2004:4). The two concepts thereby overlap, but also differ in several ways. Whereas the civilised stands for what is perceived to be culturally and morally superior, the respectable stands for a more conformist adjustment – to be good enough, rather than to be the best (Skeggs 1997:1). Furthermore, the concept of civilising differs from that of respectability by not just describing a goal, but also denoting the process that leads to changes in people's conduct over time.

On the other hand, there is one aspect where the concept of respectability is more focused than the concept of civilising: the word 'respectable' itself implies what anthropologist Richard Jenkins describes as the dialectics between internal and external identification processes; that is, the manner in which identity is influenced by how one perceives others and how one is perceived by others (2004:18–20). Being respectable is not just a matter of behaving properly, but also of being respected by others. As such, the concept of respectability is situated on a very concrete analytical level focusing on social interaction. For these reasons, I will also draw upon this concept, but when describing the process that leads to respectability, I use the concept of 'civilising', just as I discuss civilising ideals in my descriptions of the cultural norms and values surrounding the 'proper' family life. In short, I will use 'civilising' as a superordinate concept and 'respectability' in relation to conformity and countering the prejudices of others.

In Denmark, respectability is not just something, which the working class struggles to achieve. As suggested by sociologist Stine Faber, upper class, like working class, functions as a negative social signifier in egalitarian Danish society (2008:122; see chapter 7 in this volume for a discussion of this in a school context). As is apparent in the two passages cited at the beginning of this chapter, affluent families are not always seen as deserving of respect. At an early stage of my fieldwork, I came into contact with a family therapist who offered her views on the families north of Copenhagen. She described affluent parents who did not spend enough time with their children, instead leaving them to be looked after by Filipino girls, and who did not set boundaries for their children, spoiling them in terms of material goods. Via this family therapist, I became aware of the critical narrative regarding affluent families. This turned out to be a view shared by less affluent families and other child professionals, but was also expressed by some of the affluent families themselves. A number of them wanted to live in the area, but did not want to be like everyone else. Faber's findings are similar. The wealthy families she interviewed also distanced themselves from 'the rich', who they felt neglected their children (2008:122–5). Wealth is thereby something that, in one particular narrative, is in contrast to the civilised and respectable.

Although the families that this chapter focuses on were sometimes categorised as upper class by others, and in a few cases identified themselves as such, in an analytical sense they belong to the middle class, albeit at the upper end of the spectrum. Unlike a genuine upper class, such as the nobility in feudal society described by Elias (1994 [1939]:421–35), these families have not automatically inherited their privileged status; nor can they pass it on to their children as a matter of course. On the contrary, this privileged status has to be re-acquired by each generation. Although the affluent families' children do not have to start from scratch – they are, as Bourdieu puts it, advantageously predisposed by their family's various forms of capital (1987:1–6) – there is always a risk of 'falling'. As pointed out by Elias and Jenkins, modern Western societies are characterised by the absence of rigid status systems and mobility in all social strata (Elias 1994 [1939]:436–47; Jenkins 2004:11).

Elias talks about a widespread 'fear of falling' (1994 [1939]:444–5), and several of the affluent families in my study have experience of close relatives who have fallen in status. All of which means that, contrary to Skeggs' claims, no one can be sure of doing the right thing or disregard what others think about them. Coupled with the ideology of equality, which is prominent in Scandinavia, and the suspicion of money, which I have registered, this is especially true of the affluent, who therefore strive to appear civilised and respectable. As such, I do not consider the fight for respectability a working-class issue, but a more general identity issue.

The Good Childhood

The women in my study made it a priority to spend time with their children and be highly involved in their lives. They placed great importance on 'being there' for them, offering them care and intimacy, protecting them from danger and bad influence, and providing stimulation. This is in sharp contrast to the critical narrative regarding affluent families. In fact, one of the first things that struck me when meeting the families was that well-educated women had scaled back their careers in favour of motherhood. This is unlike the typical pattern in Denmark, where most women are employed in the labour market. After having children some of the women in my study had stopped working, while others worked part-time. A few worked full-time, but ran their own company or had a job which allowed them to work flexible hours and still pick up their children early. The same focus on motherhood can be seen among middle- and upper middle-class families in most of the Western world (see for example Faircloth 2008; Furedi 2002; Kusserow 2004; Lupton and Barclay 1997; Miller 1997; Tap 2007).

To understand why some women focus on motherhood, it is necessary to consider the very institution of the family. Like Elias (1998a) and newer anthropological kinship studies (e.g. Carsten 2000; Miller 1997; Schneider 1980 [1968]; Tjørnhøj-Thomsen 2007), I do not see the nuclear family as a naturally occurring phenomenon. The nuclear family as a figuration consisting of parents and their interdependent children (Elias 1994 [1939]:481–2), where the biological ties are regarded as unbreakable and entail special feelings and obligations, is a cultural product (Tjørnhøj-Thomsen 2007:78). This means that a family and a sense of relatedness is created through the actions of family members. Insight can therefore be gained by examining how families perform this figuration work. Such a study also involves exploring the understandings that make the mothers' actions meaningful. A key factor is the importance attributed to developmental psychology.

Psychology, as Gilliam and Gulløv suggest in chapter 2, has been instrumental in the development of a new understanding of children and childhood from the middle of the nineteenth century. With the spread of a psychological framework of understanding, children are increasingly perceived as fragile beings, and childhood as being crucially important for the individual's development and character formation. Experiences in childhood are thought to mark people for life. Problems are explained with reference to a bad childhood, while a good childhood is thought to lead to happiness and positive self-esteem. Sociologist Frank Furedi summarises this view of childhood with the concept of childhood determinism (2002:57–68).

This view of childhood developed simultaneously with the bourgeois nuclear family, where the task of childrearing increasingly became the responsibility of individual parents and not, as previously, a shared responsibility among all adults in the child's close proximity. The responsibility for ensuring children have a good childhood shifts to parents and parents are both credited with their successes and blamed for their failures. Psychology attributes children's problems to relationships within the family. If the children are anxious or perform poorly, the parents have failed (Furedi, 2002:134–9). As sociologist Jacques Donzelot says, Freudianism has contributed to suspicion of 'the family of origin'. He points out that discourses regarding children's behavioural 'faults' were replaced by books on children as mirroring their parents in the post-Second World War era (1979:225–33). All in all, according to Furedi, focus shifted from impossible children to impossible parents. On the other hand, normal development has increasingly come to be seen as an accomplishment that parents can be proud of (Furedi 2002:98).

Furedi sums up parents' growing importance with the concept of 'parental determinism' (2002:87) stressing the central role of psychologist John Bowlby's attachment theory in this process. Bowlby was interested in the relationship between mother and child and concluded that motherly attachment is crucial for the child's development and the foundation of lifelong well-being (Furedi 2002:68). Both childhood and parental determinism are dominant frameworks of understanding in modern parenting culture (2002:245). Several of the mothers in my study are clearly influenced by these psychological models. They prioritise contact and intimacy based on a belief that 'being there' for your child is important for the child's well-being and development. This leads them to focus on a number of things; namely, 'filling their children up with mummy', establishing a calm and cosy home, setting boundaries for their children, and stimulating them. And because children's well-being and development are regarded as a product of their parents' endeavours, these things become elements in the families' respectability strategies.

Filled Up with Mummy

For some women in my study, prioritising time with their children is a way of distancing themselves from their own childhood, since they consider themselves to have been neglected. As touched on by Furedi, psychology has led to many adults discovering a wounded child within themselves and caused many to feel that their own life is determined by their childhood (Furedi 2002:157–63). Several of my informants therefore consider their own childhood at length and use it as a counter-image in relation to the childhood, which they want to create for their children. They take a highly reflexive position in relation to the present in the form of their children's childhood – a kind of 'future past' which the children will one day pass judgement upon; a judgement which will be a judgement on themselves as parents, just as they themselves are in the process of judging their own parents.

Among my informants, Anne is probably the one who was most clearly affected by psychological models. She believed that, due to a lack of adult contact during her own childhood, her mother had become 'emotionally stunted' and had ruined Anne's childhood. Since she did not have a role model in her own parents, Anne felt that it had been difficult to become a mother: 'I just wanted to make everything so different and good. I read whatever I could find of books on developmental psychology.' This had to some extent led to her 'having gone to the other extreme and being over-protective … Because I feel I was neglected as a child, my children were not going to be neglected.'

Just as the notions of childhood and parental determinism led Anne to view herself as a neglected child, she viewed her mother in the same way: 'It was even worse for my mother. There was absolutely no adult contact … So it will be exciting to see what my children will say one day. Their mother has been ridiculously overprotective.' This quote illustrates the mothers' reflexive relationship to the present as what their children will in future look back on as their childhood. Similarly, anthropologist Relinde Tap (2007:139) mentions a father in her analysis of middle-class families in New Zealand who says that he would hate it if his children one day were to say that their father was always studying; in other words, if his studies became part of a bad childhood memory.

Anne indicated that the reason that she had chosen to put her career on hold was that she wanted to ensure her children had adult contact. When I met her, she worked from home 10–15 hours per week: 'I worked full-time with two children, and I have become aware that that has come at a cost.' The cost was that she had not spent 'enough time with' her children: 'I missed out on big, important points in their lives.' She felt that this had had a particularly adverse effect on her second child:

I can barely remember anything from her early childhood, and I think that's so terrible ... I also find that she is the one who is constantly worrying about my whereabouts. She has a fear of separation and she is the one who is most anxious and has difficulty sleeping alone.

When her oldest daughter was little, on the other hand, Anne was studying and spent more time at home: 'So she was kind of filled up.'

As can be seen, the childhood and parental determinism way of thinking meant that Anne considered her children's well-being to be a direct result of whether or not she had been a good mother; something, which, in her eyes, was a matter of having spent enough time with them. In short, the psychologically inspired way of thinking places a huge burden of responsibility on parents for their children's lives. However, this way of thinking strips the very same parents of any responsibility for their own lives; the parents themselves are just vulnerable children. The same applies to the grandparents.

Motherhood had also changed Eva's view on the world of work: 'When I was expecting Vera, I decided to switch to a public sector job. Something changed within me because I suddenly had the responsibility for a child.' And when she had her second child, it worked 'pretty well' to begin with:

But when we had to get them picked up, and Jacob was sick, that's when you start to think: 'Why am I doing this?' ... I sat there compiling local area development plans, and you think 'it's now that you have young children'. When I'm 80 and I'm sitting there reminiscing, will I think it was great to have become a departmental manager at the age of 40 and having had to work more instead of being there while my kids were small? I had a bad conscience, plain and simple ... That's why I thought: 'No, I am going to do one thing and do it properly.'

Here it becomes evident that, for these women, motherhood is an important source of identity – as it was for Faber's working-class informants (2008:200–3). It is seen as a task of great responsibility which can be performed more or less properly. Motherhood becomes an alternative path to self-realisation, which seems more important than a professional career. Julie likewise elected to focus on motherhood:

It's a paradox that you have some people who are well-educated but then have a strong moral instinct that staying at home while their children are small might be the right thing to do. Children need parental contact. After all, you're always hearing that that is what determines whether children have a good childhood.

Along the same lines as Anne, Julie talked about 'giving her kids enough mummy'. Nonetheless, 2-year-old Astrid was clingy: 'I don't understand it. She has had so much mummy time during her life, "My mummy, my mummy, myyy muuuummy", she says.' Julie wondered whether Astrid's 'clinginess' might be because she was the only one of the children whose family had had an au-pair ever since she was born: 'But I would still say that Astrid has got at least as much mummy as the other children.'

Julie's decision to reject a career and choose motherhood came up a lot during our conversations, as well as in Julie's conversations with friends. One of her friends had said that, by staying at home, she was contributing to society by bringing up 'three strong children'. According to this logic, contact with their mother creates strong children, while motherhood becomes a service to the community. The latter emphasises the family's role as a civilising institution. On the other hand, an 'absence of mummy' creates weak children. Julie spoke in horror of a girl from school whose mother was dead and whose father had a hard time coping with the task of parenthood: 'And, I mean, that leads to a weak child.' Based on this logic it therefore surprised Julie that her youngest child showed signs of weakness in the form of clinginess. According to the logic of parental determinism, a clingy child is the result of an absence of mother, and is therefore incomprehensible for a girl who has been 'filled up with mummy'. Anne also seemed to be influenced by this logic when she viewed her second child's separation anxiety as a consequence of her absence during early childhood. As such, both Anne and Julie considered being 'filled up with mummy' a prerequisite for being able to break away from one's mother and become a strong and independent individual, rather than weak and insecure. The strong and independent individual is a key objective of the civilising process for virtually all the families in my study.

Calm and Cosy

Bringing up children to be in harmony within themselves and with others is another childrearing objective among my informants. It was therefore considered essential to establish a calm and cosy home. Although Camilla thought she had had a good childhood, there were certain things which she distanced herself from: 'The only things that were hectic in my childhood were the mornings. My dad ran around like a madman because we always slept too long. I thought it must never be like that when I have children. It has to be calm.' Eva also emphasised the importance of avoiding stress. She had therefore stopped working during her third pregnancy: 'It was great to be at home instead of having to go to work and live that terrible stressful life as so many people do.'

Anthropologist Marianne Gullestad points to peace and quiet and the central position of the home as key cultural categories in Norway (1992:22). She argues that, in contemporary 'transformed modernity', Norwegian homes have lost certain functions while gaining others. In 'classic modernity', the domain of childhood was the space between the houses in the neighbourhood. Here, children were 'boundary-breakers out of their homes and bridge-builders from home to home' (1997a:27), and their time was spent on free, self-regulated play in the neighbourhood. Gullestad points out that Norwegian ideas of the good childhood are grounded in classic modernity. However, many now see this childhood as threatened by institutionalisation, as well as by neighbourhoods that are no longer considered safe and which are deserted during the afternoon (1997a:31).

The mothers in my study tried to maintain core aspects of such a classic modern childhood, which also existed in Denmark. They all make a point of picking up their children early so as to allow them to have a nice afternoon at home. The mothers had, however, embraced day-care institutions to such an extent that even the 'homemakers' sent their children to nursery and kindergarten, and regarded institutional life as compatible with a good childhood (see Gulløv 2009a). Nevertheless, all agreed that it is not good to spend too much of the afternoon in a public institution. In the afternoon, it is best to be at home. Spending the afternoon at home also creates an opportunity for relatively free play with other children from the neighbourhood. As in Norway, and unlike for the middle class in the USA (Lareau 2003:1–7), playing with friends from the neighbourhood was something that the families in my study held in high esteem. As such, the mothers felt bad if they were unable to pick up their children early. On the rare occasions when Christine was busy, she felt like 'a neglectful mother'. She told me 'that it is a horrible feeling picking up [your children] at five o'clock in the afternoon'.

Like a calm environment, a cosy atmosphere was something I noticed during my fieldwork; for example, on two occasions when I had dinner with Henriette and Martin. During the first visit, Henriette was struggling to get her new job to balance with her desire 'to come home and make a cup of tea in the afternoon, to make it home and be there, baking cakes, doing homework, and driving to riding lessons'. During my next visit, Henriette had stopped working again and the mood was much calmer. Similarly, I used the word 'cosy' in my field-notes describing an afternoon visit to Leonora's house:

> I arrive at the cosy house. Leonora's mother opens the door because Leonora is out walking the dog. Three-year-old William is sleeping. Upstairs, the girls (aged 9 and 6) are playing with a neighbour. Then Leonora shows up. She had initially thought that the interview was the following day, but it doesn't matter as they don't have any plans.

Cosiness was also something stressed by the families themselves. This is illustrated by the diary which Leonora kept for me:

> While Hannah plays tennis, I pick up Rose, and then we have a bit of cosy time at home. Hannah comes home from tennis … then I have to pick up William. Let the girls play at the neighbour's house … I come home with a tired William who wants to watch films. I let him … Then I just about have time to make pasta sauce. We have a cosy dinner together and put three tired children to bed.

As is evident from the diary's self-presentation, Leonora sought to establish an everyday life which was calm and cosy. Like the other families, she tried to avoid the stress and chaos associated with modern middle-class life (Faber 2008:197–200). However, just as some children were clingy despite being 'filled up with mummy', the threat of chaos occasionally lurked in these homes too. Despite the fact that Camilla did not work very much, some mornings were chaotic. And Cathrine, who had dropped her career, in part to be able to spend cosy afternoons, apologised after one of my visits 'that it had been a bit chaotic'. While Cathrine was being interviewed by me, she was cooking chicken drumsticks for an event at her son's after-school centre, and there had been a lot going on around us. Similarly, one Sunday Julie warned me that I would be witnessing their 'chaos day'. For once, the children had got to bed late and the youngest (aged 2) had spilt milk all over the place. Furthermore, Julie had to bake rolls for Emil's school class. These examples – like the ever-looming bad conscience – suggest that the childrearing strategy in these families, as was the case among Skeggs' working-class informants, is accompanied by defensive elements and an awareness that you do not always live up to the standards of respectability, with the result that you feel compelled to explain and apologise.

Not only are stress and chaos the opposite of calm; the same is true of 'turmoil'. Julie spoke about the amount of turmoil in Emil's school class. She was aware of which boys were causing this turmoil, because Emil (aged 7) had played with them once. This was not good for him. It had made him 'wild and confused'. So, as well as prioritising calm afternoons because they provide the children with the opportunity to play relatively freely with friends, Julie also felt that doing so created the opposite of 'wild and confused' children.

In summary, the effort made by the mothers in my study to ensure a good childhood for their children also includes an effort to civilise them, whereby a good childhood is considered a prerequisite for rearing strong, independent and calm individuals rather than weak, insecure and 'wild' ones. The affluent women can therefore, on the one hand, be seen as concentrating on motherhood for the sake of their children. On the other hand, however, they also choose to invest their time and effort in childrearing for the sake of their own reputations. The developmental psychology way of thinking contributes to the formation of a figuration characterised by a specific type of cause–effect relationship and interdependency between parents and children, in that children's well-being and behaviour are seen as indicators of parental capacity. The psychological discourse implies a notion that through their actions, parents determine their children's lives, which in turn contributes to some parents investing so much energy in their children that this interdependency is reinforced. At the same time, this appears to entail a sacrifice, whereby the women have made a compromise in terms of their careers. However, precisely the act of sacrificing makes certain relationships particularly strong, according to anthropologist Daniel Miller (1997:73). Nevertheless, it cannot be said that the women had made a choice between children and self-fulfilment, as childrearing has become an alternative path to self-realisation.

Boundaries for Self-Expression and Influence

The children in the families I studied were subject to a considerable amount of adult control. The parents regulated their children's lives in numerous ways: in regard to emotions, physical health and different kinds of bad influences. Such parental regulation was conceptualised using the psychological/pedagogic notion boundary-setting. The idea of boundary-setting (as discussed in chapters 5 and 9) can be interpreted as a civilising endeavour attempting to instil in children a sense of how much space and time it is appropriate to take up. As such, boundary-setting implies both an intention in relation to the children and a notion that this requires a specific adult endeavour. Elias points out that the ideals of authoritarian childrearing and obedience have been replaced by negotiation and democracy (Elias 1998a:191; see also chapters 1 and 2). Sociologist Anette Lareau believes, however, that this ideal has now itself become subjected to criticism in favour of the idea that children need boundaries (2003:254). According to Gullestad, the latter is a metaphorical expression of a form of authority which fits with contemporary compound civilising ideals. These ideals concern a belief that children should 'be themselves' – not too obedient but also a little naughty (1997a:34).

The parents in my study used the concept of boundary-setting interchangeably with words such as consistency, responsibility and structure. Cathrine stressed the importance of 'some boundaries being set', and that 'other people should also be given some space'. She and her husband were 'pretty consistent; a no is a no, and that's the way it is'. Julie, likewise, described herself as 'quite authoritarian' and 'incredibly strict' regarding bedtime. She told me that she was the 'tough one' at home because she knew what she didn't want. One afternoon, Julie was trying to tell me something on the way to tennis, but Emil (aged 7) also had something to say. 'You're interrupting me', Julie told him in a sharp tone of voice. Later, I was standing with Julie and Karen watching their sons and some other boys practise. The boys began to muck about, placing their hands on their penises. 'Hey you', Karen shouted to one of them in a commanding voice, 'stop doing that.' On another occasion, I was standing alongside three women watching their girls horse riding. When I told one of them about my study, she promptly said that she was 'strict'. Benedicte likewise told me that she was 'pretty firm'. At children's birthday parties she would not put up with them all mucking about. She said that other parents tolerated such behaviour, but that she is 'more controlling'.

These examples illustrate that boundary-setting is a widespread practice among the families. In my analysis of what people mean by setting boundaries, I am inspired by professor of international studies Joel S. Migdal (2004). Although his work is based on how ethnic groups relate to one another, several of his points can be applied to psychological/ pedagogic boundary-setting. Migdal points out that boundaries serves to separate the safe and secure from the perilous and chaotic: 'Boundaries signify the point at which something becomes something else, at which the way things are done changes, at which 'we' end and 'they' begin, at which certain rules for behaviour no longer obtain and others take hold' (2004:5). Migdal writes that boundaries are maintained with the help of 'mental maps' and 'checkpoints'. The former are cognitive ideas concerning how the world is organised and divide the space into home and alien territory. The latter are the checkpoints at which the division between the two spaces is monitored. These checkpoints can be concrete, such as a passport control point, but also symbolic, whereby dress, language or daily practice signify affiliation (2004:6–9).

Inspired by Migdal, one might say that the civilising ideal expressed above involves instilling in children mental maps as to how much space it is appropriate to take up (see also chapter 5) and someone who monitors the boundaries. The psychological/pedagogic idea of boundary-setting, put simply, requires both that the child recognises boundaries and that those rearing the child exercise some authority. Boundary-setting thereby also becomes an expression of responsibility and an indicator of respectability.

The parents in my study also stressed that they were not the type that overly pampered and spoilt their children. As most of the families had an au-pair, there was no practical need for the children to help out around the house. When parents required their children to do so, it was a moral issue. One morning Peter asked Christian (aged 7) to make his bed. Cathrine explained that they had introduced this chore to counter their tendency to pamper their children. Similarly, Camilla told me:

> They [aged 6, 8 and 11] have to help clear the table. Just because Lisa is here to help, that does not mean they have got a maid. That's why they do their bit and have to tidy their rooms. But, other than that, they do not have many chores; actually, incredibly few. That's kind of what I think: 'Ah, I really have to, now they really have to' ...

In these examples, one senses that the parents were conscious of the critical narrative about affluent families and, if they had a tendency to pamper, they were aware that they ought to temper such inclinations. Likewise, they didn't want to be seen as the type of parents who don't set boundaries. Here, it is notable that it did not appear to be embarrassing to rebuke children in the presence of others. On the contrary, it signals that you set boundaries and protect others from the child. As such, one can consider boundary-setting as an authoritative marking out of the child's space for self-expression. As we shall see, however, boundary-setting is at the same time a matter of protecting the child from negative influences.

Emotional Control

In most of the families, there was one child who seemed to be a particular challenge. Typically this was children who were regarded as very much themselves. For Cathrine it was Ella (aged 2–4), who had a tendency to kick up a fuss when she had to get dressed. Similarly, Julie told me that Emil (aged 6) had a temper and one morning had 'thrown a massive wobbly' because he was not allowed to play with his Game Boy. Both Julie and Cathrine responded to this behaviour with scolding and sanctions such as being sent to their rooms. Nevertheless, neither Cathrine nor Julie was unequivocally critical of their children's temper. They both saw it as a hassle, but, at the same time, Cathrine emphasised that Ella was good at setting boundaries for herself. As such, setting boundaries is also an issue of autonomy and of protecting oneself from others. Gullestad refers to campaigns where a circle is drawn around a person to teach young people to set boundaries in terms of the kinds of physical intimacy they want. She writes that: 'Firm boundaries around the person seem to be a prerequisite for social involvement in culturally correct and positive ways' (1997a:34), and that this applies to children and adults, as well as young people. It is a matter of marking out one's own individual space. Ella's and Emil's behaviour was nevertheless regarded as challenging due to the schism between individual and sociocentric values. Anthropologist Adrie Kusserow points out that many American middle- and upper middle-class parents experience a dilemma between desiring that their children be civilised and true to themselves (2004:90–91, 151). The same dilemma characterises my informants, but it is my belief that the civilised in this cultural context is seen as a balance between self-expression and respect for others. As long as children's tempers do not have an adverse impact on others, they are regarded as positive.

Negative children and children's fighting are a clearer source of irritation. Such things take up space and parents made an effort to civilise these feelings, by training their children to verbalise them. However, as Gulløv also discusses in chapter 3, verbalisation does not in itself offer recognition; that requires saying something particular in a particular way. As such, Leonora taught her children that you don't say 'you're stupid', but 'I'm angry because'. And Camilla adapted negative language to positive. If her children said 'unh, do we have to go to the weekend cottage?', then she responded: 'Really, are we going to the weekend cottage? Aren't we the lucky ones.' Although it is positive emotions that are legitimate, they do not have to be expressed loudly, thereby taking up space in an acoustic sense. One day when Julie gave Emil (aged 7) a CD, he responded with a joyous cry of 'yeah!' Julie's response was that there was no need to shout. All things considered, the parents in my study set considerable stock in teaching their children to find a balance between being considerate and self-expression. As well as instilling in them the importance of autonomy and personal integrity, they emphasised that the children should be polite. I often heard children making demands being gently reminded to 'say please' and on several occasions parents reminded their children to say hello and goodbye to the people they met.

Healthy Bodies

The mothers in my study were likewise concerned that their children were healthy. In a discussion of the cultured man in Sweden around the turn of the twentieth century, ethnologists Jonas Frykman and Orvar Löfgren (1987 [1979]) point out that the core values regarding the mastery of the body were at this point redefined as health issues. In his studies from France, historian of ideas Michel Foucault suggests that the population's health became a political matter as early as the eighteenth century (1972b), and that the family became an instrument for regulating the health of the population (1991:216). From this point on, it was no longer a matter of getting the family to produce the optimum number of children, but of managing childhood in the correct manner. As we have seen, childhood is increasingly perceived as a complicated period of maturation which requires not only parental attentiveness but also an effort in relation to hygiene, exercise and so on. According to Foucault, health becomes one of the family's most demanding goals and the family begins to function as the interface between the individual and the state. This 'medicalisation' of the family occurred throughout Europe during the eighteenth century, forming the foundation for subsequent health policy and forms of governance (1972b:96–7).

Sociologists Jacques Donzelot and Nikolas Rose demonstrate, based on developments in France and England respectively, how medicine comes to play a central role with regard to the state's way of controlling the individual through the family, including in the nineteenth century, when mothers became allied with doctors and were transformed into a kind of nurse (Donzelot 1979:18; Rose 1999 [1989]:130–2). As stated, in a Scandinavian context, Löfgren and Frykman (1987 [1979]) point out that, around 1900, health gained a central position, while historians of ideas Lars-Henrik Schmidt and Jens Erik Kristensen show that the construction of the housewife in the early 1900s was part of a comprehensive medical childrearing project in Denmark. Here it became the woman's project to create a home that is not only cosy, but also hygienic and forms the foundation for fit and healthy children (1986:128–42).

Today, as well, a child's health is considered part of the individual parent's field of responsibility (see, for example, Furedi 2002; Miller 1997; Rose 1999 [1989]; Tap 2007) and thereby acts as an indicator of distinction and respectability. Anthropologist Marilyn Strathern draws attention to the growing tendency to see children's bodies as signifiers of parental devotion or negligence. Have parents properly applied knowledge about health, hygiene and so on in their interaction with the child? In her discussion of this, Strathern talks about parents sharing bodies with their children twice: first, there is the genetic body, and second the body that parents are involved in creating through their engagement. Strathern refers to Miller's study of middle-class mothers in London. She points out that mothers cannot do much about the genetic body, but that they can do a lot in relation to health, hygiene and so on (Strathern in Faircloth 2008:2–3). And they do! As such, Miller shows how the mothers fight against first sugar, then biscuits, and then cola (1997:76). The same is true of the women in my study. They fight against sweet things and are very health conscious. In several homes, the children were given porridge for breakfast, and at Cathrine's house, the porridge was topped with banana instead of sugar.

The mothers were also conscious of what they put in their children's lunch boxes. At Cathrine's house, chocolate spread was only allowed on Thursdays. In addition to the quality of what the children ate, Julie also emphasised quantity. She told me that her children could become impossible if they did not get enough food and sleep. She therefore kept an eye on how much they ate. One evening Ida (aged 3) ate virtually nothing and Julie discussed with her husband how many pieces of crispbread she had been given before dinner. Her conclusion was that Ida had to eat an extra-large breakfast the next day. She did not want her children to be 'tired and impossible' at school or kindergarten. In short, it seemed as though, already the night before, Julie began to worry about whether or not her children had eaten enough to be well-behaved the next day. Similarly, Frederikke talked about food and sleep as necessary for 'behaving properly'. In this way, being health conscious is not just a matter of ensuring children's good health; it also implies a civilising effort to prevent bad behaviour and become well-functioning.

In many of the families, the children were also offered a healthy snack in the afternoon, and we were served nutritionally diverse meals at the homes where I joined the families for dinner. Eva did not want the au-pair to cook because she wanted to have some control over how much oil was in the food. Several of the mothers mentioned that they wanted to control what their children put inside their bodies. For the same reason, virtually all the families had designated Friday as the only day for eating sweets. The parents thereby saw the bodies of children as under threat; as a container which they needed to guard, but where it was important to gradually teach children to assess for themselves what is good for them. Once again, the parents thereby functioned as checkpoints (cf. Migdal) tasked with protecting their children against the threats surrounding them which, in relation to health, often means friends, family and acquaintances. A number of those I spoke to said that grandparents had a habit of giving the children sweet things. Eva told me that her mother-in-law gave the children Coco Pops for breakfast and that they had asked her to make porridge instead.

Schools, day care and peers could also constitute threats in the children's surroundings. One evening, Cathrine reprimanded Philip (aged 9) after he came home from swimming with a bag of toffees which the father of a classmate had given him. Similarly, Caroline told me, clearly irritated, that her daughters (aged 6 and 7) had been given a packet of chocolate biscuits by a friend just as they were setting off for lunch with one of her friends. When her eldest daughter complained about boring packed lunches, Caroline responded: 'It's because I'm taking care of you' – which was contrasted to others in the neighbourhood who were eating 'far too much junk food'.

The families also took an interest in exercise and hygiene. One of the mothers told me that she was 'very strict' with her son (aged 6) when it came to washing hands: 'I always listen out for the tap when he's in the bathroom.' Just as the families in my study had embraced the psychological way of thinking, they also followed many of the health recommendations. The intense monitoring of children's health confirms Rose's thesis regarding the increasing regulation of the family over the last 150 years, whereby middle-class families have internalised both psychological and medical norms in the socialisation of their children (1999 [1989]:130–2, 200). As suggested by Donzelot, the mothers enter into an alliance with the health-care system and act as nurses in relation to their children (1979:18).

The behaviour I describe should not, however, be construed as evidence that these families have passively internalised the health campaigns. On the contrary, it is often people from this social stratum that define the health recommendations. Rose also stresses that the increasing regulation of family life does not occur through coercion, but is increasingly in accordance with the family's own wishes. As we have seen, due to childhood and parental determinism, normal development is increasingly perceived as an achievement as a lot can go wrong in the now so 'delicate passage to maturity' (1999 [1989]:203). Rose concludes that the regulation of the population occurs through the autonomous, responsible family's wishes, hopes and fears – the wish for the normal child, the hope for the exceptional and the fear of the abnormal. According to Rose, the mothers want to act in accordance with expert norms in order to prevent disease and abnormality, and promote health and future prosperity (1999 [1989]:202). My material indicates that the mothers' motivation is also to ensure that the child is well-functioning and behaves properly in school and day care – a job they consider quite important. This is because of their interdependency with their children, where the children's behaviour reflects back upon them, and the mothers' health-related efforts are thus part of a strategy for respectability. At the same time, it is not just a matter of positioning oneself, but also that the mothers are in favour of a healthy lifestyle and keep themselves informed regarding the prevailing knowledge.

Screens and Other Evils

The families in my study also sought to limit their children's use of television, computers and game consoles. A number of researchers have pointed out that the perception of the child's innocence, which also developed during the nineteenth century (see chapter 2), has resulted in widespread scepticism towards such things. Miller demonstrates how women in north London try to prevent their 'pure and innocent' children from being corrupted by these media. He points out that this is part of a general attempt to shield children from evils (1997:81–4). Correspondingly, the families in my study sought to restrict their children's access to 'screens', but also, for example, to Barbie dolls, based on a conviction that these were bad things, which threatened children's innocence. Julie stated that children should be allowed to live in a state of innocence for as long as possible, which is why Emil (aged 8), unlike a number of his classmates, was not allowed to watch the Danish crime series *Forbrydelsen* (*The Killing*). Furthermore, Leonora found that her children (aged 6, 8 and 11) became aggressive from watching Disney Channel. The latter bears witness to television restrictions also being a matter of regulating children's emotional behaviour.

Tap (2007:192) also shows that middle-class parents in New Zealand try to limit risks and therefore prescribe limited doses for their children's consumption of television and other electronic media. Tap relates the issue to class and points out that working-class children tend to watch more television than middle-class children. Perhaps this aspect also influences my informants. In that case, part of the motivation for restricting access to 'screens' is that letting one's children be 'babysat' by the television is associated with low social status. Whatever the reason, the parents who participated in my research generally distinguished between active learning and passive entertainment, and between anti-social and social activities. They wanted to restrict anything considered passive and anti-social. When it comes to television and computer games, there is talk of activities, which are defined as opposed to an active outdoor life and to play, which is increasingly cherished as the ultimate expression of all that is childlike (Gullestad 1997a:16). As I will discuss further later, play stands simultaneously for the innocent, the educational and the social. As such, Camilla talked enthusiastically about play, while she was not 'all that crazy' about computers.

It's probably just old fashioned. But I think it's fantastic with all the bits and bobs that Chris [aged 8] sits there building. And at our weekend cottage, where we don't have a computer, how they can spend seven weeks just playing with sand and earthworms in the soil. I think that's great. On the other hand, I am aware that computers are a part of it ... But I don't think they should sit for five hours every afternoon or two hours. And I don't think it's all that social.

The relationship to 'screens' was not entirely negative, however, as they were also in some cases regarded as educational. During a visit to Julie's house, Emil (aged 6) had sat himself in the living room to watch television. Julie explained that on Tuesdays he was allowed to watch television for a whole hour as the shows *Nørd* and *Lille Nørd* (*Nerd* and *Little Nerd*) were on, which she considered 'a fantastic Children's Hour' where children 'learn about things'. And just as certain programmes were seen as making children aggressive, the television was also sometimes regarded as a form of relaxation which could positively affect behaviour. Although Henriette 'might shout very loudly and say "now we are going to take all the screens in this house" [and throw them out]', she also sometimes thought 'they need to sit down and freak out, whether it is in front of a computer or the tv or some other screen'. Julie sometimes seemed to use the television in this way too. One afternoon, Emil (aged 7) was bored and Julie had taken issue with his behaviour several times. At a certain point she said that he was allowed to watch television for half an hour. He sat and flicked back and forth between Discovery and a cartoon channel. When Julie came in, he flicked over to Discovery. She asked if it was good to watch a little television. He flicked back to the cartoons again. 'Really', she said, and he flicked back. 'You do like that too', she said.

The parents' relationship to computers was not entirely negative either. Like the parents in Tap's study they wanted their children to keep up with technological developments (2007:19). The ambivalence regarding the digital was particularly pronounced in the case of Henriette and Martin:

> *Henriette*: Now he can surf the net but it has to be supervised. Martin and I disagree on that.
>
> *Martin*: Not in terms of supervision.
>
> *Henriette*: No, but we disagree on how much time it's okay to spend in front of a screen.
>
> *Dil*: What do you reckon, how much time is okay?
>
> *Henriette*: If it was up to me then it would be an hour.
>
> *Dil*: And if it's up to Martin … ?
>
> *Martin*: I don't think I'd give a certain number of minutes, so they get a fixed dose …
>
> *Dil*: But you don't think it matters if it is more than an hour?
>
> *Martin*: No, because I can hear what he [aged 10] learns from it. He learns languages, and he has taught himself how to search with

Google. In order to be able to find something on the internet, you have to be able to spell properly, after all.

Although Martin was not in favour 'of a fixed dose', establishing principles regarding how much time children were allowed to spend in front of a screen was the way most families dealt with the ambivalence. It is therefore an activity that the children cannot just engage in but for which they need to ask permission. Philip (aged 8) told me that when he came home from school, he asked if he was allowed to play PlayStation. One afternoon, however, he just went up to his room to play. Cathrine quickly followed after him though, and said he should ask first, telling him how long he was allowed to play for. Nevertheless, Cathrine's boys had both a PlayStation and a television in their room. Cathrine gave a detailed explanation as to why that was the case and repeated that they had to ask for permission so she could control how long they played. When the neighbour's son, Mark (aged 7), came to visit, Cathrine told him and Philip that they could play for half an hour. In order to ensure that the daily dose was not exceeded, Cathrine would sometimes run across the street to Mark's house to check whether her boys had continued playing over there.

As such, the parents functioned as border guards not only in relation to sweets. In order to limit bad things in general, Cathrine and Peter also instructed the grandparents as to what gifts were acceptable and sometimes they had thrown gifts away. Cathrine believed that 3-year-old Ella was too young for a Barbie doll. Similarly, Julie pointed out, that her daughter had received a Barbie doll from her grandmother, but that it was a 'ridiculous toy' for a 3-year-old. Cathrine, Julie and Christine were also in favour of limiting the quantity of gifts, which suggests a certain ascetic and anti-materialistic attitude. This again becomes a way of countering the critical narrative about affluent families spoiling their children. All in all, it can be said that, just as the parents saw the outside world as a threat to the child's body, they also felt the home was under threat. Especially computers, the internet, and television, with its morass of foreign channels, but also grandparents with stupid gifts invade the home's boundaries and are seen as a threat to childish innocence and play.

In the preceding sections, I have dealt with various forms of regulation of children's behaviour that are encompassed by the concept of boundary-setting. This concept includes central civilising ideals; it entails the child, via a checkpoint, being instilled with a mental map of its space for self-expression. This is both to protect others from the child and the child from others. On the one hand, the child has to use the map as a guide as to how far it can go without taking up so much space that it negatively impacts others. On the other hand, it is about protecting the child from the intrusion of the unhealthy and bad. Boundary-setting is thus a matter of regulating both what goes into the child and what comes out.

Boundary-setting is also directed at the parents. The concept contains an expectation that parents act as border guards. The parents in my study have accepted this task, and the state does not have to exercise direct authority over them. Similarly, the goal of the parents' childrearing and civilising efforts is that the child – at some point in the not too distant future – will not only have internalised the mental map, but also the checkpoint itself and will have become capable of self-government (cf. Foucault 1991). In addition to this overall civilising endeavour, we have also encountered more specific civilising ideals which are prevalent in this milieu: a proper human being is someone who helps out and participates in the practical chores in a family, has a sense of health and quality, is active and social, keeps up with technological developments, and exhibits a degree of asceticism and anti-materialism.

The Stimulating Home

The parents' childrearing strategy is not just a matter of preventing illness, misbehaviour and so on. Parents are also concerned with helping their children develop the right competences, as witnessed in their ambivalent relationship to screens. The home is thus filled with stimulating elements and one might regard it as a form of educational hothouse (Donzelot 1979:20). Rose highlights a gradual shift in focus from preventing anti-social behaviour to maximising the child's potential (1999 [1989]:182). According to Rose, the spread of developmental psychology since the beginning of the 1960s has led to the middle-class mother being assigned a crucial role in maximising the child's ability to read, write, do arithmetic and so on. Just as the mother was previously, and still is, allied with the doctor, she now became an ally in educational programmes. Psychological theories of cognitive development and 'the importance of the early years' (1999 [1989]:198) have, according to Rose, transformed domestic everyday life into a complex of learning opportunities. The belief is that if the mother is doing well, then the child's chances in life will be significantly improved. If she fails, then things will not go well for the child in school or life in general.

According to Rose, the spread of these norms for intellectual growth contributed to an expansion of the market for stimulating books, toys and so on, and to a transformation of the home's intimate environment into a laboratory for cognitive growth. It was not about disrupting domestic life, but recognising that all daily routines could form the basis for a learning experience. Moreover, rather than resisting the educational and psychological norms, these are sought after by the families, just as was the case in relation to health. Rose concludes that the last 150 years of family policy have now succeeded to such an extent that families seek out experts in order to function optimally (1999 [1989]:198–201). Something similar applies to the families in my study. In the Danish context, the pedagogy launched by the educational reform movement (see chapter 2), with its emphasis on free thinking and democracy, in particular in the post-war period, has meanwhile been instrumental in ensuring a focus also on character building, and we have already seen that affluent families make an effort to develop independent and harmonious individuals.

On the basis of fieldwork with American families, Lareau reaches a similar conclusion to Rose; that is, that middle-class families do everything they can to stimulate their children. They view the child as a project that cannot be left to nature but which must be cultivated. Lareau calls this strategy 'concerted cultivation', which denotes an active partnership between families and schools. She defines this in opposition to the childrearing strategy of the working class, which she characterises as 'natural growth' (2003:2–3). Lareau identifies extra-curricular activities, communication within the family and an engagement in school as the three primary areas of cultivation. This stands in contrast to the lives of working-class children which are characterised by free play with neighbourhood friends and relatives and lots of time spent watching television (2003:1–13).

In the next three sections, I will demonstrate that the childrearing strategy of the families in my study can also be characterised as 'concerted cultivation' where domestic communication and parental involvement in school are key elements. However, unlike the US context, children's play, either alone or with friends from the neighbourhood, constitutes a key activity. Nevertheless, there is not talk of 'natural growth', as the children are not allowed to play with whatever they want, and play, like many other domestic activities, has become a learning experience. Play is regarded as a skill that one can either be good or bad at, and has become a metaphor for creative competences. That is not to say that the children in my study did not participate in extra-curricular activities. The children in all the families went to tennis, horse riding, football, music, swimming and so on; activities their parents regarded as healthy and social, and which gave the children skills that would be useful later. However, family life was not centred on these activities. Even in Camilla's family, where the eldest son (aged 11) played football for the first team, football was not a family project, and he was old enough to cycle to training by himself. Furthermore, although the parents tried to insist that the children continued with a given activity until the end of term, the children seemed to switch between activities quite frequently.

At the same time, there was also a desire among the parents that the number of extra-curricular activities should not get out of hand. As touched upon by Lareau, it is currently possible to trace certain trends which are opposed to the hectic family life she otherwise describes (2003:245), but I also believe that one finds another set of values in my material. One part of the critical narrative surrounding affluent Danish families concerns parents who are overly ambitious on their children's behalf, overloading their schedules and pushing them to achieve. Not sending one's children to a vast array of extra-curricular activities or taking it too seriously can therefore be regarded as an attempt to avoid this categorisation. At the same time, this prioritisation indicates a particular civilising ideal where being proper means not being too ambitious, but socially flexible while remaining independent and creative. This is especially evident in relation to play.

Play

Play was the key activity for the children in the families I have studied. In each of the homes, the children had stimulating toys: jigsaw puzzles, memory games, marbles, farm animals, train tracks, Lego and other construction toys. Toys which the parents categorised as good, and which they felt stimulated the children's imagination, unlike the passively entertaining 'screens'. As such, Camilla drew a contrast between playing with building blocks and playing on the computer. In her description of her son Christopher's play, it is clear that play is not just something you do, but is considered a social and creative skill:

Christopher [8 years] is so good at playing … He is good at playing with things. He has all sorts of set-ups with things of small wooden blocks. He is so creative … If he gets frustrated by the computer, I'll tell him not to use it for the next week, and he just starts playing with his toys. And he is really, really good at it. If he has friends over, they will be playing too. And when their parents come to pick them up, they'll be, like: 'God, you haven't played on the computer at all,' because their children are really, like, computer-children.

Similarly, Laura said: 'They are extremely good at playing, my kids … When you put them somewhere where there are no toys, then they come up with something.' When we talked about Laura's friend, whose daughter her own daughter Clara (aged 7) thinks is 'the absolute pits', she said: 'When she comes to visit, Clara says … "What's up, doesn't she know how to play at all?" Because she is very much like a grown-up who just wants to sit there. She is not very play-oriented.'

In this way, play helps to define 'proper' children in contrast to miniature grown-ups or 'computer-children'. In addition, some parents are quite explicit as to whether one can learn something from playing. One evening Cathrine asked me if my daughter (aged 3) did not have games such as Memory. I replied that she was mostly interested in her grocery store. Cathrine said 'yes, perhaps that's what you should do, so they can learn about business'. Along similar lines, Ida (aged 3) wanted to play picture lottery during one of my visits. Julie considered picture lottery 'a really good toy' and used it, among other things, to practise the colours. She was also conscious of the educational aspects which play in itself could contain. When Emil (aged 7) one evening was seeing how long he could get his spinning top to spin, Julie said that they had to remember to tell his teacher that he was playing something with 'more than' and 'less than'.

As mentioned, the new technologies of government referred to by Rose (1999 [1989]) function by getting people to integrate educational elements in common pursuits. As we have seen, play is seen as educational in itself, and it is also possible to add educational elements. Furthermore, educational games can be incorporated in ordinary routines. In Cathrine's family they sometimes played word games during dinner, or while out driving. The educational elements need not, however, be presented as play. One day Christian asked me how old I was. I answered 34, and he told me that he was 7. 'How many years are there between you?' asked his father.

The parents were also conscious of the fact that children can learn more implicitly. In Eva's family three children (aged 4, 7 and 9) shared two Advent calendars between them. Eva thought this was an excellent way to learn how to share. As well as being another example of the existence of a widespread awareness of what things could teach children, this is also evidence of the somewhat ascetic and anti-materialist attitude.

One of the things the mothers value about 'good play' is its creative potential. As outlined by Gullestad, play under transformed modernity is valued more highly than previously – both as an activity that children engage in and 'a metaphor for desirable human qualities of creativity and innovation' (1997a:30). I also noticed among my informants that creativity was held in high esteem. Henriette told me that Maria (aged 10) was creative, and that she hoped she would become a jewellery designer or something like that. She was considering sending her on a drawing course and showed me a homemade book which Maria had decorated. While Kusserow talks about creativity being held in high esteem among the upper middle class because it becomes part of a special kind of individuality (2004:95–7), my informants also seem to regard creativity as a competence which is beneficial in relation to future employment. So even though many of my informants are not explicitly ambitious on their children's behalf and say that they just hope their children will be happy and have fun, play and fun have become part of a way of thinking about success. That the former is the legitimate stance is also apparent in the critical narrative regarding families that have too many ambitions on their children's behalf, and it might also be related to the Scandinavian ideal of equality and the associated belief that people should be careful not to appear 'too big for their boots' (cf. Gilliam in chapter 5). The playful and creative individual can therefore be seen as part of a particular cultural interpretation of the proper person, which is in harmony with Danish reform pedagogy's emphasis on free thinking.

Communication

In the last section, we saw some examples of parents stimulating their children linguistically through play. Lareau stresses language awareness as a key element of concerted cultivation. She shows how middle-class parents stimulate their children's language by reading to them, answering their questions with questions, involving them in discussions and so on. In this way, the children develop a large vocabulary and an ability to participate in negotiations. Lareau stresses that this stands in contrast to the working class, where parents issue orders and children are rarely involved in discussions (2003:105–60).

In the families in my study, language stimulation primarily takes place through conversations where parents respect their children's comments. For example, Ella (aged 3) was allowed to interrupt a conversation between her mother and myself. Ella said that she wanted to tell 'that lady' about the exotic trip which they had just returned from. Cathrine corrected her: 'not "that lady"', but then asked her daughter what she wanted to tell. Ella told me that 'they ran after the boys in some cars'. Her father, Peter, and her brother Christian (aged 7) explained that she was talking about some toy cars that her brothers had received for Christmas. During this conversation, Cathrine and Peter also highlighted a distinction between themselves and another family at school by saying that this family often travelled outside the school holidays. As a result, the family's son had missed out on learning 'the house of sounds' – a particular method for learning what characterises different vowels and consonants. Cathrine asked Christian if he could remember the house of sounds, to which he replied 'Ahhhh' and 'long S', and so on.

In some of the families, the parents had systematised the language-stimulating conversation during dinner. At Leonora's house everyone took turns to share what they thought had been good and bad that day. This collective reflexive practice also came to light in the context of my interviews. Even though Julie sometimes tried to curb her enthusiastic children, she also included them in the interview. She told me that Ida (aged 3) liked going to the playground, and asked: 'Isn't that right, Ida?' – to which Ida replied: 'Yes'. All in all, Julie asked her children a lot of questions. One morning, while in the car en route to school and kindergarten, she asked them what they wanted in their picnic baskets for a picnic with the kindergarten that evening. Emil (aged 7) replied 'ice cream, chocolate and sweets', which Julie at first rejected: 'Ah' – after which she grasped the learning opportunity and asked him what he thought would happen to the ice cream.

The parents also stimulated their children's language more consciously by reading and singing with them. In virtually all the homes, a bedtime story was part of the bedtime ritual. According to anthropologist Charlotte Faircloth, books are objects which signal diligence (2008:4), and, in several of the homes, there were a lot of books. In Christine's home, they had a room fitted out as a library and the children (aged 2 and 4) spent both mornings and afternoons looking at books. Christine told me that the staff at the day-care institution described her children as 'highly intellectual and smart'. Moreover, just as many parents, as per the aforementioned parental determinism and family interdependency, take the blame for their children's difficulties Christine attributed her children's success to the fact that she had never used baby language when talking to them.

In a number of the families, I also found that languages other than Danish were stimulated, in part because the families travelled a lot, but also because, in a third of the families, one of the parents was not Danish. The parents generally wanted to bestow on their children a global awareness, and I noticed globes and world maps in several of the children's rooms. Eva's family, unlike many of their neighbours, did not go to holiday resorts. Instead, they went on challenging and, as they believed, more rewarding trips for the children (aged 4, 7 and 9), for example to India. Similarly, rather than beach holidays, Barbara and Alfred took their children (aged 13 and 15) on city breaks, where they visited museums and the opera. The parents also emphasised that their children should be open in relation to the few children from ethnic minority backgrounds attending schools in the municipality. Leonora welcomed Hannah's (aged 9) interest in the Middle Eastern boy in her school class, and Henriette had worked intensely to get the class's 'little Hassan' into the local sports club.

In addition to stimulating play and communication, the families introduced their children to highbrow culture, as evident in Barbara's and Alfred's travel preferences. In a number of families, the children regularly accompany parents or grandparents to museums or the theatre. Frederikke explicitly stated that she wanted to give her children (aged 4 and 8) 'a cultural awareness of theatre, museums' and so on. Similarly, to Barbara's great pleasure, Marie (aged 13) sat one day doing homework while listening to Mozart. However, trips to a flea market or the zoo were also cherished. These experiences were also regarded as potentially stimulating as, during a trip to a flea market, they believed that the children could develop a flair for antiques.

The previous examples show that concerted cultivation is partly a matter of providing children with 'good taste'. Good taste, like education, is a key element in what Bourdieu (1986) defines as cultural capital, vital in terms of dignity and respectability. In the next section, I explore the more educational dimensions of cultural capital.

Involvement in School and Day Care

Getting involved in one's children's schools is a key element in concerted cultivation. The mothers in my study are involved in their children's schooling to such an extent that they say 'we' go to school, 'we' start at 8.00, 'we do homework' and so on. This illustrates that the family is a small figuration of interdependent persons (Elias 1994 [1939]:481–2). When I asked Cathrine to describe her day, she said that, after the boys had eaten breakfast, 'then we go to school ... we try to cycle down there. We start at 8.00.' Continuing, she described how they started making dinner at 5 p.m. 'Sometimes we do homework while I prepare some food; other times we do it after dinner.' Similarly, the middle-class parents in Lareau's study are highly engaged in schoolwork (2003:165–81). As Rose suggests, the middle class have internalised many educational norms (1999 [1989]:198–201), and there is a strong continuity between the efforts of school and parents.

Professors of education Thomas Popkewitz and Marianne Bloch point out that, in the USA, a shift occurred towards parental involvement already in the 1960s. Through a series of school reforms during the 1990s, the expectation of parents' cooperation has become generalised (2001:97–101). Based on an English context, Furedi likewise describes the school's growing expectation that parents get involved. Previously, overzealous parents were often considered annoying and homework the responsibility of the child. Nowadays, homework has become a family project, and parents are brought in as unpaid teachers. It is no longer only children who are assessed by the school. Schoolchildren's results are now seen as a direct reflection of the quality of the support they receive from their parents (Furedi 2002:115). Furedi believes that schooling and homework has become an informal instrument for evaluating parents. As such, homework becomes another pointer as to whether or not parents are living up to their responsibility, and thereby an indicator of respectability. Parents' new role involves a surveillance function and an active educational role in regard to their children's schooling and homework (2002:115). These tendencies can also be found in Denmark, although they may be more ambivalent. As far back as the educational reform movement, one finds a preoccupation with ideas of participation and involvement, and several researchers stress that there is currently a heightened focus on cooperation between school and home (Dannesboe, 2009).

I have experienced in a number of homes how the dining area was transformed into a kind of classroom when parents and children did homework together, and how parents assumed a surveillance function. The mother was often the person who took the initiative with regard to homework, and it was also the mother – like the traditional teacher – who decided what was to be done and for how long. The schools in the municipality where the families in my study lived practised an experimental pedagogy, which, according to the families, meant that the children had to give themselves homework. Few of the children lived up to this responsibility and it was the mothers who had taken on the task. In the following, I will show that doing homework together can lead to both positive experiences and conflicts. One reason for conflict is that homework is among the only things that can compete with play. Cathrine sometimes said no to playdates because it could have an adverse effect on homework. However – like Camilla – she solved this problem by occasionally insisting they did their homework even though their friends were visiting. Camilla described how this also gave her an impression of how her children were performing compared to their peers:

> When they are doing homework together ... then Christopher [aged 8] sits and reads a book for early readers next to Phillip [aged 9] who is reading Harry Potter. And they don't have a problem with that ... It's the same if Christopher is doing maths with them, and he's flying through it ...

Doing homework was one reason why Julie picked Emil (aged 7) up early from school. One afternoon, Emil was constantly putting up a struggle and placed his head in the book. Julie helped him to spell his way through the text. Then he began to read, but without looking at the book, after which Julie noted that he had just learnt what it said by heart. Finally, she said that he didn't know it well enough and that he could read the first part of the book if that was what he was best at. He leafed back to the beginning, but read very little and, after about 10 minutes, the strained session was over.

At Martin and Henriette's house it was the daughter (aged 10) who took the initiative to do homework, saying after dinner: 'Daddy, we have to do homework.' Here, doing homework together seemed pretty cosy, as the following exchange illustrates:

> *Martin*: Well done Maria, you deserve a prize for that ...
> *Maria*: Yeeaah.
> *Martin*: A big wet kiss from your Dad.

As well as getting involved in their children's schooling by taking an active part in homework, a number of the parents were part of parents' boards at the schools and day-care institutions their children attended. Camilla belonged to the parents' committee for all three of the institutions her children attended. She considered it essential to play an active role in school life: 'Both for one's own sake, participating in school events to see how the class functions and meet the other fathers and mothers, but also to show the children that we too are part of this.'

As is apparent, one way to show your commitment to schools and day-care institutions is to participate in the various events which include parents. During my fieldwork, I was struck by how often the families were on their way to such an arrangement or had just been to one. As mentioned previously, Julie talked about a picnic with the kindergarten and, one Sunday morning, she baked rolls for a get-together in Emil's school class. Similarly, Cathrine spent an afternoon frying chicken for an event at her son's after-school centre. The act of bringing something edible which you have prepared yourself to such events demonstrates an investment of time and resources and thus becomes a signifier of being civilised and respectable.

In this section we have seen that the families in my study, like the American families in Lareau's study, cooperate strongly with their children's educational institutions. This should not be interpreted as passive compliance but rather as an active strategy for ensuring respectability, including that their children function optimally and behave properly. In the last three sections, we have seen that not only is the home protected against negative influences, it is also filled with stimulating elements and can be regarded as an educational hothouse. The parents' childrearing can thus be characterised as a concerted cultivation strategy, in which domestic communication and parental involvement are key elements. However, unlike Lareau's description from the USA, it is the children's play rather than extra-curricular activities which are considered most important. Nevertheless, there is no talk of 'natural growth', as play is interpreted in a learning perspective and playdates are, as will be seen, often organised by adults. All in all, these last sections have demonstrated that the parents' childrearing strategy is not just a matter of fencing in and limiting, but also of opening up and stimulating. The civilising ideal is about creating children who can both adapt to others and express themselves. In other words, people who are able to socialise with others without friction, who can 'be themselves' in a variety of social contexts, and who can strike a balance between being considerate and making themselves heard. This ideal of the proper human being is not a pipe dream, but an ideal which has been translated into a thorough endeavour to cultivate. The civilised and respectable does not come of its own accord; the parents work on the details.

Childrearing as Boundary Marker

As we have seen, the parents play a central role in relation to both regulating and stimulating their children. I have described this as a kind of border guard role. However, not all parents signalled their control. Some instead stressed a laid-back approach. Leonora told me that she and her husband were easy-going and that things were negotiated in their family. Nor was it control that jumped out at me in Frederikke's family. While visiting for afternoon cake I was greeted by two children who grabbed the digital recorder out of my hand and began interviewing their mother and me about childrearing.

I also thought, qua the civilising ideals I have identified, that Camilla signalled an easy-going style. During a visit, myself, her children and their schoolmates were offered buns and cinnamon bread. The children were also given ice cream and fruit squash, and the girls (aged 6) played with Barbie dolls. I told Camilla that I felt there were two kinds of parents: 'the easy-going' and 'the tough but fair'. She disliked this categorisation:

> We're easy-going, but I'm tough when it comes to stuff like bedtimes. I can see that some of Arthur's friends who go to bed at 11 p.m. are tired every day. And things aren't like that in our family. But at the same time, at 5 p.m. we don't know what we are going to have for dinner. And then we have a large social circle that often drop by unannounced. I don't really think we can be placed in either category.

Faircloth (2008) distinguishes between a controlling and a liberal style of parenting, but she also points out that this distinction does not entirely stand up to scrutiny. This is because parents can include elements from one style in the other, just as 'liberals' can be forced into a more controlling role if their intended approach fails, and vice versa (Faircloth 2008:3). In terms of my study, we have seen that even quite controlling mothers are open to the playful, but here Faircloth's point is that, due to the existence of 'competing normalities', parents end up making choices and are held

accountable for them (2008:3). Thus childrearing becomes an active coun-
terbalancing of liberal and controlling elements. Elias similarly points out
that civilising is a question of finding the right balance between constraint
and fulfilment of drives and needs (1994 [1939]:446–7).

My material shows a tendency for parents to position their childrearing
strategy, and thereby themselves, in relation to, and often in contrast to,
other parents – controlling or liberal. Leonora spoke critically of how her
childhood home was characterised by an inability to exercise appropriate
authority: 'I don't think we were ever set boundaries.' Similarly, we have
seen how Benedicte distanced herself from parents who tolerated 'mucking
about'; how Cathrine distanced herself from families travelling outside
of school holidays; how Caroline dissociated herself from others in the
neighbourhood who gave their children junk food; how Julie dissociated
herself from parents allowing their children to watch *Forbrydelsen* (*The
Killing*); and how Camilla distanced herself from families letting their
children stay up late. All these examples demonstrate how childrearing is
used as a signifier of distinction.

The ideal of balance means that both overly liberal and overly controlling
parenting is problematised. What is considered worst is to be too lax and
too strict at the same time. Christine distanced herself from a family at the
kindergarten that combined these extremes:

> *Christine*: Well, their boys [aged 5 and 6] were very, very self-reliant at
> much too young an age.
> *Dil*: In what way were they self-reliant, and how did you experience it as
> being at too young an age?
> *Christine*: They had made their own packed lunches ... And they haven't
> been wearing enough clothes: [their mum said] 'Okay, then they have
> to remember that in the mornings themselves; they have to become
> better at remembering it.' She constantly denied [responsibility].

I asked Christine whether the children also behaved differently:

> Yes ... They were extremely quick to approach the adults and ask 'Can I
> come home with you?' And when they were picked up, then they always
> said 'No, we want to stay, we don't want to come with you', making a fuss
> ... They were missing that thing that there is a mother who establishes
> contact to say 'Should we arrange a playdate?' ... They were completely
> without that filter of shyness that most children have ... They just said

everything: 'No, my mum's moved out, my mum and dad are arguing', and 'Now we are here', and 'No, we don't know where we're going to go to school because we don't know where we are going to live' ... They just blurted everything out.

This passage contains a number of elements related to psychological-pedagogic boundary-setting. As stated previously, it is a matter of giving the child a sense of its 'spatial' limits so that things do not spill out. Furthermore, it is a question of the existence of appropriate checkpoints. As indicated earlier, playdates – at least in relation to small children – are usually organised by adults. It is the adults who function as the home's checkpoints, and it is through their diplomacy that borders are opened and movement made possible. Should a playmate be too quick to take the initiative, it can be experienced as invasive. Christine also told me that one of the two boys was very difficult and she mentioned that the parents were not only too 'lax': 'They were all the time a bit tougher on him. So he was also more contrary.'

Anne recounted a similar story when I asked her whether there was anyone at the kindergarten who she did not want her daughter (aged 4) to play with:

> *Anne*: No ... Well yes, there is actually a mum there ... Seriously, I'm telling you, she is so strange ... She invited herself to a Christmas do at my house ... And then I was carrying my son around when he tugs at my blouse and says 'breasts'. 'Well', she says, 'it looks like it's time for him to have something to drink?' So I say, 'Good God no, he's two years old and he doesn't get anything from there any more.' 'Oh well, I'm still breastfeeding.'
>
> *Dil*: What, no, the five-year-old boy?
>
> *Anne*: 'You do what?', says Flora's mother. 'Yes, not Augusta [aged 4], but Peter Nikolai'. And then one of the other mothers says 'Really, is it true?' 'Sure it is', she replies. 'Seriously, don't you want to have your breasts for yourself?', adds a third mother. 'No ... I'll breastfeed him until his confirmation if he still wants to.' Then I just thought ... 'No way, you can't do this.'

The above underlines that boundaries are to do with personal space. Anne, the other mothers and even I were all taken aback by the symbiotic relationship between this mother and son. The boundaries around their bodies were indistinct as she still breastfed him. Sociologist Deborah Lupton writes about the 'civilised body' as the bounded body, but also that women, in connection with childbirth and breastfeeding, find that the boundary between themselves and their children becomes blurred (Lupton and Barclay 1997:30–3). The passage quoted above, meanwhile, indicates that it is only up to a certain age that such a blurring of boundaries is respectable. If you breastfeed your 5-year-old, then you are doing something shameful and undermining your honour. The limit of how much naturalness is healthy, is exceeded. You instead appear grotesque, and the other women at the Christmas do were embarrassed. Although parents are expected to spend considerable time with their children, and many parents feel interdependent with their children and strongly identify themselves with them, things should not become too symbiotic. There still have to be boundaries between parents and children. As we saw earlier, another aspect of the notion of the bad family life is the idea of clingy children, which in turn points to independence as a central civilising virtue. Anne also told me that the mother in question was very strict with her son, and again we see that the combination of 'soft' and 'hard' childrearing practices is considered the least respectable.

All in all, we have seen how families evaluate each other based on their childrearing. Childrearing comes to function as a boundary marker between the civilised and the uncivilised, whereby those who are not practising 'appropriate' boundary-setting are judged negatively and fuel the narrative regarding the bad family life. For the affluent families, however, it is not just a question of childrearing being used as a signifier of economic and cultural class which demarcates them from people in other positions. There is often talk of a moral boundary marker separating small groups of equal standing from one another: our family versus the childhood home, our family versus the neighbours, our family versus the in-laws, our family versus friends, the other families at school, at kindergarten and so on. What's more, these demarcations do not prevent interaction, but are a matter of using other families as points of orientation and mental maps in a complex childrearing landscape where what characterises the civilised person is constantly being negotiated. As such, childrearing and civilising becomes a complicated practice where it is a matter of striking the right balance between too little and too much control. On occasion, however, the moral distancing goes hand in hand with socioeconomic distance, as was the case with the breastfeeding mother who was characterised according to her lack of resources and objectively belonged to a different social segment.

Childrearing Among Affluent Families in Denmark

In this chapter, I have focused on the childrearing strategies of affluent families. The institution of family entails a twin endeavour. On the one hand are the children who have to develop certain qualities and competences. On the other hand are the parents who have to make a specific effort. A recurrent image is that of the child as a container to be filled up with all that is good. At the same time, it has to be possible to close the container, to ensure that bad things do not 'intrude', but also that they do not 'spill out'. This is because the child is at the same time regarded as innocent, playful and creative, and as wild and uninhibited. Given that play and creativity are viewed in a positive light, as parents it is a matter of developing a balanced childrearing strategy, where the 'childish' is allowed to thrive, but is also sufficiently limited. The interpretation of the civilised human being that emerges from my material is, in short, a complex one. Civilised human beings must be able to make themselves heard while, at the same time, being considerate and not taking up too much time and pace.

Despite the increasing institutionalisation of children's lives, it is the parents who are held responsible for the creation of such human beings, both by each other and by child professionals. The idea is that if parents ensure a good childhood for their children, where they are filled with cosiness and parental contact, then the result will be strong and harmonious human beings, rather than weak and wild ones. If the parents manage to set appropriate boundaries, the idea is that this will result in fit and healthy individuals who are independent and have personal integrity while also being polite and respectful towards others. And if parents succeed in stimulating their children, the expected outcome is individuals who are smart, creative, active, social and so on. In addition to these general civilising objectives, my material also includes more specific ideals whereby the right input from parents is believed to lead to helpfulness, anti-materialism, diligence, good taste, a global perspective, a sense for technological developments – and high attainment at school.

The demands made of parents in terms of civilising are, like the demands made of children, complex and highly ambiguous. For example, setting boundaries can be reconciled with both controlling and more liberal childrearing practices. It therefore has nothing to do with the practice enforcing absolute rules, but rather with the ability to balance between freedom and control in relation to the filtering of what 'comes in and out' of the child. Similarly, parents are expected to stimulate their children and to invest much time and resources in them without becoming too ambitious or having too symbiotic a relationship. This is because boundary-setting is also about drawing a line between parent and child, since independence is considered a civilising virtue. Nevertheless, not even this ideal is unambiguous, as it is not considered a good thing if children are self-reliant at too early an age.

Given that there are so many demands and expectations regarding family life, and that these are both ambiguous and imprecise, there will always be something you can criticise parents for failing to live up to or for prioritising wrongly. And given that there exists both a controlling and a liberal 'normality', parents' childrearing strategies are never just a passive internalisation of norms. The presence of competing normalities means that a childrearing strategy will always involve choices, thereby consolidating the attribution of responsibility to parents. The families in this study criticise other families and hold them responsible for their choices, and they use other families' childrearing as points of orientation with regard to their own childrearing strategies and to position themselves. Because children's behaviour, well-being and future opportunities are seen as determined by parental input, and because parents thereby are held accountable for their childrearing strategy and made interdependent with their children, childrearing becomes a distinctive practice. This also explains the degree of detail in the endeavour to promote those characteristics that are considered key in order to appear to be a civilised family figuration.

One might then ask: who it is that the affluent families are distancing themselves from with this endeavour? With their 'concerted cultivation' strategy, they are reminiscent of the middle classes, which much research places in contrast with the working class. Nevertheless, they also share some of the characteristics often linked to the working class, such as the way the mothers are oriented towards family life (2008:202–3). Like Faber's working-class women, the affluent women draw a lot of their identity from motherhood and denounce the stressful lives of most middle-class families. At the same time, the women in my study also distance themselves from the negative image of the upper class, which I mentioned at the beginning of this chapter. Here, a picture is drawn of affluent parents not spending enough time with their children and spoiling them with material goods. This is also how my informants describe many of their neighbours, and several state that, while they want to live in the area, they do not want to be like everyone else. When the affluent families speak critically about other families, there is, as we have seen, often talk of moral distinctions which separate families of equal standing from one another. By using other families as points of orientation and identification, most of the families attempt to place themselves in, if not a middle-class position, then a central position, morally speaking – the balanced and civilised position, which is neither too controlling nor too easy-going, and where the parents spend considerable time with their children without the relationship becoming too symbiotic (the tendency to seek a central position is discussed in relation to schools in chapter 7).

Precisely the fact that children and childrearing are included as moral distinctions among groups of equal standing within society's upper echelons leads me to consider respectability as a more general signifier of identity than merely something that the working class strive for and the middle class take for granted. Not only in socioeconomically hierarchical relationships, but also more equal ones, people define themselves as respectable by defining others as unrespectable. In addition, a fear of falling in status can also be observed within society's upper echelons. This may help explain the commitment shown by the mothers in relation to the cultivation and civilising of their children. Although many of the children are filled with cultural capital and presumably can look forward to a good future, things can go wrong. The intensive childrearing endeavour thus concerns both the family's standing in the here and now and its longer term position and respectability.

Not only are the parents subject to each other's and child professionals' evaluative gazes, many have internalised how their future adult children will see them. The children will probably blame their parents if they become a failure. The suspicion that is focused on parents, and not least rich parents, has the consequence that the affluent families, even though they are often vindicated in their childrearing strategy, are also on the defensive. It is easy for them to feel guilty, and they apologise and explain if what they are doing in any way goes against the norms. In short, the affluent families' considerable investment of time and resources in their children is not only part of an offensive strategy of civilising and distinction, but equally a defensive strategy of respectability. Just like the working-class families in Skeggs' study, they endeavour to counter the prejudices of others. It is about showing that they are affluent in a good enough way and avoiding being judged as bad parents. The latter also applies in relation to their own children, when they, at some point in the future, look back on their childhood.

9

Civilising Institutions
Cultural norms and social consequences

Laura Gilliam and Eva Gulløv

This book has explored childrearing and forms of interaction within Danish families, day-care institutions and schools. In this chapter, we will discuss the civilising ideals and practices across the institutions we have studied. Our intention is to interpret the priorities and character-istic traits that they share in their formative work with children, thereby creating a cultural analysis of central norms of Danish society. Though the analysis specifically concerns the Danish welfare society, we believe that it contributes to educational research and to anthropological studies on childhood, socialisation and welfare societies in general. The attempt to understand the ideological and practical implications of civilising projects in children's institutions illuminates the way social figurations, state interventions, institutional dynamics and cultural norms are integrated in everyday life and, through long-term processes, come to define the moralities, priorities and impact of such central societal institutions. Yet we also find that the particular focus on children and children's institutions adds something to the Eliasian approach, as it shows how moralities are formed, challenged and transmitted intergenerationally. Thus, despite the fact that this is a case study, we regard many of the analytical points of this chapter as having a more general nature.

In order to understand the priorities and aims of children's institutions in Danish welfare society, we open the chapter with a further look at the connection between the state, children's institutions and cultural norms. Digging into the cultural content of the civilising practices, we continue by exploring the strong endeavour to make children 'social', which has been a recurrent theme in all the institutions. By means of guidelines, boundaries and contrasts, parents, pedagogues and teachers work to incorporate in children the proper balance between being themselves and being considerate to others. Central to this effort is the perception that being able to adapt to social communities is paramount for the individual as well as for the civilised state of society.

Though we have observed a certain level of consistency in the perceptions and prioritisations of the institutions we have studied, we have also seen many examples of how institutional childrearing is complex and ambiguous. Likewise, children are not necessarily formed in the way institutions intend: civilising intentions may have unintended outcomes. In the last part of the chapter, we discuss children's reactions to the pedagogical initiatives they meet across the studies. In doing so, we intend to shed light on the consequences of civilising ideals and efforts for children in their everyday lives at the institutions – as well as, in a broader perspective, for the social constellation of Danish society. We end the book by pointing to some of the recent changes towards increased formalisation and regulation within civilising projects, and discuss whether we might be witnessing a change in the civilising standards and practices which have hitherto been so integrated in the welfare project.

The Relationship Between State and Institution

The claim that our studies of institutions' childrearing practices and civilising missions can be considered a cultural analysis is based on two assumptions. First, as we discussed in chapters 1 and 2, ideas about the civilised are expressions of culturally dominant perceptions about how people should act and interact with others. Thus, focusing on markers of the civilised provides insights into the prevailing norms for social behaviour and morality, and thereby also into criteria for evaluation and distinction. The second assumption is that children's institutions act in the interests of society by organising, maintaining and developing these specific norms of interaction. This makes these institutions particularly suitable venues for studying cultural values, dominant perceptions and social hierarchies. Examining this with a civilising perspective, we can shed light on the processes that establish specific values, perceptions and ways of acting as legitimate and dominant. This latter point is also rooted in the fact that institutions are not autonomous, delimited or homogeneous. They are both unique and a part of a larger society in which individuals relate to each other through, among other things, institutional arrangements, categories and classifications (Douglas 1986:91–111). Thus they have their own routines, hierarchies and orders, but are also based in and dependent upon a society that, with changing priorities, supports their existence and basic norms.

This fact is particularly relevant when studying educational institutions that are at once inextricably interwoven into the structure of society and small social worlds in themselves. Norms and priorities, standards and distinctions reflect and underpin more general understandings, making careful studies of daily actions and institutional routines within these institutions particularly suited to exploring cultural priorities and relations of dominance, and thus essential not merely for educational research but also useful for anthropological studies of contemporary welfare societies. As already stated in chapter 1, educational institutions reflect both dominant interests and civilising projects, yet they also influence cultural understandings of what it means to be civilised. Through the daily formative work with children, norms of social interaction are imposed and standardised as the proper ways to behave; but they are also moulded and defined in accordance with the conditions of everyday institutional life. This dual process of institutionalisation is important for understanding the way educational institutions are integrated in the reproduction and redistribution of power and norms, yet also contribute to and redefine these processes through everyday dynamics. This explains why educational institutions have become increasingly important parts of most contemporary political objectives, yet also objects of conflict and concern. They are integrated parts of the formation, articulation, consolidation and distribution of the dominant morality.

The dual work of institutions, which both reflects and contributes to the 'cultural production of the educated person' (Levinson and Holland 1996), is particularly evident in the case of Denmark, where educational institutions are widespread and all-encompassing, and where the involvement of the state is profound. Here a large portion of children's and young people's everyday lives takes place in state-financed and state-monitored childrearing and educational institutions. They conduct their business under the mandate of the welfare state, and the pedagogues and teachers have obtained authorised qualifications in order to raise and educate the children in accordance with what is prioritised and imposed by the state. Every public institution is required to report and account for its practical organisation and pedagogical performance to a regulatory apparatus. However, as we discussed in chapter 1, the state is not an unequivocal form of power. It is comprised of numerous organisational agencies and individuals, and it is continuously subject to conflicts of interest among them as well as from actors outside of the state apparatus.

Sociologist Pierre Bourdieu relates the legitimacy and authority of institutions to the emergence and propagation of the state. He argues that the power of the state is based to a large extent on the spread of shared understandings and terms, and on establishing concepts that, for example, reinforce the relevance of institutional efforts (1994:35–8). As referred to in chapter 1, Bourdieu argues that: 'One of the major powers of the state is to produce and impose (especially through the school system) categories of thought that we spontaneously apply to all things of the social world – including the state itself' (1994:35). This highlights the importance of state institutions for cultural integration through the spread of certain dominant perceptions and forms of behaviour. In this way, state-instantiated standards always reflect relations of dominance: the fact that some groups' understandings, linguistic forms and values, over time and through these groups' appropriation of the state, have gained ground over more local variations. Having been spread and broadly recognised as proper, they have gradually been incorporated into different institutional rationales and routines and thereby been standardised as norms.

Norbert Elias describes a similar relationship between the emergence of the state and the spread of norms of interaction. He describes how the state has gradually become consolidated through the establishment of a number of regulatory agencies ensuring the state's monopoly on the exercise of power as well as working to integrate an increasing number of groups into the institutional organisation of society (Elias 1994 [1939]:273–7). He argues that this development has led to an extensive and detailed coordination and standardisation of citizens' interactions, leading in turn to an increased level of stability in both the exercise of power and interpersonal relations (1994 [1939]:369). Thus, state institutions integrate, stabilise and standardise interpersonal relations.

However, it is important to elaborate these theoretical points on standardisation in relation to our discussion. Civilising endeavours surely entail a standardisation of norms for forms of interaction, but for two different reasons. As we explain in chapter 1, Elias argues that interpersonal interactions in increasingly integrated societies involve the coordination and stabilisation of expectations with regard to others' behaviour. Predictability and trust are needed when people are increasingly interdependent. From this perspective, standardisation is an effect of long-term social dynamics. At the same time, the development of an increasingly detailed and ramified welfare state apparatus, as is the case in Denmark, results inevitably in more intentional efforts to regulate. These efforts also have a standardising function in relation to people's behaviour, but in this case the standardisation is part of a project rather than an effect of a social dynamic. However, following the points above, this does not mean that ideas about children, childhood and upbringing, and norms of behaviour are merely defined and disseminated 'from above' through the state's exercise of authority or through specific policies (Shore and Wright 1997; Sutton and Levinson 2001). They are also shaped, developed and standardised through the social dynamics in children's institutions.

Children's Institutions in a Welfare Society

Children in Denmark spend much of their time outside their families as they are cared for and educated at society's nurseries, kindergartens, schools and after-school clubs from a very young age. This agreement between parents and society is an example of one such well-established and indisputable understanding that has been supported and disseminated by the Danish state. Although families have many different views about childrearing and childhood conditions, there is widespread acceptance of the idea that children should attend day-care institutions and state-funded schools, and 'have activities' in their spare time in order to be cared for, learn useful skills and 'have fun', as the parents of one kindergarten child expressed it. Parents generally agree that out-of-family care is important not only to uphold their own relation to the labour market but for the sake of a sound development for the child. The reason given is often that it is 'good for a child to be with others', as one mother explained when asked why she chose to send her daughter to kindergarten while she herself was on maternity leave with a younger sibling. Children's institutions have gradually become the proper place for children to spend their weekdays: in a sense, they have become an integrated component of the very conceptualisation of childhood in Denmark (Kampmann 2004:145–6).

The institutional organisation can be seen as a state-supported process of social integration requiring social adaptation – as a 'fabricated' civilising process in miniature, as Gilliam argues in chapter 5. This integration has developed gradually so that it encompasses ever more aspects of children's everyday lives, development and upbringing. As mentioned in chapter 2, the time that children spend in institutions has gradually increased from more or less compulsory schooling for a short number of years, to an undisputed understanding that children should spend their weekdays in a broad ramified institutional structure from the age of 1 until they are about 18. Thus, the proliferation of institutions for children has both contributed to and been the result of a comprehensive integration and homogenisation process, in which a number of actors work to integrate children into society, and to mould them in accordance with dominant civilising norms.

In chapter 2, we showed how childrearing has become a central part of the Danish welfare state. This is a general characteristic of welfare states. Seen from an Eliasian perspective, in a societal structure that is characterised by a complex social composition of different yet also internally dependent groups, segments and layers, there will be an increasing need for institutionalisation, coordination, adaptation and standardisation. This does not mean that the same level of awareness about social behaviour cannot be found in other forms of society; rather, it means that the civilising ambition in societies that are not integrated in this way and thus based on less extensive webs of interdependence does not necessarily include individuals from outside one's own group. 'The others' – being other social or ethnic groups – can live as they please as long as they keep to themselves.[1]

In this regard, it could be claimed that the range of civilising projects is determined by the structure and range of social interdependency. In closely integrated societies the pressure on individuals to adapt their behaviour to changing social contexts increases: they must recognise and master different social codes and be able to tailor their actions accordingly. This is even more pertinent in a welfare society such as Denmark, which has a complex institutional structure and a large public sector, offering universal benefits that depend on the organisation of multitudes of people and on people's payment of tax to the common fund. People must be able to rely on the accountability and social attitude of others. Furthermore, the regular interactions with people from different levels of society make it necessary to downplay differences and status markers in order to avoid acting inappropriately or losing the respect of people one is close to or dependent upon (Wouters 2004:206–9). In this context, equality and avoidance of conflict are a prerequisite for recognition and social integration. Thus, the efforts of welfare states to establish connections and consolidate peaceful coexistence have resulted in increased requirements and efforts with regard to assuring civilised behaviour and situational adaptation across society. As pointed out by Durkheim, the need for social order and cultural reproduction means that society cannot risk ignoring how children are raised (Durkheim 1975 [1922]:40, 49). Accordingly, due to the need to ensure the integration and stability of the highly interdependent Danish society, the Danish state has, with the increasing support of the public, developed an increasingly far-reaching and important process that not only monitors children's academic development but also their social skills and attitudes.

Working with 'The Social'

By adding an ethnographic and everyday-practice approach to the more theoretical and historical perspective of Elias, we have analysed a range of civilising norms and ambitions through the previous chapters. Looking across these and applying a lateral perspective to the families and public institutions we have studied, we find that a particular pattern emerges: when parents, pedagogues and teachers emphasise that they work to make children 'social', and when they assess how well a child or a group of children has been brought up based on how 'social' he, she or they are, they are reinforcing a specific way of understanding their pedagogical task as well as civilised behaviour. The objective of childrearing is not simply to teach the child to control its bodily drives or inappropriate physical expression. Nor is childrearing just a matter of the child's personal development, appropriation of manners or the realisation of his/her learning potential. The aim is more encompassing: to nurture a particular kind of fellow human being, a particular kind of interactional form and a particular kind of community.

In the following, we will further explore this idea of 'the social'. We do so by looking more closely at three traits we have found characterise the civilising work across the institutions: the first is related to the frequent use of the term 'boundaries' in adults' reflections about specific children and upbringing practices. The second is a marked focus on 'balance' and the requirement for a finely tuned situational awareness, and the third is the effort to create 'civilised communities'. We suggest that taking a further look at these traits and identifying what they involve can reveal some of the dominant cultural ideals for individuals, interactions and societal forms in Danish society.

The Meaning of 'Boundaries'

The word 'boundaries' is repeatedly used when upbringing is discussed in the families, children's institutions and schools we have studied. Parents and teachers stress that a child should: 'respect other people's boundaries'; 'not transgress other people's boundaries'; be able to 'limit oneself' and 'sense where the boundaries are'. Similarly, children are described as being 'transgressive' if they break behavioural codes (e.g. by burping, passing wind, spitting or acting in socially inappropriate ways), and when they are metaphorically criticised for 'offending others' (in Danish 'at støde andre' – literally meaning 'bruising others'), as this is interpreted as evidence of disrespect for other people's personal integrity. When working peda-gogically with children, adults attempt to teach individual children to 'sense' and 'respect other people's boundaries', and also to 'mark their own boundaries'; that is, to express and maintain what is described as 'their self'.

Our material shows that Danish parents, teachers and pedagogues seem to have a 'passion for boundaries' similar to the one that Marianne Gullestad found in her study of Norwegian childrearing (Gullestad 1997a). As seen in her work, too, the concept of 'boundaries' functions both as a euphemism for marking differences and inviolable social spaces, and, in a more psychological sense, as a way of framing the personal self, which must not be invaded. The influence of psychological science on perceptions of civilised interaction is clearly evident here (albeit the influence most probably also goes the other way, in that civilising processes also have substantial influence on notions of the self within the discipline of psychology). The idea of boundaries seems to be closely linked to the dominant idea of the self as a delimited and vulnerable entity that can be damaged and traumatised, and therefore requires careful handling; but it also reflects the idea that social relations are a common space where each person has the right to their own demarcated spot. As a metaphor, awareness of 'boundaries' works on several levels at the same time: whether one recognises relevant categorical distinctions and can assess what is acceptable to different categories of people; whether one knows how much room to take up in interactions with others, not least through body, gestures or sounds; and whether one 'knows oneself', can 'delimit oneself' and can create boundaries around oneself in order to avoid the intrusions of others. In today's Danish society, civilised interaction thus requires that individuals possess a sense of their own and others' physical and psychological boundaries, and can navigate within these boundaries with care, informality and ease. In the words of Marianne Gullestad: 'Firm boundaries around the person seem to be a prerequisite for social involvement in culturally correct and positive ways' (Gullestad 1997a:34).

Thus, children need to learn behavioural forms, but they also need to be able to orient themselves in a situation by taking stock of the markers that establish and communicate the boundaries of what is respectable. This is complicated by the fact that these boundaries are never static: they change their meaning in different social contexts as well as over time. As Gulløv describes in chapter 3, when an ethnic minority child arrives at kindergarten smelling of soap, with wet-combed hair or a pretty dress, the staff do not view this as a sign of respectability, as the parents might have intended. On the contrary, this actually challenges the institution's civilising ideal, which celebrates the childlike, natural and independent. Children should decide for themselves and express themselves, and should be allowed 'to get dirt under their fingernails' and grass stains on their knees. Wet-combed hair and pretty dresses are perceived as an expression of a repressive stance towards children, which emphasises being presentable rather than autonomous. On the other hand, when one of the mothers mentioned in Bach's chapter (chapter 8) breastfeeds her 5-year-old son, this is not viewed as a sign of naturalness or an open mind; rather, it is perceived as a worrying symbiosis between the mother and child, and a lack of boundaries between them, which – just as in the previous example – corrupts the ideal of individual independence.

The concept of boundaries also suggests that what is considered to be uncivilised is precisely that which transcends or cannot be grasped by our perceptual categories. To paraphrase Mary Douglas: We are disgusted and ashamed about bodily excretions that are neither entirely apart from the body nor an integrated part of it. In the same way, we are disgusted by forms of interaction that transgress culturally established boundaries around the individual. 'Dirt offends against order' and, as such, the uncivilised can be seen as a kind of contamination of the social and symbolic order upon which we are dependent in our interactions (Douglas 1966:2). The boundary markers change over time, and are often assigned different meanings in different social contexts. However they are not random. As Douglas shows, boundary markers are symbolic expressions of affiliations and power relations. They are the result of social processes that have loaded certain objects and ways of acting with meanings about people's status, affiliations and identities. Both of the examples described above reflect a historically well-established understanding of humans as independent individuals with an autonomous core – a self. When this idea forms the basis for interpretations, actions that challenge what are perceived as another person's boundaries – here the child's independence

– are both a fundamental denigration of the autonomy of the other and a breach of the codes of civilised conducts: a contravention of the very foundation of sociality.

Boundaries are culturally acknowledged markers between different categories and people. Therefore, children who are 'too intrusive', who 'invade other people's space', who 'are shameless', who in other ways do not accept other people's boundaries or who 'lack boundaries' appear to be uncivilised. At the same time, a child's lack of boundaries reflects parents who are unable to 'set boundaries'. They have not been able to teach their children how much space they may occupy, or how they should sense the boundaries of others. Thus, 'setting boundaries' is a euphemistic term for a requirement to assure proper social interaction between children and others. The civilised Danish child may swear and be outspoken and informal with authorities in most situations – but he/she must always have a particularly well-developed sense of proximity and distance, both psychologically and socially. This form of nuanced and subtle social sensitivity is integral to being 'social', and one of the prime objects of the civilising efforts of parents and staff.

The connection between social sensitivity and boundaries also refers to social distinctions. Having a social sense involves knowing the differences between social categories and groups and their status, their entitlement to use the social space, and being able to assess one's own position in relation to them and to act appropriately towards people of different positions. This sense of distinction is central for being civilised. When someone says anxiously that a child 'has no boundaries', they mean that the child does not have the commendable ability to sense social contexts and positions, and understand his/her own place within them, which is necessary to behave in a civilised manner.

Balanced Behaviour

In relation to the sophisticated work of establishing boundaries, children are met with an expectation of psychological and social equilibrium, which seems to express a widely recognised cultural ideal in Danish society of appropriate comportment, emotional stance and relations to others. Throughout our material, we have noted a distaste for extremes, such as children who are temperamental or loud, or children who are too quiet or self-effacing. Extremes should be avoided, especially when it comes to violence, aggression and destruction, but also when it comes to self-presentation or particular persistence as expressed by the somewhat derogatory discussions of children who are 'overconfident', 'too forward' or 'too precocious'. In general, it is not good to be too much of anything ('too nice', 'too clever', 'too quiet', 'too pretty', 'too headstrong' or 'almost too sweet'), even when the personality trait that follows is something valued by pedagogues and teachers. Thus, the civilising efforts address a particular personal as well as social balance. Children must not shout, but they should not be too quiet either. They should neither be too lively nor too physically passive; rather, they should be actively and calmly engaged in the institutional practice (cf. Palludan 2005). Moreover, they must learn to 'stand up for themselves', without 'placing themselves above others', 'putting others down' or 'pushing them to one side'. These spatial metaphors describe an almost physical balancing act between consideration for oneself and others, between the inner and the outer, the top and the bottom, the quiet and the wild, the repressive and the repressed. Therefore, behaving in a balanced manner is a matter of finding and knowing one's position in the imagined social space by neither placing oneself 'above' or 'under' others, nor pushing anyone 'out' or being on the 'outside' oneself. It was evidently an explicit part of pedagogical awareness – for example, when the grade 0 teachers (in Gilliam's chapter 5) described how they must 'hold' some children 'back', and 'push' others 'forward' in order to keep the individual in the right balance while also ensuring the harmony of the group.

While we will suggest that civilised conduct is generally related to a specific interpretation of how to balance between extremes, the institutional framework and increasing institutionalisation seems to add to this. We will thus argue that the act of balancing becomes particularly essential, yet also complex in an institutional context characterised by many people in close proximity. Institutional functionality frames interactions, implicitly demanding that everyone should adjust, balance their own needs with those of others and respect activities, tasks and time schedules. Yet it is important to emphasise that, in the Danish context, this compliance with institutional demands should ideally never be too restrictive because children should not be cowed. Thus, the institutional civilising project is itself a balancing act. The objective is socially adjusted, emotionally balanced, happy and independent children who seek out knowledge with curiosity and passion. Such balanced and joyous children affirm the adults in their efforts to create a good childhood and institutional life for the children.

The Balanced Childrearers – Norms of Power and Authority

As shown above, pedagogical work seeks to give children the opportunity to develop as unique individuals at the same time as teaching them to respect the institutional framework and constantly consider other children, staff and the accomplishment of the tasks at hand. Moreover, ideally children should not simply do what the adults say: they should do things of their own free will and out of consideration for others. This is seen, in particular, in the kindergarten and grade 0, where the pedagogues want to give the children space for their particular forms of expression, but under relatively controlled conditions. Thus, the task is to gently and without obvious authority make the children want to do what is expected. As children grow older, it becomes more legitimate to demand more of them, as long as it is 'for their own good'. Strict discipline, scolding and forceful authority are not legitimate, though as we have seen in chapter 6 and will discuss later, these methods are still practised in relation to children who severely challenge the work flow or the social cohesion of the community. This, however, raises moral scruples and much concern and debate among the teachers. As we have shown in several of the chapters, Elias points out that increasing informality, partly resulting from changes in power balances between adults and children, has resulted in greater requirements pertaining to upbringing in civilised ways (Elias 1998a). This does not mean that all pedagogues, teachers and parents use the same methods of childrearing, or that they share exactly the same perceptions and ideals. But we can see that the ideal of the civilised childrearer is a well-known figure that everyone must take into account and position herself in relation to: an adult who, without using corporeal or coercive means, makes the child aware of and adapt to social requirements without transgressing their personal boundaries.

In this interpretation of the civilising project, there is some alternation between correction and support, control and acceptance, in an attempt to encourage without cowing the child. We will argue that this ambiguity reflects a dominant attitude to power and authority within Danish society in general. In this cultural setting, demonstrations of powerful authority are illegitimate in social relations, as these should at best be characterised by equality, the good will of independent actors and informality. This illegitimacy of any display of power and the manifestation of inequality that it implies might lie beneath the encouraging smile that we have noticed as a commonly occurring expression in interactions between children and adults, both professionals and parents. It is also the reason for the frustrated expressions of pedagogues and teachers who feel that they are 'forced to be controlling' or 'strict'. As we have seen in most of the chapters in this book, the civilised ideal places high and often contradictory demands on the adults to interact in a civilised manner with children, without displaying anger or other forms of forceful authority. They are required to find a balance between setting up boundaries and giving the child freedom, and between strict and relaxed forms of childrearing.

The Civilised Middle Position

As demonstrated above, it seems to be a general trait that the civilised position is placed in the middle of different extremes, yet what varies is the extremes set up to establish the civilised norm. In the specific cultural context studied here, children should 'do what they are told', but not be 'too well-behaved'; they should be 'lively' but not 'wild'; they should not be 'inhibited' nor 'lack boundaries', just as adults should neither be too 'strict' nor too 'easy-going' or 'lax'. In many of the examples in the book, the informants describe their own position as being balanced between two constructed extremes from which they distance themselves. In this way, as in the case of the parents in chapter 8, they discursively construct their own civilised nature by devaluing the ways of life and behavioural forms that compete for legitimacy and threaten to devalue their own behaviour or childrearing methods.

It is also evident that Danish children's institutions project a dominant cultural understanding of the middle position as the most civilised in terms of class. We have registered several narratives and explanatory models in which social background was used to explain, or indeed assume, certain kinds of childrearing and child behaviour. As it is culturally inappropriate to notice or mention class and social hierarchies, in these cases class is rarely referred to in direct terms. Nevertheless, through the euphemism of resources (the healthy 'resource-strong' and the burdened 'resource-weak' parents and children), social distinctions are implicitly communicated. Moreover, it is implicitly indicated that too many resources can also be morally dubious. In this cultural model the middle-class position is the most wholesome and legitimate. This is illustrated by the way in which the wealthy mothers in chapter 8 are acutely aware of the negative perceptions of being busy, neglectful or materialistic, or of spoiling one's child, that are often associated with upper-class families. Similarly, the privileged young people in chapter 7 learn that the morally defensible position lies in between the uncivilised lower classes and the immoral rich. In chapter 6, the teachers also expect that the behaviour of ethnic minority boys from low-income families is caused by their 'resource-weak' families and describe these families as the direct opposite of a civilised family because the parents are thought to spoil or hit their children, and to neglect their duties to care for their sons. In spite of a strong focus on equality, and a widespread social awareness of unequal opportunities, the middle class is viewed as morally superior to other classes. This reflects a power balance between social groups established in Danish society since the Second World War. In this period the middle class has expanded a great deal, becoming culturally dominant (not least as professionals in welfare institutions) and is thus able to present both lower and higher classes as morally suspicious.

This exemplifies, yet again, how civilising ideals and efforts systematically draw upon contrasts. Because the civilised position is always relative, the demarcation of categories is key. The contrasts that make sense and the balances that appear meaningful and legitimate will of course vary historically and culturally. But it stands as a general aspect of civilising dynamics that civilised ideals are constructed, formulated and gain acceptance in opposition to categories, behaviours and social forms which are depicted as uncivilised, animalistic, non-integrated, violent, irrational, uncontrolled or too controlled. The high-status position is a balanced one, presented rhetorically in contrast to extreme forms which it is reasonable to dismiss as inappropriate and uncivilised.

Moulding the Civilised Group

As we have seen in several chapters, what children are taught in the institutions we have studied is that civilised forms of interaction are not only a matter of manners, but above all of relationships. Therefore, working with 'the social' encompasses both the individual child and the group of children. Appeals to be inclusive and reminders that 'everyone should feel comfortable here', that there should 'be room for everyone', that one 'should include others' and not 'leave anyone out' highlight the institutional prioritisation of the community and its social cohesion (see discussion of the rhetorical figure of 'everybody' in Anderson 2008, also referred to in chapter 5). This is also seen in the orchestral work teachers do to organise children's interactions and encourage friendships and bonds across the group. The strong focus on the way children play illustrates particularly well how this priority of the community affects ideals for the child. Being 'good at playing' is a quality that was regularly mentioned in our conversations with parents, pedagogues and teachers. This seems to denote the child's ability to be creative, imaginative, take the initiative, yet also to integrate other children and their ideas in the shared interaction; and expresses a cultural ideal of the independent, free-thinking person, who at the same time engages with others in inclusive and integrative ways. The priority of the group can also be seen in the importance that schools place on cooperation in educational projects and exercises. Here too, the focus is on cultivating a creative and empathic child who listens and is inclusive, while not repressing his/her own wishes. As indicated by phrases like 'he is not good at the community stuff', the formation of well-functioning groups is not only an objective, it is also a benchmark. There are right and wrong ways of being together with others and being 'good at community stuff' is a criterion of evaluation. In this way, 'the social child' is a child who contributes to the well-functioning and inclusive community – though on the terms that the adults at the institution have defined. As we have seen in several chapters, the institutions' own frameworks and routines are also significant in this regard. It is the appointed class, team, or group of children that should function well, not merely because the adults value a harmonious group, but also so that teaching and activities can be conducted in a smooth and non-conflictual way.

One characteristic of the ideal civilised community that is stressed across the institutions is its ability to cope with individual differences, and that people from different backgrounds can interact in a harmonious manner. For example, a sentiment that is often repeated in different variations is: 'you can still be friends, even if you are different from each other' and 'there should be space for all of us'. As we have seen, children's institutions, especially schools, make a point of uniting children from different levels of society, and teachers and parents express a special joy when a class interacts harmoniously despite internal social and ethnic differences. Indeed, it is a stated ambition that institutions should be able to include people from different backgrounds and have an integrative function in order to create social cohesion. There are, however, also limits to the inclusion. Some types of behaviour are so challenging to the standard norms that children who display them – for example by destroying things, being violent, but also by transgressing other people's psychological boundaries – are considered to be 'impossible to integrate' or 'beyond the reach of pedagogical interventions'. These children often end up being moved from the institution for their own sake, but also for the sake of the community. In this way, children are taught about social inclusion, yet they also experience that tolerance has its limits. In short, we can observe a distinction between legitimate differences, which confirm established codes and demonstrate the inclusive character of the community, and illegitimate differences that challenge the social forms and equality required in a civilised community. In the same vein, while institutions celebrate tolerance of differences, in reality these are often treated as a threat to social cohesion, as this is generally perceived to be based on similarity and equality. Based on observations in Danish schools, Anderson shows how mutuality and similarity are articulated, whereas differences tend to be practised implicitly (Anderson 2000:241). She depicts this as 'the social art of acting as if equal' (Anderson 2011). Marianne Gullestad makes a similar point when she points to a preference for similarity and argues that, among Norwegians, it is acceptable to mark social boundaries around oneself and small social groups via different distancing manoeuvres and the creation of what she calls 'symbolic fences' – as long as this is not obviously exclusive and does not undermine the highly valued experience of cohesion despite differences (Gullestad 1992:165, 174, 179). Likewise, in the observed institutions 'the social child' is able to mark boundaries subtly and without aggression, and a school class can be considered to 'be well-functioning', even if some individual children or groups of children do not interact with each other, as long as they do not highlight these differences and as long as the class is not explicitly polarised and thus exposed as an uncivilised community.

As such, communities require a certain level of cohesion and equality, and there is an ongoing task to emphasise that which unites and avoid fragmentation by integrative efforts, but also by establishing the relevant boundaries and balancing the ways in which they are marked. In this, we see the Scandinavian ideal that Gullestad describes as 'equality defined as sameness' (Gullestad 1992:191–5). Equality can be seen as a social form: an interactional practice that should be learned in the children's institutions of the welfare society as well as in other places.

The distinction between non-problematic and problematic ways of marking differences reflects institutional categories. As Anderson puts it: 'exclusion seems to mean exclusion from a group of which one would usually expect to be a member' (2000:157). Thus, excluding someone by referring to institutional divisions – such as groups, rooms, classes, teams, or accepted lines of demarcation such as age or gender – does not undermine the community. This means that a rejection in the form of 'you can't join in because it is actually only the girls who are playing in here' is acceptable, because it is based on a well-established categorical distinction which the pedagogues and teachers also utilise when, for example, they form groups or choose teams. Such categories are endowed with an acceptable exclusivity. Other distinctions are not affirmed and are instead criticised if the staff hear them: for example, those that are personal ('I don't want to play with you'); those that divide categories considered to be a unit (girls who play together often and do not incorporate the other girls in the community are referred to as a 'clique'); or those that undermine the cohesion of the group or stress illegitimate boundaries within it ('we don't want Pakistanis to play with us'). Marking these kinds of differences challenges the ideal of inclusion and also undermines the expected inclusivity of the categories.

Therefore, an implicit but important aspect of the formative work seems to be that the children experience which categories and differentiations are considered to be legitimate and which are perceived as wrong, challenging or undermining of group cohesion (just as it is important for children to learn in which situations this does not apply). Likewise, it is a crucial part of the civilising project that the children learn to reject others and mark differences in appropriate ways. The children are allowed to say 'not right now' or 'no, not now, as we are playing really well' to a child asking to join in a game, and they are allowed to retreat to the exclusive 'cushion room' as described in chapter 4, but not to expel someone aggressively or indeed just explicitly.

When we look at the material as a whole, we are thus able to discern the contours of a specific cultural ideal of the properly civilised person. This is the 'social' individual, who is psychologically balanced and aware of his/her own limits in relation to others. It is someone who is able to adapt without submission, who can interact with different people without 'losing him- or herself'. It is a person who can use his or her imagination and creativity without appearing to be selfishly concerned with his or her own interests and at the same time be a part of and contribute to the development of the harmonious community by employing the inclusive and acceptable exclusive practices which this entails. Furthermore, it is a person who can express him- or herself, but not at the expense of others; rather, he or she should possess an almost physical sense of other people's psychological boundaries, and an awareness of the present social community. And last, it is someone who tolerates differences, yet stresses similarities in order to maintain harmonious interaction.

The Relationship Between Institution and Society

When the grade 0 teachers in chapter 5 insist that they do not see any difference between teaching children how to be a good human being, a good pupil and a good citizen, they highlight the connection between school and society. Thus, the requirements for social interaction of the community within the school or the kindergarten become a concrete expression of the abstract requirements pertaining to interaction in the closely integrated society outside of the institutions. Peaceful coexistence, selflessness, democratic participation and downplaying class and ethnic differences are concrete pedagogical goals in everyday life as well as ideals for the society that one hopes to create.

As Gilliam describes in chapter 5, communities in institutions function as both models of and models for the broader community in society (cf. Geertz 1993 [1973]). Child and adult communities in institutions are perceived as reflections of the greater community in society, a training ground for learning civilised society's recognised forms of interaction. Thus, institutional communities are not only significant in their own right, they are also a harbinger of the society of the future. Children and their interactions are generally interpreted through a future perspective, which both preconceives a potential developmental trajectory for the individual child and paints a picture of the conditions and future of society. From this point of view, it is understandable that the formative work and efforts to promote community cohesion are such a highly prioritised and consistent task in all the institutions we have studied. It is here that the new generation must learn what it means to be part of a community. At the same time, the family, the kindergarten group, the class and the school all become models for how one should structure and interact within other communities – neighbourhoods and workplaces as well as in the Danish welfare society.

This metonymic relation is seen in the clear prioritisation of inclusion: institutional education is meant to counteract inequality and differences, and children should be raised to participate. 'Inclusion', 'community', 'participation', 'involvement' and 'responsibility' are commonly-used phrases in state policies, municipal educational plans and staff meetings, and the intention to include children in decision-making processes is widespread among both the families and public institutions we have studied. Although we have also observed counter-tendencies, the main goal is still to make the individual child an engaged and integrated participant in society. To 'participate' is to 'do democracy' in a way that links the individual to the national community. From this perspective, enrolling children in societal institutions is a civilising effort to turn everyone into participants in society. Therefore, it becomes especially important to enrol marginalised groups, such as ethnic minorities, into these institutions, while the immigrant parents who choose an ethnic or Muslim 'free school' are seen as endangering the integrated civilised society.

In the first part of this chapter, we described how the welfare state has contributed through children's institutions to the standardisation and establishment of particular norms and categories of understanding. The democratic ideal is a good example. When children's institutions try to mould social communities, this is a concrete way of organising the group of children, and preventing conflict and overt expressions of superiority and dominance. However, it is also a way to socialise the individual child into a particular form of democratic thinking – a societal formation that is thereby naturalised and standardised. As such, democracy becomes an icon of what counts as civilised sociality. On a day-to-day level it stands as an ideal for either small-scale or large-scale social relations, but on a more general level it has the effect of incorporating a specific cultural under-standing of the nature of the state and society.

Like other civilising ideals, the ideal of the democratic community is also constructed through contrast, for example in comparison with societies which do not listen to children or have authoritative educational methods or school systems. While tolerance towards and understanding of other ways of life are highly valued and also practised, in our material there are several instances where the Danish', the 'Christian' or the West are contrasted with people, countries, societal forms and religions that are, for example, portrayed as being violent, despotic and oppressive to children and women. In the material from families and teaching in schools, there are examples of contrasts based on class, ethnicity and religion, whereby the civilised ideal is explicitly compared to groups that are perceived not to master the correct balance in their behaviour, emotional expression or social interactions, or dosage of individual freedom. 'The civilised community' is presented as an equal harmonious community of possibly different, yet like-minded, balanced, democratic and rational people, who both support individual freedom and work for the best interests of the individual and the group. Thus, the focal point of pedagogical efforts seems to be the civilised community – not only as a social form, but also as a moral benchmark for respectable interaction. In this way, the community is both inclusive and marks moral boundaries for who is inside and who does not belong due to their lack of social and moral understanding.

Children's Reactions to the Demands of Civilisation

The families, kindergartens and schools we have studied are generally characterised by a pleasant and 'child friendly' atmosphere. Children and adults interact in informal and generally friendly ways, and children are, as we have described, given much leeway to follow their interests and express their emotions. Moreover, children generally seem to learn to be inclusive and attentive to others. In all the contexts we also find children who do as expected and cooperate with adults. But there are also always children who behave in other ways and express other attitudes, either because their attention and interest is directed towards something else, or because they do not understand the expectations, or because other behavioural norms apply between them, or in outright protest. As we have seen throughout the chapters, and in line with the anthropology and sociology of childhood, children – like all other social actors – respond actively to their surroundings. They do this based on their personal experiences and habituated dispositions, as well as on their own rationales for acting in the social situations of which they are part. Thus, institutional civilising is not a simple process of transmission. Rather, it is the result of 'many single plans and actions of people', as Elias depicted the civilising process (Elias 1994 [1939]:336). Some of these actions are performed by children who actively respond to, incorporate, participate in or oppose the civilising ambitions of their surroundings, though, as the analyses in this book have shown, rarely in unambiguous ways. Moreover, children more or less consciously draw a range of conclusions based on the experiences they gather from patterns in their everyday lives: they interpret and react to the childrearing practices of the adults in order to grasp the social and moral constitution of their world. In our view, including children's actions and reactions to the norms and expectations they meet improves our theoretical understanding of the social processes that influence and result from the civilising endeavours in educational institutions.

We have seen that children are generally aware of the existence of demands and norms, and they generally view adults as the custodians of these norms. Despite the informal interactional style, rules and regulations are part of daily life, though in a rather down-played form. Even our youngest informants talked about what they were 'allowed to do' and 'not allowed to do'; they were aware that their actions are judged and that they, via their actions, manoeuvre in a moral space and a space of varying social statuses. When the children assert themselves in relation to other children by pointing out that they are 'nice', 'quiet' and 'well-behaved', or speak condescendingly about the children who are 'badly behaved' or who 'do things they are not supposed to', this suggests that they also realise that this is a moral space where people can be placed into a human hierarchy of more or less civilised. Similarly, we saw children who actively corrected each other and even used the adults' admonishing phrases to scold or position themselves in relation to others: 'Small voices!', 'you mustn't argue', 'you should be friends'; 'you should tell a grown-up'. Children seem to test these normative statements and see how they work in relation to different others in order to confirm and consolidate their own under-standings, as well as to assert themselves. On the whole, demands and regulations are gently articulated, negotiable and vary from one adult authority to another. Children can easily list rules, such as 'you must not hit other children' or 'you must not shout indoors'. But understanding when a boundary has been transgressed and knowing which pedagogue or teacher appreciates free expression, and which prefers a more disciplined child, are experiences that the child must gain by constantly observing reactions or testing situations. One can see that this is the case when a child has not understood that it is actually regarded unfavourably if he or she is too quiet, or does not understand how lively or joyful he or she is allowed to be, how often he or she may sit on a pedagogue's lap, how loudly he or she may brag about winning at badminton or to what extent he or she is allowed to pee with the door open. Norms for interaction are always socially adapted and, as such, are changeable, even though they are based on certain values and ideals. As shown in several chapters, not all children are aware of these informal yet demanding norms for social interaction. Neither are they all socialised in a way that makes them live up to the standards or want to do so. Some attempt to increase their status among the other children by challenging and transgressing norms instead of conforming to them.

The Paradox of Civilising – Consequences for Categories and Communities

In our empirical material, we can see a clear tendency that children use the institutions' basic norms to position themselves socially and to create alliances within the group of children. Adhering to or transgressing the institutional norms is often central to what children regard as defining social categories such as being a 'girl', 'boy', 'Dane', 'immigrant'. Although many children find strength and a shared identity in doing what the adults say they should do – thereby being popular pupils, the good girls and boys – there is also a tendency to use transgression of the institutional norms and rules for behaviour to create alternative children's communities. In chapter 4, the young people happily recall communities based on daring each other to deviate from the norms (for instance making sandwiches so large that they could not fit in their mouths). In this way, the types of groups and communities that children form do not always correlate to the ones the professionals try to mould and promote. On the contrary, alternative forms of interaction are often consolidated by a shared distancing from the dominant values and power that the adults seem to possess. As discussed in chapters 3, 5 and 6, children sometimes gain status and are united by resistance against the normative requirements they do not master or from which they distance themselves or feel excluded. Pertaining to this, we observed a tendency whereby forms of resistance target the symbols of civilised behaviour with which the children are met – and children often use an exact reversal of the civilised forms when establishing their own social forms. They play with their food and use the toilet as a place to hang out, as Olwig describes; or they shout, swear, fight, tease and exclude other children. They also consider aggression and rough language to be a sign of strength.

In accordance with the understanding of especially young children as uncivilised, many adults tolerate troublemaking and the transgression of boundaries as something naturally childlike, and even as a practice that boys in particular are almost obliged to participate in (Ann A. Ferguson describes 'the good bad boy' as a norm [2001]; see also Gilliam 2009). Olwig shows how kindergarten children take advantage of their status as 'not-yet-civilised' to explore and transgress boundaries. These experiments remain within the framework of what is acceptable, which the pedagogues in turn expand in order to make room for natural and childlike behaviour. As long as the children demonstrate that they understand the boundaries of what is truly challenging and respect the authority of the adults, their actions are treated with lenience. But while day-care institutions can and will tolerate a certain degree of uncivilised behaviour, as children get older schools make different and greater demands with regard to civilised interactions. In their first year of school, children are met with a stronger reaction if they do not do what the teacher says. Teachers are able to accept 'uncivilised' behaviour to some degree in young children, but they attempt to moderate it by using a 'positive approach' until the real process of schooling begins in grade 1. Their lenience and positive approach also seems to depend on the category of children who display the uncivilised behaviour. If the conduct is perceived as a sign of faulty or uncivilised upbringing, the children seem to be met with more concern and civilising measures. As Gilliam describes in chapter 6, in grades 4 and 6, the teachers do not view the 'bilingual boys' disruptive behaviour as natural childishness or typical boyish behaviour. Instead they see it as a sign of failed childrearing in Muslim homes and respond with much firmer discipline than we have seen in the other cases. The teachers regret that they have to employ these tough and illegitimate measures, but find that the boys need it to develop 'social competences' and 'inner control'. It is worth noting here that the boys themselves do not perceive their troublemaking and resistance as being defined by their position as children at school, but rather as an expression of their social category – their identity as 'foreigners', 'immigrants' and 'Muslims', and as resistance against 'the Danes'.

Thus, we see that the individual children, pedagogues and teachers – as well as the categories, norms, tasks, institutional conditions and local circumstances – are significant in terms of how behaviour is perceived, explained and reacted to. In institutions with only ethnic majority children, as in Nordlund School described in chapters 5 and 7, it is the labels of gender, social class and individual circumstances that are drawn upon in explanations of the groups of children who engage in norm-breaking behaviour. The backgrounds of the pedagogues and teachers themselves, and the extent to which they socially and ethnically identify with the children, also seem to be significant in relation to which models of explanation they use to understand why some children resist their formative efforts. Nonetheless, there is a clear pattern that girls and ethnic Danish children from middle- or upper-class backgrounds in particular occupy the civilised category. It is definitely not part of the pedagogical intention that some children should feel more included or correct than others – on the contrary. But the children seem to infer this lesson from the situations and explanations they encounter.

While Bourdieu and Passeron explained a similar pattern in relation to the assessment of skills in the French school of the 1970s (Bourdieu and Passeron 1990 [1977]), we find that the reading of Elias combined with the ethnographic insights of Paul Willis (1977) provide us with a more detailed explanation concerning the processes of distinction and reproduction taking place in educational institutions. Including in the analysis – as Bourdieu and Passeron did not do – the active contribution of children and young people and their various modes of reactions sheds light on the complex ways in which social positioning, institutional ideals and assessments, and various kinds of social categories (not least ethnicity, class, gender) are intertwined in everyday interactions in ways that have significant consequences for the educational and moral outcome for the individual as well as for groups. As we have discussed several places, this can be seen as the result of an implicit paradox within the civilising project. It seems to be a general characteristic that dominant – in Eliasian terms 'established' – groups aim to integrate the groups they perceive as uncivilised in their lifestyles – that is the outsider groups – while simultaneously maintaining their own position as more civilised. When this concurrent inclusion and exclusion is communicated (be it ever so subtly), it often leads to a counter-reaction in the individuals portrayed as not-yet-civilised or simply uncivilised. In the process, the outsiders tend to internalise the moral space in which they are judged, but they also learn to identify themselves with and utilise the position they are assigned within this space (see Fanon 1982 [1952]). As we have shown in the analyses, the intention is to get the children to participate in particular forms of interaction, and to teach them the norms for social interaction. But in doing so, the often middle-class ethnic Danish – and, it should be noted, female – pedagogues and teachers emphasise which acts and attitudes to others cannot be accepted. Some children experience that both their behaviour and they themselves do not measure up. They become the object of civilising offensives and, at the same time, they are told that they do not live up to what is expected of them. Reacting to this, we have observed in kindergartens as well as in schools (see chapters 3 and 6) children who come to identify with the uncivilised image and find alternative strengths in opposing adaptation to the norm. As teachers and pedagogues tend to respond to this with stricter discipline, the ball is set in motion and a counter-cultural form may develop around the category that was targeted by civilising offensives. In this way the youngsters, like Willis's 'lads', play an active part in their own marginalisation (Willis 1977; see also Gilliam 2009, 2015). A pattern of ethnicity, gender and class can be identified in these dynamics. The institutions are part of a national state project, which aims to reproduce and integrate new members in a national community, and to mould them in relation to a civilising ideal that is usually defined by the ethnic majority and the classes that possess a large amount of cultural capital. Thus we see how the inclusive pedagogy of Danish children's institutions, despite its good intentions, also tends to reproduce specific norms of interactions and communication with the consequence that the middle-class child most often occupies the civilised category.

Civilising Between Private and Public Institutions

In this book, we have regarded civilising as both an ideal and a practice, a goal and a process. We have viewed civilising projects in a power perspective – as ideas about what is 'proper', which are driven by shifts in human figurations; and we have viewed them in the social balances between different groups with varying degrees of impact and influence. We argue that perceptions of civilised conduct – reflecting relations of dominance – are established and upheld not least through the daily work of the childrearing institutions in society. This applies in particular to welfare societies like Denmark, which are highly organised into a range of formal institutions with the prime task of educating and ensuring peaceful coexistence between citizens. Although the family and educational institutions such as day-care institutions and schools are normally classified as two separate social domains, an approach involving the notion of civilising enables us to find overlapping interests and objectives. We have demonstrated that ideals about peaceful interaction, inclusion, equality, cooperation, self-control, balance, community and democratic participation recur in our material across the divide between state-run and autonomous institutions, and that they blur the separation between the private and public spheres. In this sense we regard the study as a cultural analysis pointing out the dominant norms and values in Danish society expressed and disseminated through central institutions as part of wider social power dynamics.

However, the similarities and connections we have noted between norms in public institutions and in the private sphere should be read with the reservation that we have only systematically studied an affluent segment of parents. Among this segment, the extent to which parents concur with the formative work that is conducted in institutions is striking. They seem to both agree to entrust their children to the institutions' project, and to contribute in precisely defined ways, for example by supporting shared arrangements and activities in kindergarten, in the school class and in other extra-curricular organisations such as horse-riding clubs and Scouts meetings (see chapter 8). However, though we have not studied less privileged parents in nearly the same detail, they are part of our empirical material as well. In all of our ethnographic fieldwork we have talked with, interviewed, heard about and observed less privileged parents. Most of them tend to share the norms and ambitions of the institutions' civilising project, but some express that they cannot cope with all of the institutional expectations, while a minority express frustration with the pedagogues and teachers, and disagree with their corrections of the children's behaviour or their assessments of the children (Bundgaard and Gulløv 2007, 2008a; Gilliam 2009). Thus, parents' reactions can take another form among groups of parents whose background differs from that of the teachers or pedagogues, or in cases where parents – and this also happens to middle- and upper-class parents – often encounter negative reactions or expectations. However, although the case of the ethnic minority parents in chapter 6, who were criticised for not giving priority to their children's contribution to the community, shows that it might not be generally shared, the elaborate ideal of 'the social child' seems to be familiar to and accepted by most of the parents in our studies.

As such, the analyses in this book do not reveal any severe discrepancies or tensions between the private and public spheres. On the contrary, they indicate an interconnection between domains and a consistency in values that is sustained by the fact that children move between them and link them together. For example, it is clear in Bach's analyses that the efforts to integrate children in harmonious social groups in day-care institutions, schools and extra-curricular activities involve entire families, who both willingly adapt and define their actions and childrearing values in relation to the institutional expectations. In the other institutions studied, parents are also involved in institutional life. They invite children home, they engage in and arrange social activities for the class or groups of children, and they exchange views and advice with each other as well as with the professionals. In this way, the different societal spheres are continuously linked together via daily interactions between individuals who move around and exchange values and priorities with each other. Thus, the work of institutions is both aligned with and related to actual parents and children who participate on a daily basis. The formative objective is aimed at teaching both the individual child and his/her parents a particular sense of the routines, requirements and performative practices of various social contexts. At the same time, the formative work is oriented towards social integration, linking different spheres via the exchange of children. Children pass from their family to a day-care institution and then to a school; from one educational setting to the next, and from a formal, obligatory institutional system to the extra-curricular organisations' leisure activities. Via their actions and interpretations, the children establish connections between one place and the next. Thus, children are not only objects of exchange between different, separate institutions; they also create cohesion symbolically (as a category) and concretely (as actors) through their practical participation in different institutions. So one can argue that the integrative development of the welfare society is partly driven by the children who, when participating in different societal spheres, must be given space and learn to be like and interact with others in proper ways. In this way, the focus on children adds to our knowledge of the integrative dynamics of a welfare state society.

Both as actors and as symbols, children also have a key role in the quest for social positions. For example, parents seem to be acutely aware that their parenting skills and social reputations are judged in relation to how they raise their children, and how their children behave in institutions and in the civic space. In this way, children reflect their parents' civilised status and are therefore a kind of walking and – (as they are segregated from their parents in children's institutions throughout most of the day) – potentially uncontrollable marker of distinction. However, their behaviour in public is also interpreted as an expression of the civilised character of the institutional and national communities. This symbolic position gives them a particular role in the relationship between the state, civil society and the private sphere, and also partially explains why working with their behaviour receives so much attention and effort, and why this work is so closely coordinated by state institutions. Investigating children's actions and possibilities, their understandings and the perceptions and reaction they are met with, as well as the symbolic meanings attributed to them, thus reveals not only values and norms but also processes of transmission, reproduction, cohesion, social distinctions and mobility.

Lessons of Social Hierarchies

As we describe above, the civilising projects of Danish children's institutions reflect widespread and dominant cultural understandings about appropriate interaction, the respectable individual and the good society. Throughout the book, we have elucidated how these ideas are expressed in the different types of institutions, and how various actors – professionals, parents and children – affect and are affected by specific forms of interaction and communities. Looking at the material as a whole, it is, however, clear that, though there may be variations in the individual childrearer's ideals and approaches, most children pass through a rather uniform childrearing system. The prioritisation of harmonious social communities crosses institutional divides; therefore, despite the wide variety of institutional tasks, it is reasonable to talk about a coordinated civilising effort mirroring central cultural values of the Danish welfare society.

This does not mean, however, that the civilising projects manifest themselves consistently or are experienced in the same way by all children. As we have demonstrated, pedagogical initiatives can be perceived in a different way than intended, and can have consequences other than those that are anticipated. For example, the great emphasis on social consideration and harmonious groups does not mean that the pedagogical outcome can be said to be unequivocally inclusive. Children may draw different conclusions to those that were intended, and may experience that distinctions are an important aspect of everyday institutional interactions, despite the rhetoric of inclusion.

Children learn that some categories and communities are open and inclusive and others are not, and that they can comment on and mark some differences but not others. They are taught what it entails to be part of a well-functioning social group, and how they should be tolerant and inclusive. However, they also experience that children who continuously break the norms or prefer to engage outside the established groups of the institutional community raise concerns and are met with various measures (scolding and firm regulations, consultations with child experts, and sometimes removal to other institutional settings). They come to understand that behaviour is continuously assessed in relation to moral standards; that despite the inclusiveness and the value of tolerance and equality, there are different kinds of people, and some are less acceptable and rank lower in social and moral hierarchies, and, not least, that they themselves belong among some of these kinds of peoples and not others. Our analyses show that some children feel that they fulfil the expected forms of behaviour and interaction while others do not; and that they often associate this with their affiliation with various social categories, such as age, gender, ethnicity, class and religion, even though they also experience that such distinctions should not be marked.

As we have described, the civilised ideal is most often described through contrasts, and thereby through pinpointing who and what is uncivilised. In institutional interactions, this has social consequences. Some children come to 'occupy' the civilised position, so to speak, while others take on the role of the 'uncivilised' and define their social relations and categories accordingly, hereby achieving an alternative status via the inversion of the civilising ideals. In this indirect way, we see that childrearing institutions are significant to children's self-perception and ideas about what is normal, proper and right, their participation in communities, expectations about the educational system – and, in a broader perspective, their under-standing of the social order of society. People's experiences of these early communities remain with them, and teach them how to recognise and create new associates and communities, distance themselves from behaviour that challenges the harmony of the community, cope with differences and reject others in appropriate ways. These experiences may also teach them to avoid communities or contexts that seem too different, where the ideal of equality cannot be upheld, or where they have the uncomfortable or even shameful experience of overt expressions of either superiority or inferiority (Gullestad 1992; Wouters 2004). In other words, children's institutions, and not least the practical conditions to which they have to adapt, influence what it means to be civilised; that is, the moral order that classifies people in relation to each other and the behaviours associated with it. As discussed in further detail in chapters 1, 2 and 5, this influence is best understood as a result of a historical and ongoing dialectic between the social norms of children's institutions of the welfare state and Danish society. As generations of Danish citizens have passed through nurseries, kindergartens and schools, the kind of behaviour and social forms that are needed as well as celebrated as civilised come to influence the way they perceive proper conduct and their 'models for' appropriate ways of acting in groups and organising society. At the same time, the institutions mould the children and their communities with reference to cultural 'models of' the good civilised society, which they carry with them from broader society (cf. Geertz 1993 [1973]; see chapter

5). We will thus argue that children's institutions and Danish society shape each other by a continuous exchange of social norms and forms, and that the dominant social norms that people live by in Danish society in a sense have 'institutional' traits. We need further studies to assess whether this is a broader characteristic of welfare state societies in which children are brought up and educated in institutional contexts demanding adaptation to tight-knit groups and institutional structures.

The Exclusiveness of Being Equal

As shown throughout the chapters of this book, children's institutions are important not only for the individual child's appropriation of fundamental cultural values, norms and categories, but also for the social and cultural order of society. By means of the institutions, specific understandings of interactional norms, handling of conflicts, modes of expression and social categories have been established and propagated as the obvious social order. Judging from the interactional forms and attitudes and understandings of children in early childcare and schools, and the relatively equal, peaceful and democratic nature of Danish society, they have been quite successful. In a way one could say that institutions for children have been key to the stability, integration and sense of community in Danish society.

Yet as we have pointed out, the institutionalised moral order also has consequences for perceptions of distinctions and deviances, and the handling and reproduction of inequality. As Gullestad remarks in her discussion of Norwegian society, symbolic boundaries between social units (individuals, groups and even nation-states) have become more important in contemporary open society, in order to ensure internal sameness between those belonging to the same category. From this perspective, the integrating measures of children's institutions may lead to a reinforcement of 'invisible fences' separating into distinct categories those who do not appear to be of the same kind (Gullestad 2002:45–63). In a paradoxical way, the ideal of equality may in fact lead to a reinforced though subtle marking of boundaries keeping at a distance those not familiar with or not sharing the same understandings.

This dynamic is particularly pertinent when it comes to institutional organs of the welfare state, commissioned to maintain social stability by means of conformity and standardisation. The more vigorous the endeavour to uphold specific understandings of civilised life, the more exclusive and distinctive it also risks being. This is the case when individual children who do not live up to the expected requirements are met with more forceful interventions and, at times, with subtle modes of exclusion. However, it is also the case in relation to entire social groups being targeted in order to make them adapt to the moral and social order. In order to keep up the cultural norms of the civilised individual and community, people who challenge this – ironically by making it impossible to uphold the image of equality, acceptance of differences and integrated harmonious interaction – tend to be kept out. Thus, despite Danish society's generally tolerant and democratic character, it is not surprising that it raises its border barriers towards refugees and immigrants in order to 'protect the welfare society'. Such protective measures and 'civilising offensives' (van Krieken 1999; Powell 2013) are often part of a negative spiral where transgressions of norms are met with mistrust and interventions, leading to more mistrust, counter-reactions and polarisations. When such dynamics become integrated in the operation of state institutions, the result may be a decivilising process eroding the very trust that the civilised welfare society is based on.

Civilising Institutions and Decivilising Tendencies

When considering current public debate and the political statements of recent years, it seems that the understandings of civilised conduct and social values that we have identified in our empirical material are under considerable pressure. Inclusive ideals and efforts to develop harmonious and tolerant communities are challenged by the increasing focus on optimising individual competences, and professionally and culturally preparing individuals for an era characterised by individualisation, competition and globalisation, which we described in chapter 2. This can be seen, for instance, when political initiatives seek to downscale unstructured play in order to give more time for formal teaching in day-care institutions, establish special placements for gifted children, and introduce formalised methods for teaching children social skills. Yet, rather than regarding such measures as an erosion of the hitherto well-established understanding of the task of children's institutions to ensure well-functioning inclusive communities, these tendencies could also be interpreted as efforts to sustain this civilising project, and thus as part of continuous yet now more forceful efforts to maintain the civilised Danish society, which is currently perceived as being challenged by shifts in global power balances. Instead of interpreting these tendencies either in the light of an erosive process of globalisation or as the result of an almost omnipresent movement of 'neo-liberalism', we consider it important to recognise the civilising endeavours involved in contemporary developments: they reflect enhanced efforts by politicians and dominant groups to stabilise social order and moral ideals through civilising projects. Following this line of thought, the faith that welfare institutions can ensure the civilising of the up-coming generation as well as the social cohesion of society has not declined. On the contrary, many political initiatives and regulations seem to address a perceived need to strengthen children's social conduct and commitment through enhanced efforts by children's institutions as well as by parents. From this perspective, the increased attempts to get children into public children's institutions from an early age and the increased efforts to formalise the work with children's skills, knowledge, interactions and expressions can be seen as an intensified civilising project directed at all children, yet in particular concerned with those perceived as positioned at the edge of the civilised community. It takes the form of clear-cut civilising offensives when directed at groups with the least educational, cultural and economic capital – especially 'outsiders' such as refugees and immigrant children and their parents.

Thus, rather than witnessing radically new political agendas or regarding the role of the welfare state as played out, we might see in this a continuous societal effort to make children conform to social expectations and develop an emotional identification with one another, with the institutional project and, in a longer perspective, with society as a whole. What has changed in recent years is not the ambition and civilising ideals. But power balances within Danish society have shifted, granting the – never absent – criticism and mistrust of the child-centred pedagogical approach more voice. Though the norms of the social child and the inclusive community, and the approach of gradually incorporating these norms in the child through careful guidance are, as shown in this book, still widespread, concern has been raised that this approach does not work for all children or all groups; that some children need things spelt out and formalised in a more structured manner. Likewise, we see more mistrust in the ability of pedagogues, teachers and parents to do the required formative work – resulting in demands for documentation and formalised plans. And, finally, the implementation of pupil plans, goal-oriented teaching, standardised pedagogical methods and other formats for the teaching and assessment of individual conduct and social competences show a tendency towards a formalisation of hitherto informal interactional forms, and much more detailed attention to and regulation of institutional civilising projects.

Although Danish society is generally characterised by prosperity, a high level of integration and trust and a low level of violence, the fear of disintegration, economic decline and violence has surged with the prospect of increased immigration, global competition, terror and a more polarised world. This seems to have augmented pre-emptive and regulatory measures, leading to a demand for more external means of control. In contrast to the civilising efforts that characterised the post-war period, as described in chapter 2, a strong, regulative state, national sentiments and formalised measures seem to have ceased to be regarded as a threat to civilised society or to the possibilities for free expression. On the contrary, in contemporary Danish society the welfare state tends to attempt to ensure social stability and civilised conduct in increasingly authoritative ways. Though the civilising project has not lost its strength, this might indicate what Elias described as a decivilising spurt, as trust in the civilised behaviour and predictability of others has somewhat decreased, while regulation, control, surveillance and nationalism have gained ground (Elias 1994 [1939], 1996). Only time will tell whether this is just a minor fluctuation or if what we are seeing is a shift in the balance between self-constraints and external controls, and thus an evolving change in the civilising norms of Danish society and in the tasks and efforts of Danish children's institutions.

Notes

Introduction

1. We have chosen to use a translation of the Danish emic term '*pædagoger*' for the child professionals who work in the nurseries and kindergartens, to stress that these have a special pedagogical training and are distinguished from teachers working in schools.
2. Apart from *Folkeskolen*, which are funded and governed by the state, parents can choose publicly subsidised private or independent schools (so-called 'free schools') established by parents and teachers usually on the basis of specific educational or religious ideas (see chapter 2).
3. To avoid the connotations of a 'higher stage' and stress our focus on normative aims, practices and processes, we mainly use the term 'civilising' instead of 'civilisation'.
4. All persons and institutions are anonymised; any proper names used are pseudonyms.
5. Direct quotes from the empirical material are in quotation marks; these are often single words or phrases that came up repeatedly.

1 On Civilising: a Perspective on Childrearing, Conduct and Distinctions

1. In spite of the definite form here, this is not one single process but many processes that, over the centuries, have resulted in contemporary understandings of what characterises civilised behaviour.
2. Bourdieu elaborated Elias's work through analyses of the role of the king and the state's monopolisation of a broad range of capitals, such as cultural capital redistributed through educational institutions (Bourdieu 1994, 2004).
3. The concept of habitus plays an important role in Elias's theory. The concept denotes a taken-for-granted way of thinking, perceiving and acting; it refers to embedded dispositions for interpreting situations and for acting. As noted, Elias's use of this term is more or less parallel to Pierre Bourdieu's use of it in subsequent work (Paulle et al. 2011).
4. As our aim is not to make a full presentation of Elias's work, we will not go into further details about the theoretical scientific sources of inspiration for Elias's theory, which include Max Weber, Emile Durkheim, Sigmund Freud and Karl Mannheim. For an expanded description of this, we refer to van Krieken (1998) and Mennell and Goudsblom (1998).

5. In this case, 'strategic' does not necessarily mean purposeful targeted action; rather, it refers to behaviour that is driven by a habituated practical sense of what is socially important (Bourdieu 1977).

6. Elias does not expand upon this concept as much as Bourdieu, but they both attempt to avoid an analytical separation of the individual and society, actor and structure as distinct or even opposed entities. Although Bourdieu has shown that Elias inspired him in many respects, his concept of habitus was probably developed independently of Elias (Mennell and Goudsblom 1998:43, note 44).

7. Note that not all groups are subject to civilising efforts. In all societies, there are groups that fall outside of civilising efforts because they are external to the classificatory order of the inhabitants. As we briefly describe in the final chapter, welfare states are principally characterised by an inclusion of all citizens in the human order (thereby making them the object of civilising projects). Nevertheless, even in these societies, there are groups that are in fact outsiders, such as asylum seekers, people who have been granted leave to remain and certain groups of addicts and homeless people.

2   Society's Children: Institutionalisation and Changing Perceptions of Children and Upbringing

1. Cultural radicalism was an intellectual, modernist and critical cultural-political movement, inspired by the ideas of the Danish scholar and literature critic Georg Brandes. It held an understanding that enlightenment and reason were the route to individual emancipation and empowerment (of women, children and workers, for example) and thus the development of society.

3   Civilising the Youngest: an Ambiguous Endeavour

1. See: Ehn (1983); Åm (1992); Andersen and Kampmann (1996); Gulløv (1999); Nielsen, R.D. (2001); Nielsen H.W. (2001); Rasmussen and Smith (2001); Ellegaard (2004); Palludan (2005); Markstrøm (2005); Bundgaard and Gulløv (2008a, 2008b); Karrebæk (2009); Seland (2009); Larsen (2010).

2. My translation of the Danish swearwords: *pikslikker, røvhul, lort, lortespasser, kusse, jeg smadrer dig.*

3. In the present context, I do not have the space to discuss why the majority of the children who end up in a position of resistance are boys from ethnic minority groups. I refer to chapter 6, where Gilliam shows that it is no coincidence. The opposition is a reaction to an unequal power position, either in the specific relation or structurally on a societal level. In its collective form, the opposition can generate a sense of coherence, which is nourished by the rejection of the perceived requirements or symbols of dominance (see discussion by Willis 1977; Ferguson 2001; Youdell 2003; Gilliam 2009; and the discussion in chapter 6).

Even if the social groupings have a much more volatile and transient nature in the kindergartens than in institutions for older children, it is observable that even among these quite young children, oppositional coherence is stimulated by a collective rejection of or challenge to those behavioural requirements which the institution primarily emphasises, that is, adherence to civilised virtues.

4   The Not-Yet-Civilised: Negotiating the Kindergarten's Civilising Project

1. This chapter is a revised version of an article published in *Social Analysis* 55(2):121–41, 2011.
2. In a Scandinavian context, Gullestad (1997b:203) has related these notions to an important shift in the social role of children. Whereas formerly children were brought up to be obedient – and useful to their parents – they are now expected to find their true authentic selves, in other words to 'be themselves' as children. Gullestad links the emergence of this ideology to the need for flexibility and creativity in the modern economic system.
3. Rasmussen and Smidt's study describes similar rules and structures (see, for example, 2001:152, 160).
4. This phrase is an abbreviation of '*vær så god*' – 'be so good'.
5. This phrase can be translated loosely as 'I hope the meal agreed with you.' Both *værsgo* and *velbekomme* are commonly used, especially when having guests for dinner.

5   Social Children and Good Classes: Moulding Civilised Communities in the First Year of School

1. Apart from the children who attend *folkeskoler*, 16 per cent of children go to state-subsidised and -inspected 'free schools' or private schools (see chapter 1), and the remaining children go to various youth schools and special needs schools.
2. Of the young people who finished ninth grade in 2014, 93 per cent were expected to complete a 2–3 year youth education, and 62 per cent a further education of 3–5 years duration (Undervisningsministeriet 2014; Uddannelses- og Forskningsministeriet 2015).
3. Second Step is an American programme developed to teach children empathy, anger management and problem-solving techniques. It has been adapted to the Danish context by the Centre for Social and Emotional Learning and is called 'Trin for Trin'.
4. Since the most recent school reform in 2014, the average school day for children in grade 0 has been extended to 2 p.m.

5. It is difficult to assess the relation between psychological diagnoses and the high demands placed on pupils in terms of their social adaptation at school. However, it is interesting to note that several of the diagnosed pupils at Nordlund School go without medication during school holidays. According to their parents, they do fine without it, but the teachers demand that they go back on medication when they return to school, in order for them to adapt to the daily routines of school life.

6   The Impossible Bilingual Boys: Civilising Efforts and Oppositional Forms in a Multi-ethnic Class

1. 'Giraffe language' was developed by Marshall B. Rosenberg as a form of communication and approach to conflicts intended to avoid an escalation of the conflict (Rosenberg 1999).

7   The Decent Citizens: Lessons on Moral Superiority and the Immorality of Wealth in a Class of Privileged Youth

1. Continuation school (in Danish *'efterskole'*) is a boarding school for pupils in the 8th to 10th grades which offers lessons in the regular school subjects as well as alternative subjects and activities such as sports, art or outdoor activities. It is often an option for pupils who want to postpone upper secondary education or need to improve their academic skills.
2. The conversations here are represented as closely to the original dialogues as possible. However, since they are recorded by hand and not digitally, not all formulations are presented verbatim and not all statements are included.

9   Civilising Institutions: Cultural Norms and Social Consequences

1. The political desire to 'clean up' the ghettos and interfere in how people live in them is an expression of the pronounced civilising ambition of the Danish welfare state. However, this ambition does not involve all groups. For example, the lack of interest in the lives of asylum seekers in asylum centres reflects the way they are not perceived as part of society in the same way as others. Indeed, they are almost considered to be outside the category of fellow human beings.

References

Aftaletekst om skolereform (2013) Aftale mellem regeringen (Socialdemokraterne, Radikale Venstre og Socialistisk Folkeparti), Venstre og Dansk Folkeparti om et fagligt løft af folkeskolen. http://www.kl.dk/ImageVault/Images/id_62271/scope_0/ImageVaultHandler.aspx

Andersen, P.Ø. and J. Kampmann (1996) *Børns legekultur*. København: Gyldendal.

Anderson, S. (2000) *I en klasse for sig*. København: Nordisk Forlag.

Anderson, S. (2008) *Civil Sociality, Children, Sport, and Cultural Policy in Denmark*. Charlotte, NC: Information Age Publishing.

Anderson, S. (2011) 'Civil sociality and childhood education'. In: B.A.U. Levinson (ed.) *Blackwell Companion to Anthropology of Education*. Malden, MA: Wiley-Blackwell.

Ariès, P. (1962) *Centuries of Childhood: A Social History of Family Life*. New York: Vintage Books.

Augé, M. (1995) *Non-places: Introduction to an Anthropology of Supermodernity*. London: Verso.

Åm, E. (1992) *På jakt etter barneperspektivet*. Oslo: Universitetsforlaget.

Bach, D. (2014) 'Parenting among wealthy Danish families: a concerted civilising process'. *Ethnography and Education* 9(2): 224–37.

Bach, D. (2015) *Overskudsfamilier: Om opdragelse, identitet og klasse blandt velstående familier i Nordsjælland*. Aarhus: Aarhus Universitetsforlag.

Bauer, M. and K. Borg (1986 [1976]) *Den skjulte læreplan*. København: Unge Pædagoger.

Bayer, S. and J.E. Kristensen (2015) *Pædagogprofessionens historie og aktualitet*, Bind 1 and 2. Copenhagen: U-Press.

Berger, P. and T. Luckmann (1966) *The Social Construction of Reality*. London: Penguin.

Billig, M. (1995) *Banal Nationalism*. London: Sage.

Borchorst, A. (2000) 'Den danske børnepasningsmodel – kontinuitet og forandring'. *Arbejderhistorie* 4: 55–70.

Borchorst, A. (2005) 'Nøglen i de rigtige hænder. Lov om børne- og ungdomsforsorg 1964'. In: J.H. Petersen and K. Petersen (eds) *13 reformer af den danske velfærdsstat*. Odense: Syddansk Universitetsforlag.

Bourdieu, P. (1977) *Outline of a Theory of Practice*. Cambridge: Cambridge University Press.

Bourdieu, P. (1984) *Distinction: A Social Critique of the Judgement of Taste*. New York: Routledge.

Bourdieu, P. (1986) 'The forms of capital'. In: J.G. Richardson (ed.) *Handbook of Theory and Research for the Sociology of Education*. New York: Greenwood Press.

Bourdieu, P. (1987) 'What makes a social class: on the theoretical and practical existence of groups'. *Berkeley Journal of Sociology* 32: 1–17.

Bourdieu, P. (1994) 'Rethinking the state: genesis and structure of the bureaucratic field'. *Sociological Theory* 12(1): 1–18.

Bourdieu, P. (2004) 'From the king's house to the reason of state: a model of the genesis of the bureaucratic field'. *Constellations* 11(1): 1–16.

Bourdieu, P. and J.-C. Passeron (1990 [1977]) *Reproduction in Education, Society and Culture.* London: Sage.

Bourdieu, P. and L. Wacquant (1992) *An Invitation to Reflexive Sociology.* Chicago: University of Chicago Press.

Bowles, S. and H. Gintis (1976) *Schooling in Capitalist America.* New York: Basic Books.

Bruun, M.H., G.S. Jakobsen and S. Krøijer (2011) 'The concern for sociality: practicing equality and hierarchy in Denmark'. *Social Analysis* 55(2): 1–19.

Bundgaard, H. and E. Gulløv (2007) 'Children of different categories: educational practice and the production of difference in Danish day-care institutions'. *Journal of Ethnic and Migration Studies* 32(1): 144–55.

Bundgaard, H. and E. Gulløv (2008a) 'Targeting immigrant children: disciplinary rationales in Danish pre-schools'. In: N. Dyck (ed.) *Exploring Regimes of Discipline: The Dynamics of Restraint.* New York: Berghahn.

Bundgaard, H. and E. Gulløv (2008b) *Forskel og fællesskab. Minoritetsbørn i daginstitution.* København: Hans Reitzels Forlag.

Carsten, J. (2000) 'Introduction: cultures of relatedness'. In: J. Carsten (ed.) *Cultures of Relatedness: New Approaches to the Study of Kinship.* Cambridge: Cambridge University Press.

Carsten, J. (2004) *After Kinship.* Cambridge: Cambridge University Press.

Coninck-Smith, N. de (2002) *Skolen, lærerne, eleverne og forældrene. 10 kapitler af den danske folkeskoles historie i det 19. og 20. århundrede.* Aarhus: Forlaget Klim.

Coninck-Smith, N. de, L.R. Rasmussen and I. Vyff (2015) *Da skolen blev alles. Tiden efter 1970. Dansk skolehistorie bind 5.* Aarhus: Aarhus University Press.

Connell, R.W. (2000) 'Cool guys, swots and wimps'. In: *The Men and the Boys.* Cambridge: Polity Press.

Connell, R.W., G.W. Dowsett, S. Kessler and D.J. Ashenden (2000 [1981]) 'Class and gender dynamics in a ruling-class school'. In: B.A.U. Levinson, M. Eisenhart, M. Foster, A.E. Fox and M. Sutton (eds) *Schooling the Symbolic Animal: Social and Cultural Dimensions of Education.* Lanham, MD: Rowman & Littlefield.

Connolly, P. (1998) *Racism, Gender Identities and Young Children: Social Relations in a Multi-ethnic, Inner-city Primary School.* London: Routledge.

Corsaro, W. (1997) *The Sociology of Childhood.* Thousand Oaks, CA: Pine Forge Press.

Dale, R. (1977) 'Implications of the rediscovery of the hidden curriculum for the sociology of teaching'. In: D. Gleeson (ed.) *Identity and Structure: Issues in the Sociology of Education.* Driffield: Nafferton Books.

Danish School Act 1814.

Dannesboe, K.I. (2009) 'Skoletasker og skolebørn. Når skole gøres fraværende og nærværende i socio-materielle sammenviklinger i børns hverdagsliv'. *Nordnytt. Nordisk tidskrift for etnologi og folkloristik* 106/7: 63–76.

Dannesboe, K.I, N. Kryger, C. Palludan and B. Ravn (2012) *Hvem sagde samarbejde? Et hverdagslivsstudie af skole–hjem relationer.* Aarhus: Aarhus Universitetsforlag.

Dencik, L. (1989) 'Growing up in the post-modern age: on the child's situation in the modern family, and on the position of the family in the modern welfare state'. *Acta Sociologica* 32(2): 155–80.

Dolan, P. (2010) 'Space, time and the constitution of subjectivity: comparing Elias and Foucault'. *Foucault Studies* 8: 8–27.

Donzelot, J. (1979) *The Policing of Families.* New York: Pantheon.

Douglas, M. (1966) *Purity and Danger.* London: Routledge & Kegan Paul.

Douglas, M. (1986) *How Institutions Think.* Syracuse, NY: Syracuse University Press.

Dunning, E. and S. Mennell (1998) 'Elias on Germany, Nazism and the Holocaust: on the balance between "civilizing" and "decivilizing" trends in the social development of Western Europe'. *British Journal of Sociology* 49(3): 339–57.

Durkheim, E. (1975 [1922]) *Opdragelse, uddannelse og sociologi. En bog om opdragelsens og uddannelsens funktion i samfundet.* København: Finn Suenson Forlag.

Ehn, B. (1983) *Ska vi leka tigar?* Stockholm: Liber Press.

Elias, N. (1970) *What Is Sociology?* New York: Columbia University Press.

Elias, N. (1992) *Time: An Essay.* Oxford: Blackwell.

Elias, N. (1994 [1939]) *The Civilizing Process.* Oxford: Blackwell.

Elias, N. (1994 [1977]) 'Introduction: a theoretical essay on established and outsider relations'. In: N. Elias and J.L. Scotson, *The Established and the Outsiders.* London: Sage.

Elias, N. (1996 [1989]) *The Germans: Power Struggles and the Development of Habitus in the Nineteenth and Twentieth Centuries.* Cambridge: Polity.

Elias, N. (1998a) 'The civilizing of parents'. In: J. Goudsblom and S. Mennell (eds) *The Norbert Elias Reader.* Oxford: Blackwell.

Elias, N. (1998b) 'Informalization and the civilizing process'. In: J. Goudsblom and S. Mennell (eds) *The Norbert Elias Reader.* Oxford: Blackwell.

Ellegaard, T. (2004) *Et godt børnehavebarn? Daginstitutioners kompetencekrav, og hvordan børn med forskellig social baggrund håndterer dem.* Doctoral thesis, Department of Psychology. Roskilde University.

Engebrigtsen, A.I. (2006) 'Norbert Elias: Makt, skam og sivilisering – Somaliere i eksil og det norske samfunnet'. *Tidsskrift for samfunnsforskning* 47(1): 109–23.

Epstein, D., J. Elwood, V. Hey and J. Maw (eds) (1998) *Failing Boys? Issues in Gender and Achievement.* Buckingham: Open University Press.

Faber, S.T. (2008) *På jagt efter klasse.* Doctoral thesis, Department of Sociology and Social Work, Aalborg University.

Faber, S.T., A. Prieur, L. Rosenlund and J. Skjøtt-Larsen (2012) *Det skjulte klassesamfund.* Aarhus: Aarhus University Press.

Faircloth, C. (2008) 'Imagined futures and limited presents: engaging parenting and inequality in contemporary North America'. Paper presented at American Anthropological Association conference, San Francisco.

Fanon, F. (1982 [1952]) *Black Skin, White Masks*. New York: Grove Press.

Ferguson, A.A. (2001) *Bad Boys: Public Schools in the Making of Black Masculinity*. Michigan: University of Michigan Press.

Fordham, S. and J.U. Ogbu (1986) 'Black students' school success: coping with the "burden of 'acting white'"'. *Urban Review* 18(3): 176–205.

Fortes, M. (1984) 'Age, generation, and social structure'. In: D.I. Kertzer and J. Keith (eds) *Age and Anthropological Theory*. Ithaca, NY: Cornell University Press.

Foucault, M. (1972a) *The Archaeology of Knowledge*. London: Tavistock.

Foucault, M. (1972b) 'The politics of health in the eighteenth century'. In: *Power/Knowledge: Selected Interviews and Other Writings, 1972–1977*. New York: Pantheon.

Foucault, M. (1977) *Discipline and Punish: The Birth of the Prison*. New York: Vintage.

Foucault, M. (1980) *Power/Knowledge: Selected Interviews and other Writings 1972–1977*, edited by C. Gordon. New York: Pantheon.

Foucault, M. (1982) 'The subject and power'. In: H.L. Dreyfus and P. Rabinow (eds) *Michel Foucault: Beyond Structuralism and Hermeneutics. With an Afterword by Michel Foucault*. Hemel Hempstead: Harvester Wheatsheaf.

Foucault, M. (1991) 'Governmentality'. In: G. Burchell, C. Gordon and P. Miller *The Foucault Effect: Studies in Governmentality*. Chicago: University of Chicago Press.

Frosh, S., A. Phoenix and R. Pattman (2002) *Young Masculinities: Understanding Boys in Contemporary Society*. Basingstoke: Palgrave.

Frykman, J. and O. Löfgren (1987 [1979]) *Culture Builders: A Historical Anthropology of Middle-class Life*. New Brunswick, NJ: Rutgers University Press.

Furedi, F. (2002) *Forældrefælden: den unødvendige bekymring*. København: Gyldendal Uddannelse.

Gebauer, G. and C. Wulf (2001) *Kroppens sprog. Spil, ritualer, gestik*. København: Gyldendal Uddannelse.

Geertz. C. (1993 [1973]) *The Interpretations of Cultures: Selected Essays*. London: Fontana.

Gilliam, L. (2009) *De umulige børn og det ordentlige menneske. Identitet, ballade og muslimske fællesskaber blandt etniske minoritetsbørn*. Aarhus: Aarhus Universitets Forlag.

Gilliam, L. (2010) 'Den gode vilje og de vilde børn. Civiliseringens paradoks i den danske skole'. In: Skole. *Tidsskriftet Antropologi* 62: 153–74.

Gilliam, L. (2015) 'Being a good, relaxed or exaggerated Muslim: religiosity and masculinity in the social worlds of Danish schools'. In: M. Sedgwick (ed.) *Making European Muslims: Religious Socialization among Young Muslims in Scandinavia and Western Europe*. New York: Routledge.

Gilliam, L. and E. Gulløv (2014) 'Making children social: civilising institutions in a welfare state'. *Human Figurations* 3(1): 1–15.

Gitz-Johansen, T. (2003) 'Representations of ethnicity: how teachers speak about ethnic minority students'. In: D. Beach, T. Gordon and E. Lahelma (eds) *Democratic Education: Ethnographic Challenges*. London: Tufnell Press.

Gitz-Johansen, T. (2006) *Den multikulturelle skole – integration og sortering*. Roskilde: Roskilde Universitetsforlag.

Gjerløff, A.K. and A.F. Jacobsen (2014) *Da skolen blev sat i system 1850–1920*. Dansk skolehistorie bind 3. Aarhus: Aarhus University Press.

Gleeson, D. (1977) *Identity and Structure: Issues in the Sociology of Education*. Driffield: Nafferton Books.

Goffman, E. (1961) *Asylums: Essays on the Social Situation of Mental Patients and Other Inmates*. London: Penguin.

Golden, D. (2004) 'Hugging the teacher: reading bodily practice in an Israeli kindergarten'. *Teachers and Teaching: Theory and Practice* 10(4): 395–40.

Goodman, N. (1978) *Ways of Worldmaking*. Indianapolis: Hackett.

Goody, J. (2002) 'Elias and the anthropological tradition'. *Anthropological Theory* 2(4): 401–12.

Gubrium J.F. and J.A. Holstein (eds) (2001) *Institutional Selves: Troubled Identities in a Postmodern World*. New York: Oxford University Press.

Gullestad, M. (1991) 'The transformation of the Norwegian notion of everyday life'. *American Ethnologist* 18(3).

Gullestad, M. (1992) *The Art of Social Relations: Essays in Culture, Social Actions and Everyday Life in Modern Norway*. Oslo: Scandinavian University Press.

Gullestad, M. (1996) 'From obedience to negotiation: dilemmas in the transmission of values between the generations in Norway'. *Journal of the Royal Anthropological Institute* 2(1): 25–42.

Gullestad, M. (1997a) 'A passion for boundaries: reflections on connections between the everyday lives of children and discourses on the nation in contemporary Norway'. *Childhood* 4(1): 19–42.

Gullestad, M. (1997b) 'From "being of use" to "finding oneself": dilemmas of value transmission between the generations in Norway'. In: M. Gullestad and M. Segalen (eds) *Family and Kinship in Europe*. London: Pinter.

Gullestad, M. (2002) 'Invisible fences: egalitarianism, nationalism and racism'. *Journal of the Royal Anthropological Institute* 8(1) March: 45–63.

Gulløv, E. (1999) *Betydningsdannelse blandt børn*. København: Gyldendal.

Gulløv, E. (2003) 'Creating a natural place for children: an ethnographic study of Danish kindergartens'. In: K.F. Olwig and E. Gulløv (eds) *Children's Places: Cross-cultural Perspectives*. London: Routledge.

Gulløv, E. (2009a) 'Om institutionalisering af børneopdragelse'. In: C. Aabro and S.G. Olesen (eds) *Individ, institution og samfund*. Værløse: Billesø & Baltzer.

Gulløv, E. (2009b) 'Barndommens civilisering: om omgangsformer i institutioner'. In: S. Højlund (ed.) *Barndommens organisering i et institutionsperspektiv*. Roskilde: Roskilde Universitets Forlag.

Gulløv, E. (2012) 'Kindergardens in Denmark: reflections on continuity and change'. In: A.-T. Kjørholt and J. Qvortrup (eds) *The Modern Child and the Flexible Labour Market: Exploring Early Childhood Education and Care*. London: Palgrave Macmillan.

Gulløv, E. and S. Højlund (2005) 'Materialitetetens pædagogiske kraft'. In: K. Larsen (eds) *Arkitektur, krop og læring*. København: Han Reitzels Forlag.

Haavind, H. (2003) 'Masculinity by rule-breaking: cultural contestations in the transitional move from being a child to being a young male'. *NORA* 2(11): 89–100.

Hall, S. (1996) 'Who needs identity?' In: S. Hall and P. du Gay (eds) *Questions of Cultural Identity*. London: Sage.

Hardman, C. (1973) 'Can there be an anthropology of children?' *JASO: Journal of the Anthropological Society in Oxford* 4(2): 85–99.

Hendrick, H. (1990) 'Constructions and reconstructions of British childhood: an interpretive survey, 1800 to the present'. In: A. James and A. Prout (eds) *Constructing and Reconstructing Childhood: Contemporary Issues in the Sociological Study of Childhood*. London: Falmer Press.

Hermann, S. (2007) *Magt og Oplysning. Folkeskolen 1950–2006*. København: Unge Pædagoger.

Hoffmeyer, H. (1978 [1952]) 'Den fri opdragelses ansvar'. In: C.E. Bay (ed.) *Dialog. En antologi*. København: Nordisk Forlag.

Højlund, S. (2002) *Barndomskonstruktioner. På feltarbejde i skole, SFO og på sygehus*. København: Gyldendal.

Højlund, S. (2009) 'Barndommens organisering – i et dansk institutionsperspektiv'. In: S. Højlund (ed.) *Barndommens organisering i et dansk institutionsperspektiv*. Roskilde: Roskilde Universitetsforlag.

Hviid, P. (1999) *'Til lykke' – børneliv i SFO og skole*. København: Danmarks Pædagogiske Institut.

Jackson, P.W. (1986 [1968]) *Life in Classrooms*. New York: Holt, Rinehart & Winston.

James, A. and A. Prout (1997) *Constructing and Reconstructing Childhood*. London: Falmer Press.

James, A., C. Jenks and A. Prout (1998) *Theorising Childhood*. Cambridge: Polity Press.

Jenkins, R. (2004) *Social Identity*. London: Routledge.

Jenkins, R. (2011) *Being Danish: Paradoxes of Identity in Everyday Life*. København: Museum Tusculanums Forlag.

Kampmann, J. (2004) 'Societalization of childhood: new opportunities? new demands?'. In: H. Brembeck, B. Johansson and J. Kampmann (eds) *Beyond the Competent Child: Exploring Contemporary Childhoods in the Nordic Welfare Societies*. Roskilde: Roskilde University Press.

Kampmann, J. (2007) 'Pædagogisk-kritiske og kritisk-pædagogiske traditioner'. In: P.Ø. Andersen, T. Ellegaard and L.-J. Muschinsky (eds) *Klassisk og moderne pædagogisk teori*. København: Hans Reitzels Forlag.

Karrebæk, M.S. (2009) *At blive et børnehavebarn: en minoritetsdrengs sprog, interaktion og deltagelse i børnefællesskabet.* Doctoral thesis, Department of Nordic Studies and Linguistics, University of Copenhagen.

Kjørholt, A.-T. and H. Lidén (2004) 'Children and youth as citizens: symbolic participation or political actors?' In: H. Brembeck, B. Johansson and J. Kampmann (eds) *Beyond the Competent Child: Exploring Contemporary Childhoods in the Nordic Welfare Societies.* Roskilde: Roskilde University Press.

Knudsen, H. (2010) *Har vi en aftale? Magt og ansvar i mødet mellem folkeskole og familie.* Frederiksberg: Nyt fra Samfundsvidenskaberne.

Kofoed, J. (2003) *Elevpli. Inklusion – eksklusionsprocesser blandt børn i skolen.* Doctoral thesis, Department of Educational Psychology. Danish University of Education.

Korsgaard, O. (1999) *Kundskabs-kapløbet. Uddannelse i videnssamfundet.* København: Gyldendal.

Korsgaard, O. (2004) *Kampen om folket. Et dannelsesperspektiv på dansk historie gennem 500 år.* København: Gyldendal.

Krejsler, J. (2014) 'Når de nye sociale teknologier sætter kursen'. In: J.B: Krejsler and L. Moos (eds) *Klasseledelsens dilemmaer. Fortsatte magtkampe i praksis, pædagogik og politik.* København: Dafolo Forlag.

Kryger, N. (2004) 'Childhood and "new learning" in a Nordic context'. In: H. Brembeck, B. Johansson and J. Kampmann (eds) *Beyond the Competent Child: Exploring Contemporary Childhoods in the Nordic Welfare Societies.* Roskilde: Roskilde University Press.

Kryger, N. (2007) 'Firing a national canon against the global challenge – questions of pedagogy in Denmark'. In: N. Kryger and B. Ravn (eds) *Learning Beyond Cognition.* København: DPUs Forlag.

Kusserow, A. (2004) *American Individualism.* New York: Palgrave Macmillan.

La Fontaine, J. (1979) *Sex and Age as Principles of Social Differentiation.* London: Academic Press.

Lareau, A. (2003) *Unequal Childhoods: Class, Race and Family Life.* London: University of California Press.

Larsen, C., E. Nøhr and P. Sonne (2013) *Da skolen tog form 1780–1850.* Dansk Skolehistorie, bind 2. Aarhus: Aarhus University Press.

Larsen, V. (2010) *Nationale praktikker i børnehaven. Om relationen mellem forskelsstrukturer i småbørnspædagogikken og en nationalstatsorganisering.* Doctaral thesis, Department of Psychology and Educational Studies. Roskilde University.

Levinson, B.A. and D. Holland (1996) 'The cultural production of the educated person: an introduction. In: B.A. Levinson, D.E. Foley and D.C. Holland (eds) *The Cultural Production of the Educated Person: Critical Ethnographies of Schooling and Local Practice.* Albany: SUNY Press.

Lewis, A.E. (2003) *Race in the Schoolyard: Negotiating the Color Line in Classrooms and Communities.* New Brunswick, NJ: Rutgers University Press.

Lien, M., H. Lidén and H. Vike (2001) *Likhetens paradokser: antropologiske undersøkelser i det moderne Norge.* Oslo: Universitetsforlaget.

Liep, J. and K.F. Olwig (1994) 'Kulturel kompleksitet'. In: J. Liep and K.F. Olwig (eds) *Komplekse liv: Kulturel mangfoldighed i Danmark.* København: Akademisk Forlag.

Lov om Børne- og Ungdomsforsorg (1964), no. 193.

Lov om Dagtilbud (2015), LBK no. 167.

Lov om Folkeskolen (1993), LBK no. 509.

Lov om Folkeskolen (2016), LBK no. 747.

Lov om Social Service (1997), LBK no. 454.

Loyal, S. (2004) 'Elias on class and stratification'. In: S. Loyal and S. Quilley (eds) *The Sociology of Norbert Elias.* Cambridge: Cambridge University Press.

Lupton, D. and L. Barclay (1997) *Constructing Fatherhood: Discourses and Experiences.* London: Sage.

Mac An Ghaill, M. (1994) *The Making of Men: Masculinities, Sexualities and Schooling.* Buckingham: Open University Press.

Mannitz, S. (2004) 'Regimes of discipline and civil conduct in Berlin and Paris'. In: W. Schiffauer, G. Baumann, R. Kastoryano and S. Vertovec (eds) *Civil Enculturation: Nation-state, School and Ethnic Difference in the Netherlands, Britain, Germany and France.* New York: Berghahn Books.

Markstrøm, A.-M. (2005) *Förskolan som normaliseringspraktik: en etnografisk studie.* Doctoral thesis, Department of Educational Sciences, Linköping University.

Mennell, S. (1990) 'Decivilising processes: theoretical significance and some lines of research'. *International Sociology* 5(2): 205–23.

Mennell, S. (2006) 'Civilizing processes', *Theory, Culture & Society* 23(2–3): 429–31.

Mennell, S. and J. Goudsblom (1998a) 'Introduction'. In: S. Mennell and J. Goudsblom (eds) *On Civilization, Power and Knowledge.* Chicago: University of Chicago Press.

Mennell, S. and J. Goudsblom (1998b) *On Civilization, Power and Knowledge.* Chicago: University of Chicago Press.

Merton, R.K. (1957 [1949]) *Social Theory and Social Structure.* London: Free Press of Glencoe.

Migdal, J.S. (2004) 'Mental maps and virtual checkpoints: struggles to maintain state and social boundaries'. In: *Boundaries and Belonging: States and Societies in the Struggle to Shape Identities and Local Practices.* Cambridge: Cambridge University Press.

Miller, D. (1997) 'How infants grow mothers in north London'. *Theory, Culture & Society* 14(4): 67–88.

Moos, L. (2014) 'Styringslogikker og diskurser i kampen om effektiv undervisning og demokratisk dannelse'. In: J.B. Krejsler and L. Moos (eds) *Klasseledelsens dilemmaer. Fortsatte magtkampe i praksis, pædagogik og politik.* København: Dafolo Forlag.

Myrdal, A. (1935) *Stadsbarn. En bok om deres fostran i storbankammare.* Stockholm: Koorperativa förbundets bokförlag.

Nielsen, H.W. (2001) *Børn i medvind og modvind: En relationel analyse af børns livtag med det refleksivt moderne*. Doctoral thesis, Institut for Samfundsvidenskab og erhvervsøkonomi. Roskilde Universitetscenter.

Nielsen, R.D. (2001) *Livet i barnehagen: Et etnografisk studie av socialiseringsprocessen*. Doctoral thesis, Norwegian Center for Child-Research, NTNU, Trondheim.

Nordentoft, I.M. (1944) *Opdragelse til demokrati*. København: Eget forlag.

Nørgaard, E. (2005) *Tugt og dannelse. Tre historier fra kulturkampens arena*. København: Gyldendal.

Ogbu, J. (1987) 'Variability in minority school performance: a problem in search of an explanation'. *Anthropology & Education Quarterly* 18: 313–34.

Øland, T. (2010) 'A state ethnography of progressivism: Danish school pedagogues and their efforts to emancipate the powers of the child, the people and the culture 1929–1960'. *Praktiske grunde. Nordisk tidsskrift for kultur- og samfundsvidenskab* 1–2.

Olwig, K.F. and E. Gulløv (eds) (2003) *Children's Places: Cross-cultural Perspectives*. London: Routledge.

Ortner, S.B. (1992) 'Reading America: preliminary notes on class and culture'. In: R.G. Fox (ed.) *Recapturing Anthropology: Working in the Present*. Santa Fe: School of American Research Press.

Ortner, S.B. (1998) 'Identities: the hidden life of class'. *Journal of Anthropological Research* 54(1): 1–17.

Ortner, S.B. (2006) 'Updating practice theory'. In: *Anthropology and Social Theory: Culture, Power, and the Acting Subject*. Durham, NC: Duke University Press.

Palludan, C. (2004) 'Bevægelse i pædagogiske institutioner – illustration af en pædagogisk-antropologisk forskningsinteresse'. In: U.A. Madsen (ed.) *Pædagogisk antropologi: Refleksioner over feltbaseret viden*. København: Hans Reitzels Forlag.

Palludan, C. (2005) *Børnehaven gør en forskel*. København: Danmarks Pædagogiske Universitets Forlag.

Paulle, B., B. van Heerikhuizen and M. Emirbayer (2011) 'Elias and Bourdieu'. In: S. Susen and B. Turner (eds) *The Legacy of Pierre Bourdieu*. London: Anthem Press.

Pedersen, K.O. (2011) *Konkurrencestaten*. København: Hans Reitzels Forlag.

Phelan, A.M. (1997) 'Classroom management and the erasure of teacher desire'. In: J. Tobin (ed.) *Making a Place for Pleasure in Early Childhood Education*. New Haven, CT: Yale University Press.

Popkewitz, T.S. and Bloch, M. (2001) 'Administering freedom: a history of the present – rescuing the parent to rescue the child for society'. In: K. Hultqvist and G. Dahlberg (eds) *Governing the Child in the New Millennium*. New York: Routledge Falmer.

Powell, R. (2007) 'Civilising offensives and ambivalence: The case of British Gypsies'. *People, Place & Policy Online* 1/3.

Powell, R. (2013) 'The theoretical concept of the "civilising offensive" (Beschavingsoffensief): notes on its origins and uses'. *Human Figurations* 2(2): 112–23.

Rasmussen, K. and S. Smidt (2001) *Spor af børns institutionsliv. Unges beretninger og erindringer om livet i børnehaven.* København: Hans Reitzels Forlag.

Rattansi, A. and A. Phoenix (1997) 'Rethinking youth identities: modernist and postmodernist frameworks'. In: J. Bynner, L. Chisholm and A. Furlong (eds) *Youth, Citizenship and Social Change in a European Context.* Aldershot: Ashgate.

Reay, D. (2001) '"Spice girls", "nice girls", "girlies", and "tomboys": gender discourses, girls' cultures and femininities in the primary classroom'. *Gender and Education* 13(2): 153–66.

Rifbjerg, S. (1969) *Børnepsykologi og opdragelse.* København: Folkeuniversitetsudvalget.

Rogoff, B. (2003) *The Cultural Nature of Human Development.* New York: Oxford University Press.

Rose, N. (1999 [1989]) *Governing the Soul: The Shaping of the Private Self.* London: Routledge.

Rosenberg, M. (1999) *Non-violent Communication: A Language of Compassion.* Encinitas: Puddle Dancers Press.

Salamon, K.L.G. (1992) '"I grunden er vi enige". En ekskursion i skandinavisk foreningsliv'. *Tidsskriftet Antropologi* 25.

Scheff, T.J. (2004) 'Elias, Freud and Goffman: shame as the master emotion'. In: S. Loyal and S. Quilley (eds) *The Sociology of Norbert Elias.* Cambridge: Cambridge University Press.

Schiffauer, W., G. Baumann, R. Kastoryano and S. Vertovec (eds) (2004) *Civil Enculturation: Nation-state, School and Ethnic Difference in the Netherlands, Britain, Germany and France.* New York: Berghahn.

Schmidt, L.-H. and J.E. Kristensen (1986) *Lys, luft og renlighed: Den moderne socialhygiejnes fødsel.* København: Akademisk Forlag.

Schneider, D. (1980 [1968]) *American Kinship: A Cultural Account.* Chicago: University of Chicago Press.

Scott, R.W. (2001) *Institutions and Organisations.* Thousand Oaks: Sage.

Seland, M. (2009) *Det moderne barn og den fleksible barnehagen. Et etnografisk studie av barnehagens hverdagsliv i lys av nyere diskurser og kommunal virkelighet.* Doctoral thesis, Norwegian Center for Child-Research, NTNU, Trondheim.

Shore, C. and S. Wright (1997) 'Policy: a new field of anthropology'. In: C. Shore and S. Wright (eds) *Anthropology of Policy: Critical Perspectives on Governance and Power.* London: Routledge.

Sigsgaard, J. (1947) 'Samfunds-Børnehaven'. I: *Norsk Pædagogisk Årbog 1946–47.*

Sigsgaard, J. (1978) *Folkebørnehaver og social pædagogik. Træk af asylets og børnehavens historie.* København: Forlaget Børn og Unge.

Skeggs, B. (1997) *Formations of Class and Gender: Becoming Respectable.* London: Sage.

Skeggs, B. (2004) *Class, Self, Culture.* London: Routledge.

Skovgaard-Petersen, V. (1985) *Danmarks Historie,* vol. 5. København: Gyldendal.

282   Children of the Welfare State

Smith, D. (1999) 'The Civilizing Process and The History of Sexuality: comparing Norbert Elias and Michel Foucault'. Theory and Society 28(1): 79–101.

Statistics Denmark (2015) Nyt fra Danmarks Statistik nr. 162, 1. april 2015.

Staunæs, D. (2004) Køn, etnicitet og skoleliv. Frederiksberg: Forlaget Samfundslitteratur.

Sutton, M. and B.A. Levinson (2001) 'Introduction: policy as/in practice: developing a sociocultural approach to the study of educational policy'. In: B.A. Levinson and A.M. Sutton (eds) Policy as Practice: Towards a Comparative Sociocultural Analysis of Educational Policy. Westport, CT: Ablex Press.

Swaan, A. de (2001) 'Dyscivilization, mass extermination and the state'. Theory, Culture & Society 18(2): 265–76.

Tap, R. (2007) High-wire Dancers: Middle-class Pakeha and Dutch Childhoods in New Zealand. Doctoral thesis, The University of Auckland.

Thing, M. (1996a) 'Af velfærdsstatens tilblivelseshistorie'. Social Kritik 44.

Thing, M. (1996b) 'Negre, børn og orgasme. Overvejelser omkring kulturradikale frigørelsesstrategier'. Nordisk Sexologi 4.

Thorne, B. (1993) Gender Play: Girls and Boys in School. New Brunswick, NJ: Rutgers University Press.

Tireli, Ü. (2003) 'Forestillinger om "muslimsk børneopdragelse"'. In: L. Paulsen Galal and I. Liengaard (eds) At være muslim i Danmark. København: Forlaget ANIS.

Tjørnhøj-Thomsen, T. (2007) 'Barnløses billeder af rigtige familier'. In: L. Andersen and P.P. Christiansen (eds) En rigtig familie: Mellem nye og gamle idealer. København: C.A. Reitzels Forlag.

U90. Samlet udddannelsesplanlægning frem til 90'erne. Undervisningsministeriet 1978.

Uddannelses- og Forskningsministeriet (2015) Profilmodel – andelen af unge som forventes at fuldføre en videregående uddannelse. www.ufm.dk

Undervisningsministeriet (2014) Status for opfyldelse af 95 pct. målsætningen. www.uvm.dk

Undervisningsvejledning for Folkeskolen 1960. Betænkning nr. 253 afgivet af det af Undervisningsministeriet under 1. september nedsatte udvalg, S. L. Møllers Bogtrykkeri, København (1960).

van Krieken, R. (1986) 'Social theory and child welfare: beyond social control'. Theory and Society 15(3): 401–29.

van Krieken, R. (1998) Norbert Elias. London: Routledge.

van Krieken, R. (1999) 'The barbarism of civilization: cultural genocide and the "stolen generations"'. British Journal of Sociology 50(2): 297–315.

Wacquant, L. (2004) 'Decivilizing and demonizing: the remaking of the black American ghetto'. In: S. Loyal and S. Quilley (eds) The Sociology of Norbert Elias. Cambridge: Cambridge University Press.

Waller, W. (1961 [1932]) The Sociology of Teaching. New York: Russell & Russell.

Willis, P. (1977) *Learning to Labour: How Working-class Kids Get Working-class Jobs*. Aldershot: Gower.

Wouters, C. (1977) 'Informalisation and the civilizing process'. In: P.R. Gleichmann, J. Goudsblom and H. Korte (eds) *Human Figurations. Essays for aufsätze für Norbert Elias. Amsterdams Sociologisch Tijdschrift* 437–56.

Wouters, C. (1986) 'Formalization and informalization: changing tension balances in civilizing processes'. *Theory, Culture & Society* 3(2): 1–19.

Wouters, C. (1992) 'On status competition end emotion management: the study of emotions as a new field'. *Theory, Culture & Society* 9(1): 229–52.

Wouters, C. (2004) 'Changing regimes of manners and emotions: from disciplining to informalizing'. In: S. Loyal and S. Quilley (eds) *The Sociology of Norbert Elias*. Cambridge: Cambridge University Press.

Wouters, C. (2011) 'How civilizing processes continued: towards an informalization of manners and a third nature personality'. In: N. Gabriel and S. Mennell (eds) *Norbert Elias and Figurational Research: Processual Thinking in Sociology*. Malden, MA: Wiley-Blackwell.

Youdell, D. (2003) 'Identity traps or how black students fail: the interaction between biographical, sub-cultural and learner identities'. *British Journal of Sociology of Education* 24(1): 3–20.

Index